EPIC JOURNEYS OF FREEDOM

RUNAWAY SLAVES OF THE AMERICAN REVOLUTION AND THEIR GLOBAL QUEST FOR LIBERTY

Cassandra Pybus

BEACON PRESS, BOSTON

Beacon Press
25 Beacon Street
Boston, Massachusetts 02108-2892
www.beacon.org

Beacon Press books
are published under the auspices of
the Unitarian Universalist Association of Congregations.

09 08 07 06   8 7 6 5 4 3 2 1

This book is printed on acid-free paper that meets the uncoated paper ANSI/NISO
specifications for permanence as revised in 1992.

Text design by George Restrepo
Composition by Wilsted & Taylor Publishing Services

Library of Congress Cataloging-in-Publication Data

Pybus, Cassandra.
  Epic journeys of freedom : runaway slaves of the American Revolution and their global quest
for liberty / Cassandra Pybus.—1st ed.
    p. cm.
  Includes bibliographical references and index.
  ISBN 0-8070-5514-X (cloth : alk. paper)
  1. Fugitive slaves—United States—History—18th century. 2. Fugitive slaves—Australia—
New South Wales—History—18th century. 3. Fugitive slaves—Sierra Leone—History—
18th century. 4. Fugitive slaves—England—London—History—18th century. 5. United
States—History—Revolution, 1775–1783—African Americans. 6. New South Wales—
History—18th century. 7. Sierra Leone—History—To 1896. 8. London (England)—
History—18th century. I. Title.

E450.P99 2006
323.3'225'09033—dc22   2005013093

For Marcus Rediker,
who made me see how much this story matters

WE HAVE NOT THE EDUCATION WHICH WHITE MEN HAVE
YET WE HAVE FEELING THE SAME AS OTHER HUMAN BEINGS
AND WOULD WISH TO DO EVERYTHING WE CAN FOR TO
MAKE OUR CHILDREN FREE AND HAPPY AFTER US...

Petition from black settlers in Sierra Leone, 1793

CONTENTS

FOREWORD

Ira Berlin

Revolutions generally benefit those who have the least to lose and the most to gain. In the middle of the eighteenth century, few had less to lose and more to gain than the black men and women held as slaves in the American colonies. Black men and women understood this, and when the simmering dispute between imperial Britain and its American colonies flared into open warfare and that war began to unravel the fabric of colonial life, they seized the moment. The result was a massive transformation that propelled thousands of black people from slavery to freedom, introduced a new ideology that presumed universal equality, and began the reconstruction of African American life as black people married, established families, secured waged employment, built churches and schools, and organized societies and associations. The spectacular increase in the number of free blacks dissolved the easy equation of slavery and blackness.

Revolutions that go forward can also go backward, and the men and women who seize the moment often have it wrestled from their grasp. Black men and women, much to their horror, also learned of the force of counterrevolution. If some black people gained their freedom during the American Revolution, many more were consigned to a dismal captivity, as slave masters consolidated their power atop the new state and initiated a massive expansion of the plantation system. There would be more black people enslaved at the end of the Revolution than at the beginning. Even as the Republic wrapped itself in the cloak of equality, new ideologies emerged that excluded black people from its democratic promise. Finally, as former slaves began to reconstruct their society, they found themselves excluded from all but the most menial employment, barred from established churches, denied access to education, and deprived of many of the rights of citizens.

But whether the Revolution smashed the shackles of slavery or tightened the manacles, it transformed black life in the eighteenth century as fully as the Civil War would in the nineteenth and the civil rights movement would in the twentieth. Indeed, the Civil War and the civil rights movement could not have taken place without the changes in black life initiated by the Revolution. The American Revolution divided the nation into free and slave. It unleashed the radical egalitarianism upon which the abolitionist movement, the wartime emancipation, the promise of Reconstruction, and the long struggle against Jim Crow rested. The contest between civic nationalism—which demanded the extension of the Declaration's principles to all—and racial nationalism—which sequestered those principles for a chosen few—had its beginnings in the Revolutionary settlement. That dispute continues to resonate in American life.

None of this would have been possible had not black men and women seized the Revolutionary moment to challenge slavery. Scholars have recognized the importance of that challenge and have created a rich history of African American slavery and freedom in the Revolutionary era. In *Epic Journeys of Freedom*, Cassandra Pybus joins a long line of distinguished historians of the so-called revolution in black life beginning with William Cooper Nell in the middle of the nineteenth century and extending through Herbert Aptheker, Luther P. Jackson, and Benjamin Quarles in the middle of the twentieth century and to Sylvia Frey and Gary Nash at century's end.

Cassandra Pybus adds greatly to the work of these scholars in part by, as she modestly put it, her "diligent excavation in the vast archival collections of the Revolutionary era" and in part by insisting that slaves stand at the center of their own history. In doing so, she makes two significant contributions to the study of African American life in the Revolutionary era.

First, Pybus personalizes the slaves' story. She does not merely speak of slaves escaping, compute their numbers, or map their flight, although she has addressed more fully the contentious matter of the number of fugitives and provides the best geography of slave escape. Instead, Pybus tells of the flight of Mary Freeman, David George, Boston and Violent King, George Liele, Thomas Peters, Harry Washington, and dozen of others. By embedding the larger transformation of black life in lives of individual men and women, Pybus deepens historical understanding of the process of Revolutionary change by revealing the reciprocal relationship between the slaves' willingness to risk all and the policies of British and American officials. Her "biographies" of flight expose the dangers that escape entailed and the courage it took to risk all for freedom. Only by measuring those dangers can the exhilaration of success be comprehended and the unspeakable misery of failure be appreciated.

Pybus makes a second important contribution to the study of the revolution in black life by globalizing its history. Perhaps because some of the black fugitives from revolutionary America found their way to her native Australia, Pybus emphasizes the vastness of the diaspora that the American Revolution set in motion. *Epic Journeys of Freedom* stretches the revolution in black life from the Canadian Maritimes to the Antilles, imperial Britain to continental Europe, and finally to the west coast of Africa. Historians have studied each of these migrations, and the histories of the individual migrations are known in greater or lesser degree. However, drawing them together and viewing them as a whole gives a sense of the epic force of the African American diaspora. Pybus reveals how the return of people of African descent to the larger Atlantic world after centuries of American captivity transformed it. Carrying ideas of evangelical Christianity, commercial capitalism, and political republicanism on their transit eastward from America, they remade the Atlantic world just as their transit westward from Africa once remade them.

Like the black Americans who spread all over the globe—refugees from a revolution in the name of liberty that would not tolerate their freedom—*Epic Journeys of Freedom* affirms how an old story can be given new life when viewed from a different perspective.

PROLOGUE

From the vantage point of his farm on the mountain slopes east of Freetown in Sierra Leone, Harry Washington could see the exodus out of the town on September 26, 1800. He knew there was terrible trouble in Freetown and that the boy the company installed as governor had offered one hundred dollars for the capture of several settlers he accused of "an act of open and unprovoked rebellion."

For the last few nights the drums from the neighboring African village had become more and more insistent, suggesting that the local Koya Temne sensed unrest in Freetown and were massing for an attack on the Sierra Leone Company.

The native drumming bothered Harry, but he paid no heed to the governor's offer of a reward. The men named as rebels were like brothers to him. Since the day twenty-four years before that he had run off from the plantation of General George Washington in Virginia, they had been together in a close-knit community of slave fugitives; first in New York and then in Nova Scotia, before making the tortuous trip to West Africa in 1792. He was now sixty years old, as best he could judge. Years of struggle and hardship had finally been rewarded with a flourishing farm that could support his family and free him from dependence on the company store. The last thing he needed at this time in his life was to get involved in a rebellion against the Sierra Leone Company's rule. Still, the way it looked to him, the land tax the company demanded would reduce his children to perpetual bondage, all over again. And it was right that the black settlers should choose their own representatives to govern them. The children of Israel had left Egypt for the Promised Land; so they had abandoned America for Sierra Leone, to find the true meaning of liberty, not to be free in name only.

Washington left his farm the next day and went down to the plain below, where he found that some forty rebel settlers had created a rough camp beside a fast-flowing brook that cut the road to Freetown. Spanning the turbid water was a narrow, swaying suspension bridge made of palm trunks lashed together with vines. Their presence beside the bridge established control of communications in and out of the town. Three days later they received a visit from two settlers acting as intermediaries who carried astonishing news: a transport ship had arrived unexpectedly in Freetown, packed with British soldiers from the Twenty-fourth Regiment as well as hundreds of Maroon warriors deported from Jamaica. A letter from the governor was read to the assembled men, in which he threatened to send a large military force against them. If they would surrender, the governor promised, the punishment would not extend to the loss of life. Blood would be spilled, the letter warned, unless a response was given by ten o'clock that night.

The men by the bridge were suspicious. How could they be sure that this was not a trick? They had learned to distrust the words used by white men in authority. Time and time again black settlers had been misled when the words read to them were later revealed to mean something different from what had been heard. From bitter experience they knew that words on paper were all that counted with the British, not words that evaporated in the air. No one in the camp could read what had been written to them. After lengthy consultation they agreed that they must have one of their own to tell them what the letters said and to write down the words that would explain the reasons for their actions. The one man who could read and write was not with them that day; they would have to fetch him. The emissaries from Freetown were instructed to tell the governor he would have an answer in writing in the morning.

Nothing would happen during the night; the weather was against it. A low mass of clouds the color of India ink cast a dark shadow over the plain, imparting an uncanny intensity to the emerald green of the elephant grass. By nightfall, jagged shards of lightning lit the sky, illuminated palm fronds whipped into the air, and the trees bowed to the ground. The rain was unrelenting for most of the night, abating just before first light. At dawn, companies of black-faced monkeys scampered back from the safety of the mountain forest, their excited gibbering adding to the cacophony of frogs and crickets drawn to the surface of the steaming, saturated ground. As the fiery ball of sun appeared in the east, so too did Captain Alexander Macaulay, advancing at a trot with a detachment of Maroons who had disembarked at the nearby bay on the previous day. The rebel settlers, sodden and scattered after the storm, were in no position to make a defense. Terrified by the pugnacious enthusiasm of the Maroons, they ran for the forest, several of them wounded, leaving two men dying where they fell. Harry Washington was among thirty men who surrendered to the governor the following day.[1]

As he faced a hastily convened military tribunal in Freetown on October 10, Harry Washington may not have appreciated the irony that his bid for freedom from enslavement to the leader of the rebellious forces in colonial America had led inexorably to this trial for rebellion in distant Sierra Leone. Whereas General Washington triumphed against the British rule in America and was subsequently reified as the president and father of the independent United States, Harry Washington lost everything in his attempt to forge an independent and self-determining community in West Africa; he was exiled from his home, with his ultimate fate unknown. The contrast between these two rebellious men named Washington could not be greater. In his lifetime George achieved near immortal status. Since his death the accumulation of papers and publications about him can fill libraries. Harry has been relegated to a brief footnote in one or two books. There can be no surprise here. In the massive literature on George Washington it is rare to find any of his slave property distinguished even by a name, let alone accorded the life history of a person motivated by complex reasoning and capable of acting on his or her own volition. An unlettered African man whom George Washington acquired in a mundane business transaction could have no role to play in the foundation narrative of the American Republic. Or could he?

Surely, it is not utterly incongruous to set beside the story of the revered father of America an alternative story of the African man he had purchased to dig ditches. At the heart of both narratives lies a commitment to the transforming ideals of liberty and self-determination, even though the drama of forging ideals into a tangible reality played out very differently for a paragon of the colonial elite than for his runaway slave. We must have competing narratives of liberty fought for and won in the

American Revolution in order to comprehend the enormity of the impact of the Revolution, as well as the ideas it spawned, in radically re-
shaping America and the wider Atlantic world. Yet is it even possible to
recover the story of Harry Washington from the callous indifference of
history? Few fugitive slaves have left an indelible impression on the historical record, and far fewer historians have ventured into the recesses
of the archive in search of them. Nevertheless, diligent excavation in the
vast Revolutionary-era archival collections, both American and British,
does reveal traces of Harry Washington: the name on a bill of sale, on the
list of taxable property, on a British military muster, on the embarkation
list of a transport ship, on a register of land titles, and in the verdict sum-
mary of a court-martial. From these insignificant scratches and tattered
bits of administrative flotsam, the lineaments of a life can be recon-
structed. And not only for the man known as Harry Washington.

One of the most remarkable archival documents, which can be found
in both American and British annals, is a compilation of the names of
three thousand black men, women, and children, among them Harry
Washington, who were evacuated from New York between April and
November 1783, all but a few carrying certificates of freedom signed by
a British general. This document, known as the Book of Negroes, provides a brief description of each person, along with the name of their former owner. It accounts for about one-third of those who left America as
free black people during the British withdrawal and stands as the most
substantial piece of evidence of the alliance between fugitive slaves and
the British military during the Revolution.[2]

From the moment that hostilities commenced in 1775, enslaved men
and women took to their heels, with rhetoric about the inalienable rights
of free people ringing about their ears, entrusting their aspirations for
liberty not to their Patriot masters, but to the king's men. Historians
know this. They were first alerted by Herbert Aptheker in his 1940 pam-
phlet *The American Revolution*, in which he highlighted the flight of as
many as one hundred thousand enslaved people to the British as one
of the most dramatic features of the American Revolution. Benjamin
Quarles's masterly 1961 study, *The Negro in the American Revolution*,
while more realistic in estimating numbers to be "tens of thousands,"
showed how significant the flight of enslaved people was to the British.

His research was further amplified by Sylvia Frey in *Water from the Rock: Black Resistance in a Revolutionary Age* in 1991.[3]

It is not my purpose to continue in that tradition. My concern, in what follows, is to recover the lives of individuals from the faceless and nameless "tens of thousands" that characterize a good deal of the historical discussion of black runaways during the Revolution. Rhys Isaac has memorably written that enslavement may be "most deeply defined as being compelled to act not out of one's own story, but the story imposed on one by another, a master." Far too often historians are content to tell the story of the enslaved as the story imposed on one by another. I don't want to do that. I want to show people in the process of entering their own stories and creating their own destiny; to explore, in as much as the sparse evidence will allow, the experience of people who emancipated themselves from enslavement and struggled tenaciously to make the rhetoric of liberty a reality in their own lives.[4]

I have tried to recover from scattered fragments in the archives the stories of individuals engaged in the tortuous process of negotiating their freedom during the Revolution. In order to remain free, they had to leave America and forge a problematic new life in far-flung corners of the British Empire. In doing so, these black refugees constituted a diaspora within a diaspora, with widespread distribution throughout the Atlantic world and beyond. The majority went to Nova Scotia and to England. Some were sent to the Bahamas, Jamaica, and St. Lucia in the Windward Islands, while a few hundred fetched up in the unregulated territory of the Mosquito Shore and the Bay of Honduras (present-day Guyana and Belize). Several dozen went as far as Germany.[5]

In this book I follow the path some black refugees took to the British imperial center of London and then into two bizarre colonial experiments that began in 1787: the Province of Freedom in Sierra Leone on the west coast of Africa, and the penal settlement of Botany Bay on the east coast of Australia. In howling wilderness, at opposite ends of the globe, their struggle to find dignity and self-determination provides an insight into the human dimension of that slippery concept, freedom.

A NOTE ON SOURCES

How does one even begin to recover the lives of illiterate people who left no more than a faint trace on the historical record? I was not even sure what I was looking for five years ago, when my curiosity was aroused by Ian Duffield's essay "Constructing and Reconstructing 'Black' Caesar," which told me there were a dozen men of the African diaspora among the convicts sent to create a penal colony in Australia in 1788. To discover who they were and where they came from would be like looking for needles in a haystack, that much I knew; as it transpired, the task was even more laborious because there were multiple haystacks, located in four different countries thousands of miles apart, one of them inaccessible because of a brutal civil war.

I began at the obvious place, the National Archives Office in Kew, England, which held prison and transportation records in the files of the Home Office. Sadly, the sparse, one-line entries in prison hulk lists and transportation indents provided no clues to the history of the black convicts. Turning to documents of the clerk of the Assize Courts, I located some trial records in the heavily creased and barely legible parchment, and others I found in the volumes of Old Bailey Session Papers, available at Guildhall Library. Still, these records gave no account of how these black men came to be in England, other than the fact that they had all been arrested in the period between 1782 and 1786, which I knew through reading books and newspapers of the period in the British Library saw a dramatic increase in the black population in London.

The vital clue that propelled me toward the United States—and the project that became this book—was found at the Archives of New South Wales in Sydney, where I read a petition for land from a black convict in which he claimed he was a veteran of the British army. A small detail in this claim arrested my attention: he said that during the American Revolution he worked as a spy for Lord Cornwallis's army at Yorktown.

Having read Benjamin Quarles's classic study on the Revolution, I knew that this man's self-aggrandizing claim was plausible, that he was most likely a runaway slave who had defected to the British and gone to England as part of the Loyalist evacuation of America.

Fascinated by the potential in this story, I flew back to the National Archives to search for evidence in the correspondence of the secretary of state for North America, muster lists of British regiments in the war office, ships' logs and evacuation reports in the Admiralty records, and the personal papers of Lord Cornwallis and Sir Guy Carleton, as well as the memorials to the Loyalist Claims Commission. It was a hugely ambitious undertaking, completely out of my area of knowledge. I was greatly assisted by the multivolume survey *Documents of the American Revolution,* and my task in tackling the hefty records of the Loyalist Claims Commission was facilitated by the research of Mary Beth Norton, who had located most of the black claimants for her 1973 article "The Fate of Some Black Loyalists of the American Revolution." Those few she had missed were identified in the meticulous research of Stephen Braidwood, whose book *Black Poor and White Philanthropists* directed me to the minutes of the Committee for the Relief of the Black Poor in the voluminous files of Treasury. When the archives in Kew were closed, I searched London newspapers in the British Library and pored over hundreds of pages of raw data on black adult baptisms extracted from parish records by the London Metropolitan Research Office.

Even later at night as I was surfing the Web, I found the Institute for Advanced Loyalist Studies, where astonishing detective work by Todd Braisted and Nan Cole in American and Canadian archives had identified all kinds of scattered documents on the black allies of the Loyalist cause. E-mail conversations with Todd Braisted sent me to Halifax, Nova Scotia, where I trawled through the archives for records of the thousands of black refugees resettled in that province in 1783. A momentous breakthrough came when a researcher at the Nova Scotia Museum informed me that the Book of Negroes, which I had previously seen handwritten in the Carleton Papers in London, was now transcribed and could be downloaded onto my laptop. I was then able to search by name, place, and date to locate several of the people I was seeking, although I was puzzled that they were listed as evacuated to Nova Scotia, when my research placed them in England. I was able to resolve this conundrum with the help of a research assistant, who diligently searched through all the Nova Scotia military and civilian musters, tax lists, land grant approvals, and court and prison records from 1783 till 1792. She established that these men had either failed to arrive in Nova Scotia or, having arrived, were so dismayed that they caught the first available ship to England.

With the help of another research assistant I was able to do a demographic analysis of the Book of Negroes, cross-referencing the names with musters from Nova Scotia, the data on black adult baptisms from parish records in London, the names of applicants to the Loyalist Claims Commission, and the lists of recipients compiled by Committee for the Relief of the Black Poor. Once I had identified a specific cohort of black refugees, it remained for me to track their history back into the American colonies, which required tackling the daunting archive of revolutionary sources in the United States.

A Fulbright Senior Fellowship in 2002, followed by two more research fellowships in 2003 and 2004, allowed me to work my way through the major documents of the revolutionary period, a great many of them, thankfully, reproduced in excellent scholarly editions. At the Clements Library, the sprawling, uncatalogued papers of Sir Henry Clinton yielded fragmentary evidence of my subjects, as did several smaller collections of papers from other British officers. Other tantalizing fragments were extracted from runaway slave notices, petitions from slave owners, and reportage in colonial newspapers. Contained in these fragments were narratives that enthralled me, flying in the face of much of the historiography on the American Revolution that I was voraciously reading. However incomplete, these were stories that demanded to be told. Before me I had the model of how this might be done in Gary Nash's marvelous essay "Thomas Peters: Millwright and Deliverer." For all my digging in the musty archives, it was his vivid historical reconstruction that allowed me to see how a book could be made.

In consulting a huge range of eighteenth-century sources I found no consistency whatsoever in the use of capital letters and ampersands; it drove me crazy. So I made a decision to standardize the quotes to modern usage in the matter of capitalization and ampersands, but to keep the idiosyncratic spelling. Anyone who wants to read the quote exactly as written should consult the original document or a definitive edited version, as cited in the notes.[1]

PART I

CHAPTER I

LIBERTY OR DEATH

It was early spring at Mount Vernon, the seven-thousand-acre estate of Colonel George Washington in Fairfax County, Virginia. Vestiges of winter snow lingered on the expanse of lawn that swept down to the Potomac River, while along the lovingly tended cherry walk, plump buds showed the first hint of spring blossom. The early-morning air was still raw on March 15, 1775, when the enslaved hostler at Mount Vernon prepared the colonel's horse for his trip to the Second Virginia Convention in Richmond, a three or four days' ride to the south. Like all the Mount Vernon slaves, Harry had only the tattered woolen jacket and the short breeches that he had worn since last summer to ward off the chill. Harry felt the cold keenly; he was from West Africa, where such bitter weather was unknown.

Harry probably came to Virginia in one of several shipments of slaves from the Senegambia imported into the Upper Potomac by Thomson Mason, the brother of Washington's close friend George Mason. Washington acquired Harry in 1763 from the estate of a deceased neighbor, one of a job lot of four people Washington purchased to be his contribution to an enslaved workforce of the Great Dismal Swamp Company. Washington was the prime mover and manager of this scheme, whereby twelve "adventurers" each contributed five slaves to the workforce in order to drain sixty square miles and establish a rice plantation. Nan was another of Washington's acquisitions for the Dismal Swamp, and she may have been Harry's wife, as Washington had scruples about permanently separating couples. There was also a boy, Toney, who could have been her son, as he was additional to the five adult slaves that Washington was required to contribute. By 1766, both Harry and Nan were taken from the Great Dismal Swamp to work at Mount Vernon. If they were a couple, they were not permitted to live together at Mount Vernon; Harry was employed around the Mansion House, while Nan labored on one of the outlying farms at Muddy Hole.[1]

In the spring of 1775, Washington was leaving his handsome estate to attend the Second Virginia Convention as the elected representative for Fairfax County. Despite the beguiling promise of incipient cherry blossom, these were uncertain, turbulent times in Virginia. The threat of war with Britain loomed, a prospect Washington dreaded. He was already the elected commander of a number of independent militias raised across northern Virginia, and he knew that if war came he would be the one to lead the American forces into a conflict bloodier than he had ever before witnessed. By the time Washington left Richmond to return home, a fortnight later, black frost had burned the blossom from all his fruit trees and his prospect for continuing with rustic pleasures at Mount Vernon was equally blighted. With a heavy heart he wrote his brother, "It is my full intention to devote my life and fortune to the cause we are engaged in, if need be."[2]

The Second Virginia Convention chose to meet in the small town of Richmond rather than the colonial capital of Williamsburg in order to avoid the wrath of the royal governor, John Murray, Earl of Dunmore. They selected the Henrico County church on a hill above the village because the recent addition of a north wing to the pleasant wooden building made it the largest in the town. Even so, the church could barely contain all the 127 delegates who converged on Richmond from all over the colony on March 20. For the townsfolk of Richmond to have the colonial elite debating matters of great urgency in their church was cause for much excitement. Word must have spread like wildfire about Patrick Henry's electrifying performance on March 23, when he urged that the reluctant delegates must prepare to resist the British.

With his face flushed with passionate intensity, Henry laid out the choice Virginians faced between freedom and enslavement. "Is life so dear, or peace so sweet, as to be purchased at the price of chains and slavery?" he demanded, his voice rising to a crescendo. "Forbid it, Almighty God! I know not what course others may take; but as for me . . ."—he allowed an exaggerated pause while he held an ivory letter opener poised above his heart—"give me liberty or give me death!" With this emotive allusion to Addison's play *Cato*, which had a profound influence on so many of the Virginia gentry, Henry invited his fellow delegates transform their provincial lives into a theater of heroic resistance and republican virtue. Washington, too, was a devotee of *Cato* and he shared

Henry's assessment of the stark choices facing the colonists, even though he remained silent in the debate that followed Henry's thunderbolt. In his more prosaic style, he had said much the same thing six months earlier when he wrote to his friend Bryan Fairfax, "The crisis is arrived when we must assert our rights, or submit to every imposition that can be heap'd upon us; till custom and use, will make us as tame, and abject slaves, as the blacks we rule over with such arbitrary sway."[3]

Henry's rhetorical flourish gave a heroic gloss to sentiments reverberating through the colony for more than a year. The cries of "liberty" heard at rowdy gatherings at the county courthouse, and in the ardent talk swirling about the streets of every town, were discreetly absorbed by enslaved people who mingled unobtrusively in the excitable crowd. Passionate chatter about liberty and despotism, which animated the dining tables and drawing rooms of Virginian plantations, was not lost on the footmen and cooks, the valets and maids, who were as much a fixture of the plantation house as the furniture. At Mount Vernon, Harry may well have listened with more than idle interest to the colonel's views about the tyranny of the British masters and the inviolable concept of liberty. He had briefly managed to achieve the condition of liberty when he ran away on July 29, 1771, after being transferred from the Mansion House to work on the construction of a mill nearly three miles away, near the newly acquired Ferry Farm. He was soon caught, in response to advertisements Washington had placed, and returned to Ferry Farm. After a year, he was again put to work at Mansion House in 1773. Though he made no further attempt to abscond, Harry had not abandoned the idea of liberty that now so animated his master.[4]

Even if Washington had been canny enough to send his slaves out of earshot, it would not have been possible to quarantine the ideas that he discussed with his friends and neighbors. Snatches of talk overheard were almost instantaneously channeled from plantation to plantation through the complex networks of the enslaved community. In the Tidewater region, dominated by long-established plantations with a large slave workforce, the slave quarters would house twenty or more people who were related, and they were likely to have other siblings, spouses, uncles, aunts, and cousins living within the neighborhood. These people had intricate means of communication, barely understood by the master. Under the cover of darkness, they would congregate together for songs

and storytelling, and the word would spread. On Sunday, they would
come together from all over the county to sell the produce raised in their
family plots and to trade information. "The Negroes have a wonderfull
art of communicating intelligence among themselves," two southern
planters explained to John Adams. "It will run severall hundreds of
miles in a week or a fortnight."[5]

The Mansion House at Mount Vernon employed an enslaved workforce of up to fifty people who lived communally in a large, two-storied
frame structure across the lane from the blacksmith's forge, known as
the House for Families. Here the volatile political events that so engaged
Colonel Washington were rehearsed in talk, song, and dance. In early
May, when Washington rode off in his carriage to attend the Continental Congress in Philadelphia, the House for Families must have been
humming with news from Massachusetts about pitched battles with
British regulars at Concord and Lexington. Speculation, too, perhaps,
that the master had packed his militia uniform in the expectation that he
would be asked to command the Patriot forces against the British. News
of the elevation of the master to General Washington, Commander in
Chief of the Continental Army, would surely have triggered celebrations
in the House for Families and gleeful anticipation of his bloody confrontation with the three British generals who had arrived with the
British army in Boston. The message Harry extracted from all this heady
revolutionary tumult was that if King George III was now the master's
enemy, then it was to the king's men that he would entrust his aspirations
for freedom.

The young James Madison intuitively understood that there was a
potential for danger in the revelry in the slave quarters. A few months
earlier, Madison had warned a friend that if hostilities did break out
the British would promote a slave revolt. Trouble of this sort had already
been instigated, he confided. "In one of our counties lately a few of those
unhappy wretches met together and chose a leader who was to conduct
them when the English troops should arrive—which they foolishly
thought would be very soon and that by revolting to them they should be
rewarded with their freedom." He was pleased to report that the plot had
been discovered and "proper precautions taken to prevent the infection."
Madison, who regarded slaveholding with distaste, chose not to elabo-
rate about the "proper precautions" taken in this instance. Very likely, the

"unhappy wretches" were savagely flogged and mutilated, although some may have been dispatched to the West Indies, a common practice for dealing with refractory slaves. As a final caution, Madison advised, it would be "prudent such attempts should be concealed as well as suppressed." By the summer of 1775, he must have realized what a Herculean and grisly task it would be to arrest the contagion of liberty, since the air was thick with infection issuing from the mouths of impassioned slave owners. A great deal more in the way of "proper precautions" would be required.[6]

Anxiety about a slave insurrection was heightened when the embattled royal governor of Virginia removed all the gunpowder from the magazine in the colonial capital at Williamsburg on April 20, 1775. Confronted by an outraged citizenry, who believed Lord Dunmore had acted in order to expose them to the mercy of their slaves, the governor inflamed passions by announcing what he would do in the case of any retaliation: "I shall be forced to arm my own Negroes and receive all others that will come to me, who I shall declare free." Given that the planters of Virginia held some 180,000 people enslaved, to even hint at such a thing was truly shocking. Prominent Loyalists insisted that the governor would use such tactics if attacked, but their reassurance did nothing to diminish the terror of white Virginians for whom, it was said, "even the whispering of the wind was sufficient to rouze their fears."[7]

At that time, a group of unidentified slaves had taken their lives in their hands to call on the governor and offer their service in support of the king, only to have him turn them away. In his besieged position in the governor's mansion, Dunmore was not prepared to risk more fury from the Williamsburg populace. His threats to free the slaves had "stirred up fears in them which cannot easily subside," he explained to the secretary of state in England; "as they know how vulnerable they are in that particular." By June, however, he had been forced to take refuge on a British warship in the James River (and to send his wife back to England) and he was only too happy to take advantage of the offer of service from fugitive slaves. From the relative safety of HMS *Fowey*, Dunmore began to assemble a squadron to strike back at the rebellious Virginians, welcoming any runaways that were able to make their way across to his fleet.[8]

At first the British response was equivocal; some runaways were returned to their outraged owners, but the British consistently refused to hand over a runaway pilot who knew the waterways of Chesapeake intimately. Throughout the summer tenders from the ships cruised up and down the river, openly inciting slaves to come on board, spreading indignation and alarm throughout the Tidewater. In late October, the town of Hampton came under fire from a small collection of British boats, providing stark evidence that the British fully intended to use enslaved people against white Virginians, and the news raised the country "into perfect phrensy," so Thomas Jefferson reported.[9]

By this time the "proper precautions" to prevent slave defections were well in place. Throughout the Tidewater slave patrols were increased and exemplary punishment was applied to runaways. A fifteen-year-old girl who had fled from her master and tried unsuccessfully to reach Dunmore received a flogging of eighty lashes followed by hot embers poured on her lacerated back. Enslaved Virginians understood that the terrible risks involved in running away had never been greater, yet still they went. In August 1775, Edward Hack Moseley, a prominent planter of Princess Anne County near Portsmouth, placed a notice for three runaways between the ages of sixteen and eighteen that he named Jack, Daniel, and Peter. Since Moseley was a friend of Lord Dunmore, and had just been appointed Lieutenant of Princess Anne County, his runaways probably did not head for Dunmore's nearby fleet. More likely they did as Moseley supposed and took refuge in one of the towns of Portsmouth, Hampton, or Norfolk. Planters were consistently angered by the willingness of white artisans and tradespeople in the towns to shelter runaways rather than return them. Jack appears to have found work with Captain John Cunningham, an Irish sea captain who was a regular visitor to the James River and whose ship was in Portsmouth in order to mend a mast that had been damaged on the voyage from Ireland.[10]

Even if Moseley's runaways were not making a beeline for Dunmore's ships, plenty of fugitives were. About a hundred had reached his fleet by November 1775. This was exactly the kind of "tampering with the slaves" that James Madison had most feared. "To say the truth," he confided to his friend, "that is the only part in which this Colony is vulnerable ... we shall fall like Achilles by the hand of one that knows that secret." Lord Dunmore knew that secret. Made bold by the idea of what might be accomplished should the trickle of runaways become a flood, Dunmore declared martial law on November 14, 1775, and published a proclamation that freed "all indented Servants, Negroes, or others . . . that are able and willing to bear Arms." He made no distinction between Patriot or Loyalist property.[11]

Here was every white Virginian's nightmare. The proclamation came as such a shock to Loyalist William Byrd III that he immediately offered his services to the Patriots. When Thomas Jefferson was drafting the Declaration of Independence the following summer, he was still so outraged by Dunmore that he wrote into the document his most impassioned charge against George III, accusing the king of "exciting those very people to rise in arms . . . and to purchase that liberty of which *he* has deprived them, by murdering the people upon whom *he* also obtruded them: thus paying off former crimes committed against the *liberties* of one people with crimes which he urges them to commit against the *lives* of another." George Washington, in his capacity as commander in chief of the Patriot forces, labeled Dunmore an "arch-traitor to the rights of humanity." Dunmore must be crushed, he warned, or the momentum of slave defections would be "like a snow ball in rolling."[12]

When Dunmore's proclamation was published in the *Virginia Gazette,* it was accompanied by a grim warning to slaves "weak enough to believe that Lord Dunmore intends to do them a kindness" to consider "what they must expect to suffer if they fall into the hands of the Americans." At the meeting of the Fourth Virginia Convention, the president of the convention, Edmund Pendleton, spelled out the "necessity of inflicting the several punishments upon those unhappy people, already deluded by [Dunmore's] base and insidious arts." The punishment for those who defected to Dunmore was death, and a fugitive caught while attempting to reach Dunmore was to be sent to work in the lead mines. A pardon was promised to those who voluntarily returned to "their duty." This combination of punitive threat and compassionate promise did not work. "Letters mention that slaves flock to him in abundance," Pendleton wrote glumly to Richard Henry Lee.[13]

Any stampede to the British was against huge odds. As Harry well knew, running away was extremely difficult. The danger of recapture and savage punishment was terribly real, and also militating against irrevocable flight were the bonds of family, from which the enslaved community drew its fortitude. By 1775 most enslaved people in the Tidewater lived in families, certainly children with their mothers and young siblings, and sometimes with their fathers, grandparents, aunts, uncles, and cousins. Mount Vernon was typical in this respect, with most enslaved people living in family units either in the House for Families or the slave quarters of the other farms. By a process of natural increase there had been a fourfold rise in the enslaved population on that estate between 1765 and 1775. While Washington encouraged stable unions within his enslaved workforce and was loath to break up families by sale, separation by distance did not concern him. Husbands and wives could be physically separated by work allocations in quite different places, as Harry and Nan appear to have been. When children reached adolescence they were often sent away to work on one of Washington's remote farms under the direction of an overseer. While the close-knit kin networks did facilitate short-term runaways by providing hospitality and shelter over a considerable distance, the bonds engendered were a powerful pull against making a decisive break from which there could be no return. Unless whole families ran away together—almost unheard of— a lifetime of separation from close kin was the consequence.[14]

Added to the psychological pressures of abandoning family, there was the fundamental difficulty of reaching Dunmore's small fleet in the mouth of the James River. Enslaved people could only move about the country with signed passes, and plantation owners kept a close watch on their watercraft. Slave patrols were doubled throughout the region, and armed militia were stationed along the Chesapeake shores. Notwithstanding the surveillance and intimidation, hundreds made a determined attempt, some running from far away. On November 18, 1775, a slave owner in remote Stafford County reported the "long premeditated" escape of "a shrewd sensible fellow" and three accomplices from other plantations in "a determined resolution to get Liberty." Several months later these four fugitives crept aboard a small schooner moored at a wharf on the Potomac. As they did not know how to sail the vessel, they told the surprised crew to steer the boat to a place on the Virginia side they identified as Coon River. Instead the white crew steered toward Maryland and organized to have the fugitives arrested. Two of the runaways were sentenced to be whipped and mutilated, while the other two were sent to certain death in the lead mines. Their owners were compensated for their loss at seventy-six pounds apiece.[15]

At the end of November, Dunmore could report, "Between two to three hundred [runaways] already come in and these I form into a Corps as fast as they come." They came mostly from Hampton, Norfolk, and Portsmouth and were often maritime workers, especially pilots. Others ran off with British forces when they cruised along the James River, while still more absconded from plantations close to navigable waterways. They mostly came on small craft, though some came on foot, propelled by sheer willpower, and swam out to Dunmore's ships. Soon after the proclamation, planter Edmund Ruffin lost five highly valuable slaves, including a carpenter, a wheelwright, and a blacksmith, who went off in a boat to Dunmore. When one of his fugitives was caught and imprisoned, Ruffin was outraged that rather than being returned, his property was left to die in the infamous conditions of the slave section of the Williamsburg jail. Ruffin's loss was typical in that those who initially fled to Dunmore tended to be young men who possessed skills of use to the British. Correspondents to the newspapers unwittingly reinforced the flight of valuable males by insisting that Dunmore would retain only able-bodied men and would sell the rest. Nevertheless, enslaved women were among those who managed to reach the governor's fleet during November.[16]

Recruits for Lord Dunmore's Ethiopian Regiment, as the governor styled his new corps, were provided with weapons and taught how to use them. Alarmed Patriots reported that several hundred of the black corps were working to fortify a strategic area of Great Bridge, at the head of the southern branch of the Elizabeth River, twelve miles above Norfolk. Rumor had it that they were outfitted in a uniform bearing the provocative inscription "Liberty to Slaves." In reality Dunmore spent months desperately begging army headquarters to send any sort of clothing for his recruits, estimating his need to be "compleat clothing for four or five thousand men." Wearing an assortment of ragged and cast-off clothing, the Ethiopian Regiment composed about half of the "ragged crew" that engaged the Virginian militia commanded by Colonel Woodford at Great Bridge on December 9, 1775. During the battle, the British commander was killed, along with about sixty of his men, and eighteen wounded prisoners were taken into custody.[17]

Those taken at Great Bridge included three members of the Ethiopian Regiment: Peter Anderson, whose forearm had been shattered; Caesar, who sustained a serious leg wound; and an unidentified man, who died of his wounds. Anderson and Caesar were extremely lucky not to have been put to death immediately. Colonel Woodford reported that "the unanimous opinion of the officers would have been to make an immediate example of them," but he felt it prudent to postpone an execution until he received advice from the Fourth Virginia Convention about the action to be taken against captured runaways. In due course they were sent to Williamsburg and held in custody in order to be valued and tried. Caesar was sentenced to the lead mines, whereas Anderson, who was deemed to have borne arms, was to be hanged. The execution of condemned slaves was held over for consideration by the Fifth Virginia Convention, so Anderson was left to endure the appalling conditions of the slave section of the jail, where captured slaves regularly died of disease and mistreatment. After about six months, so Anderson later explained, he managed to escape and hide out in the woods.[18]

The rout of Dunmore's forces at Great Bridge encouraged white Virginians to subsume their fears about slave insurrection into ridicule of the British effort to create a regiment of black recruits. Lund Washington, who was managing Mount Vernon in his cousin's absence, reported, "Lord Dunmores Negroe soldiers are, it is said, commanded by Scotchmen—proper officers for slaves for they themselves possess slavish principals." Regardless of the contempt the Virginia elite showered on the Ethiopian Regiment, their property continued to flee to Dunmore's floating base camp, even when it moved into Chesapeake Bay. Lund Washington could sneer at Dunmore, but he could not avoid the realization that people were driven to Dunmore's side by the very same passion that animated the Patriots to oppose him. In his evaluation of the loyalty of Mount Vernon's bonded workforce, both indentured and enslaved, Lund was concerned: "There is not a man of them, but woud leave us, if they believe'd they could make there escape . . . yet they have no fault to find. Liberty is sweet."[19]

As the slave exodus increased, so the backlash against Virginia Loyalists intensified. In the absence of an executive head of the colony, the

Virginia Convention in August 1775 set up a Committee of Safety, chaired by Edmund Pendleton, to act as the legal arm of the de facto government. In December 1775 the Committee of Safety ordered that Edward Hack Moseley and his son be arrested and sent to Williamsburg to be examined. John Willoughby Sr., the royal lieutenant of neighboring Norfolk County, was also detained. Captain John Cunningham too came under suspicion. His ship *Fanny*, loaded with British army provisions, was seized as a prize. Cunningham managed to convince the Committee of Safety that he had been coerced into carrying supplies for the British, and he was compensated for his loss of wages even though his cargo was auctioned off. Soon after, he applied to leave Virginia. This could have been the time that Moseley's young runaway Jack decided to throw in his lot with the king's men. Eight years later, a man calling himself John Moseley, age twenty-five, was working for the Wagon Master General's Department in New York. In giving an account of himself, he said he had left the employ of John Cunningham in Portsmouth and joined the British in 1776.[20]

In due course Edward Hack Moseley and John Willoughby Sr. were able to persuade the Committee of Safety that they were not acting against the interests of Virginians and were granted parole, even though suspicion about their relationship to Dunmore lingered. As a consequence of this suspicion, they were required to move at least thirty miles away from the shore, and to enforce submission, the Committee of Safety ordered their slaves to be taken by the militia. This provided both motivation and opportunity for the rest of Moseley's slaves to run to Dunmore. They were part of a very large group of fugitives from Princess Anne and Norfolk counties, including eighty-seven people from the plantation of John Willoughby Sr. Two years later, John Willoughby Jr. attempted to get compensation from the Virginia legislature, protesting that the loss of slave property was a direct result of the resolution of the Committee of Safety to remove his father and of "the vigorous way in which it was about to be executed."[21]

Although the legislature rejected the petition, there was some truth in Willoughby's claim. The Moseley and Willoughby slaves may well have feared being seized by the Patriots and being sent to work in the lead mines or sold away. The new government of Virginia was much in need of money, and the sale of seized slaves was one way to raise it. In June

1776 eleven enslaved people whom Lord Dunmore had left behind at the governor's mansion in Williamsburg were sold at public auction. Another eight seized slaves of defecting Loyalists had been sent to work in the lead mines. An even more distressing prospect was that seized slaves could be sold to the West Indies, as was the intended fate of one of the Moseley runaways who had been caught before he got to Dunmore. In May 1776 he was put aboard a ship to be transported to Antigua for sale, together with several others.[22]

Those who ran from the Moseley and Willoughby plantations included elderly people, as well as young women with children. A woman in her midfifties from Moseley's plantation took with her several children between the ages of eleven and three, while her husband and son ran from another plantation. The list of "Negroes gone to Dunmore" that Willoughby attached to his petition gave the names of sixteen men with ages ranging from sixteen to sixty, as well as twenty-one women with ages ranging from eighteen to fifty-five, who had with them fifty children. This pattern of slave flight was typical of the defections to Dunmore from January through June 1776, though quite unlike what had happened before the Revolution, when it was almost always young men who ran. Women ran with their children; families who were separated by different masters ran together. Despite the negative accounts the Virginians had circulated about the British intention to sell any runaways who could not bear arms, the majority of the runaways in 1776 were husbands and wives or mothers with children or even grandparents; all of them taken aboard Dunmore's fleet.[23]

A significant individual within the group from Willoughby's plantation was Mary, a woman in her late thirties, who ran with her ten-year-old daughter, Patience. At some stage in her enslavement Mary had learned to read the Bible and she was inspired by the preaching of the Wesleyan Methodist circuit riders who were active in the Tidewater. Many years later in Sierra Leone, Mary told how, at night when Willoughby was asleep, she would strap her daughter to her back and walk ten miles into the country to meet other enslaved people in order to sing praises to the Lord and exhort her fellow sufferers to open their hearts to salvation so their spirits could be freed from bondage. She may have sung a version of the hymn of Charles Wesley:

Long my imprisoned spirit lay
Fast bound in sin and nature's night;
Thine eyes diffused a quickening ray—
I woke, the dungeon flamed with light;
My chains fell off, my heart was free.

When her meeting ended, she would trudge the ten miles' return journey in order to be at work before Willoughby woke. Mary did this grueling round trip to her clandestine meeting at least once a week until a preacher was found to guide her converts.[24]

Years later, when Dunmore's fleet beckoned, Mary seized the chance to liberate her body as well as her spirit. Doubtless some of those she had been meeting in the woods did the same. Methodist runaways who made it to Dunmore sometime between December 1775 and May 1776 included Nathaniel Snowball, who absconded from a plantation in neighboring Norfolk County, his wife, Violet, who came with her son, Nathaniel, from Princess Anne County, and his brother Timothy, who slipped away from another master in Norfolk. From the plantation of prominent Patriot Mills Wilkinson, in Nansemond County, came a Methodist preacher called Moses. It is very possible that this powerful and charismatic preacher, later known to his many followers as "Daddy Moses," was following the precedent of his biblical namesake and leading his followers across the water to freedom.[25]

Blatant recruitment of their slaves by the deposed governor provided the Patriots with the perfect argument as to why they could no longer give allegiance to the Crown. Patrick Henry protested at the Fifth Virginia Convention, held in Williamsburg throughout May and June 1776, that for representatives of the Crown to be "encouraging insurrection among our slaves, many of whom are now actually in arms against us," revealed the king to be a "tyrant instead of the protector of his people." The only honorable response, Henry argued, was "an immediate, clear, and full Declaration of Independency." A resolution to that effect was carried unanimously on June 29, 1776. A new constitution was formally adopted and Henry was elected the first governor. As the head of the independent Commonwealth of Virginia, Henry proved ineffectual in stemming the tide of slave defections to the enemy. Sometime during his stay in Williamsburg, one of his enslaved servants, a man in his early twenties named Ralph, slipped away to join Lord Dunmore.[26]

Along the length of Chesapeake Bay alarmed plantation owners and managers did their best to staunch the defections by promoting benevolent paternalism over the precarious dangers of freedom. At Mount Vernon, Lund Washington was confident that the enslaved community understood that General Washington's care and protection was the best option for them. He had "not the least dread" that the slaves might make a bolt for Dunmore's fleet, Lund told his cousin, although he could not vouch for the white indentured servants, some of whom had already gone. Just how this paternalistic confidence translated in the House for Families, he had no way of knowing. None of the enslaved workers took the risk of running off, at least not at that time.[27]

Farther down the Potomac, Robert Carter called together all 350 of his slaves to explain that if the king won the war Dunmore would be unlikely to keep his promise of emancipation. Left unspoken was the threat of what would happen if the king were to lose. Several counties away, on the Rappahannock River, his irascible uncle, Landon Carter, saw no reason for such proactive intervention. As far as Landon was concerned, Dunmore's proposal to emancipate slaves who fought for him was "a thing so inhuman" that it could only appeal to "thoughtless africans." When one man ran off in February 1776, Landon was dubious about his motive. "I should have thought he was gone to increase the black regiment," he wrote in the advertisement he placed, "but in reality he is too weak and idle to be desirous of going where he must work for his freedom, as it is called." On June 26, 1776, he was surprised, and profoundly wounded, to discover that eight of his enslaved workforce had run away—"to be sure, to Lord Dunmore." Not only had they run away, but they had gotten into his steward room before dark and stolen guns, shot, and powder. The flight was clearly premeditated, as two enslaved people from an upriver plantation had gone with them in Landon's large canoe. After weeks of hearing contradictory stories about his runaways, Landon sent his apprentice manager on a circuit to get information from both sides of the Rappahannock. When the man returned with no information, Landon turned eagerly to local gossip. A tavern keeper recounted a story of returning runaways who said they had seen slaves

fleeing from Lord Dunmore; supposedly among them was a runaway
from Landon's plantation, who swore that "if he could get back, he
would return to his master; for Dunmore had deceived all the poor
slaves." Increasingly vengeful, Landon continued to seek out gossip
about the fate of his people. In July he recorded with sardonic glee a story
that Dunmore had reenslaved the runaways and sent them off to be sold
in the West Indies. Even as he slept he visited misery upon his absconding chattel. They appeared to him in a dream, "most wretchedly meagre
and wan," living in a cave in the ground, eating "what roots they could
grabble." In his dream these poor, deluded souls, now reduced to the
condition of wild animals, longed for the intervention of their indulgent
master, pleading that if he would "endeavour to get them pardoned,
should they come in." During the waking hours it must have been
galling that no such plea was ever made. As if to heap coals upon his
head, even more ungrateful slaves ran off to join Lord Dunmore.[28]

What Landon Carter's gossip mill had failed to convey was that if his
absconding chattel had succeeded in reaching Lord Dunmore, they may
well have died, not from ill-use or starvation, as he fervently wished, but
from disease. Smallpox had invaded North America late in 1774, and by
January 1776 the disease had made its appearance in Virginia. Although
smallpox had been present in the colony at times before—Williamsburg
had been decimated thirty years earlier—there had never been such a serious and widespread outbreak. Inoculation was common in England in
the eighteenth century, but it had been so bitterly resisted in Virginia
that the procedure was all but banned in the colony. When the disease
first appeared in Dunmore's overcrowded flotilla, the British were
largely immune and the Virginians highly susceptible. The disease hit
the black recruits especially hard. They died by the hundreds. Reporting
the epidemic with relish, *Purdie's Virginia Gazette* noted that bodies were
"tumbled into the deep, to regale the sharks." With advice from the naval
surgeons, Dunmore moved his forces to a small neck of land near
Portsmouth, where he created "pretty good barracks for [the] Ethiopian
corps." An influx of new recruits kept the contagion alive, wreaking
havoc on Dunmore's military ambitions and killing off "a great many
fine fellows." In order to isolate the sick after his the surgeons had inoculated his recruits en masse, Dunmore moved his base to Gwynn Island

in late May. He left behind him the graves of almost three hundred people.[29]

Of all epidemic diseases, smallpox held particular horror. From the moment the distinctive rash appeared, it rapidly covered the entire body, sometimes hemorrhaging under the skin, causing bleeding from the gums, eyes, nose, and other orifices. Most cases broke out with ugly pustules on the palms of the hands, the face, forearms, neck, and back. After two weeks of acute suffering, scabs started to form and flesh came away in evil-smelling clumps, with the victims emitting such a pungent smell healthy people could not tolerate the stench. Sixty percent of cases died, usually after ten to sixteen days of suffering, although patients remained contagious until the last scab fell off. Survivors carried numerous scars and some were blinded and lame, but they were immune for life. Inoculation, in which live variola was implanted under the skin, caused a milder version of the disease, with much less scarring yet the same level of subsequent immunity. It was risky business, as the inoculation process caused debilitating sickness that left the inoculated vulnerable to epidemic typhus and typhoid fever.[30]

The dreadful condition of Dunmore's forces was not understood by the enraged Patriots, who continued their contemptuous ridicule, with one newspaper announcing that the diminutive ex-governor celebrated the landing on Gwynn Island by throwing "a promiscuous ball, which was opened, we hear, by a certain spruce little gentleman and one of the black ladies." In truth, the scene of mass inoculation on Gwynn Island was anything but festive, with hundreds of sick men and women enduring the awful progress of the disease in hastily constructed huts. Dunmore reported to his superiors that "there was not a ship in the fleet that did not throw one, two or three or more dead overboard every night." Virginia Patriots found diseased bodies drifting ashore on the tide the next day, as many as a dozen at a time. On Gwynn Island the dead were buried in shallow mass graves. Tragically, Dunmore continued to draw fresh black recruits at the rate of six to eight each day, most of whom succumbed to the disease as soon as they arrived. Those who recovered from the inoculation fell victim to an outbreak of "fever" that "carried off an incredible number of... people, especially the blacks," Dunmore lamented. Had this not happened, he told the secretary of state, he would have had two thousand men under arms in his Ethiopian Regiment. In this dreadfully weakened condition, Dunmore's force was easily driven from the island in early July 1776, and they took refuge on the fleet once again. The British commander of the fleet reported that the "distress and confusion" of the hasty evacuation was beyond his powers to describe.[31]

The Virginia militia encountered a gruesome sight when they entered the hastily evacuated camp. The Dixon and Hunter *Virginia Gazette* of July 20, 1776, reported "the deplorable situation of the miserable wretches left behind" found dying of fever: "In one place you might see a poor wretch half dead making signs for water"; elsewhere more were "endeavouring to crawl away from the intolerable stench of bodies lying by their side." Another report in Purdie's *Virginia Gazette* indicated that bodies "in a state of putrefaction" were strewn about an area of two miles, "without a shovelful of earth upon them." One person claimed to have found 130 graves, many of them large mass burials, near the site of the camp. The fear of contamination led the Patriots to set fire to the flimsy brush huts, which still held sick runaways, so even more people burned to death. Eyewitnesses concurred that the death toll on the island from one cause or another was "near 500 souls." The Virginia press was determined to make capital of this horror. "Dunmore's neglect of those poor creatures," Purdie's *Virginia Gazette* chided, was "one would think enough to discourage others from joining him." It failed to do so. By the time Dunmore's fleet of nearly a hundred ships had taken up its near position in the mouth of the Potomac River, it was already receiving runaways.[32]

On July 19, 1776, a much smaller fleet of eight vessels made a foray up the Potomac for the purposes of gathering fresh water. On July 24, while entangled in an armed skirmish with the local militia, the British force was joined by another small craft that had come down the river from Fairfax County. Those on board offering their services to the British were "three of General Washington's servants," who were then taken aboard HMS *Roebuck*. Lund Washington always suspected that more of the general's white indentured servants would prove disloyal. Whatever his poor opinion of the white bondsmen, Lund remained supremely confident of the loyalty of the general's slaves, yet the three aboard the craft from Mount Vernon must have included Harry, the enslaved hostler. When Harry Washington was evacuated from New York in July 1783, he said that he had run away from General Washington seven years before.[33]

Dunmore found his floating town assailed by Patriot militia on all sides, and his options for making landfall were completely cut off. On July 31, he sent a pathetic letter to the secretary of state, admitting, "Where we are to go, or what we are to do next . . . I own I am puzzled to know." Being penned up on a ship with no hope of being relieved by British forces had become intolerable. With his forces "too few to stay off Virginia having lost so many by Sickness," the dispirited Dunmore gave the order to abandon Virginia. In the fleet that sailed out of the Chesapeake toward New York on August 7 was Harry Washington, together with between two hundred and three hundred surviving members of the Ethiopian Regiment and their families. At least ten people who ran from Edward Hack Moseley were on board, including the youth Jack. Among the dozen survivors from the plantation of John Willoughby was Mary, her daughter, Patience, and three other children she adopted when their parents died. The preacher Moses must have fallen victim to smallpox, but he had survived, although he was blind and unable to walk unaided. Among those who arrived in New York with him were Nathaniel Snowball, his wife, Violet, their children, and his brother Timothy. There was also Ralph, the runaway slave of Patrick Henry, another American who had taken the fiery Virginia orator at his word.[34]

CHAPTER 2

CROSSING OVER TO
FREEDOM'S SHORE

Scipio Handley was a self-employed black fish seller in Charleston when he was caught carrying messages for the embattled royal governor of South Carolina, Sir William Campbell, late in 1775. As far as the rebellious colonists were concerned, Handley's capture was clear evidence that the British were set upon undermining the social order in the slave colony. Campbell had been regarded with deep suspicion from the moment he stepped ashore in Charleston in June that year, rumored to be bringing a huge cache of arms to inspire a slave uprising against them. Six months later, incendiary stories of a British-inspired insurrection continued to percolate through the white population.

Handley could expect a grisly fate. Possibly he had witnessed the horrible execution of another free black fisherman, Thomas Jerimiah, six months before. Jerimiah was accused of encouraging a slave rebellion, supposedly telling slaves that in the event of war they should join the British, since "the war was come to help the poor Negroes." Even as he strenuously denied the charge of sedition, Jerimiah was hanged and his body burned to ashes in front of a large crowd. The newly arrived governor did all in his diminished power to intervene, until the South Carolina Committee of Safety warned him that if he interfered any more, Jerimiah would be hanged from the doorpost of the governor's mansion. Appalled at the flimsy evidence against Jerimiah, Campbell wrote to the secretary of state in England, "My blood run cold when I read on what grounds they had doomed a fellow creature to death." He bluntly concluded: "The man was murdered."[1]

Handley was more fortunate than Jerimiah. While waiting execution in the Charleston jail, he was smuggled a file to sever his iron manacles, he jumped two stories from his cell window and escaped to Sullivan's Island, a small area in Charleston Harbor under the control of

British warships. On Sullivan's Island he joined a small community of runaways sheltering in flimsy huts they had thrown together from found materials. For months enslaved people in Charleston had been absorbing the mounting hysteria about British intentions and impending war. They knew that the English army had landed in Massachusetts and was preparing to do battle with their masters, and that there had been fighting in the backcountry between the Patriot and Loyalist militia. When word of Dunmore's proclamation freeing those prepared to bear arms for the king reached Charleston, the British ships in Charleston Harbor were transformed into a symbol of hope. Those who sought refuge with the British took a calculated risk, under no illusions about the cruel death they might expect should they be caught.[2]

William Ashe thought the risk was worth taking when he ran to Sullivan's Island with his infant daughter, Esther, both enslaved to the same man in Charleston, in order to effect a reunion with his wife, Mary, who had been sold far away to the Indian Lands. In the turmoil caused by the fratricidal fighting in the backcountry she had managed to escape. Ashe was a slave mason, one of the large number of enslaved artisans hired out to work in Charleston, who consequently enjoyed a relative degree of autonomy and freedom from surveillance. The same may have been true for the black carpenter Isaac Anderson, a single man in his early twenties who had taken refuge on the island in December 1775. Years later in New York, when Anderson was asked to account for himself, he claimed to have been a "born free man in the house of Robert Lindsay," which implied that he, like Scipio Handley, belonged to the free black population in Charleston. However, Anderson was born in Angola, as he later admitted. He must have come to America in a shipment of slaves and almost certainly he was the property of either Robert Lindsey, a wealthy Charleston slave owner, or Robert Lindsay, a free black man in the city who also owned slaves. Like Ashe, he had seized the opportunity of an alliance with the British to emancipate himself from bondage.[3]

The presence of a fugitive slave community in the middle of Charleston Harbor was seen as a grave threat. South Carolina's elder statesman Henry Laurens, chairman of the Committee of Safety, complained bitterly to the British naval commander about harboring "negroes who fly from their masters" and actively encouraging these fugitives to make armed raids on plantations along the seacoast. Profoundly shaken by the subversive specter of the camp of runaways on Sullivan's Island, Laurens authorized a dawn raid on the island on December 18, 1775. Fifty-four men disguised as Indians burned the shelters of the runaways, killed three or four, and captured another four. Laurens regretted the loss of life, but he ordered the attack in the hope that it would serve to "mortify his Lordship . . . [and] humble our Negroes in general." Certainly the incident convinced Governor Campbell that he had better quit South Carolina until he had an army to reinforce his authority. He sailed out of Charleston Harbor on January 6, 1776. With him went a small number of runaways, including Scipio Handley, the Ashe family, and Isaac Anderson.[4]

Campbell sailed north to Cape Fear, in North Carolina, to rendezvous with the British commander in the region, Major-General Henry Clinton, who had arrived from Boston in February with twenty British warships and several troop transports. Even before this fleet arrived, runaways were defecting to the British commander at the mouth of the Cape Fear River, near the town of Wilmington. This was a region where enslaved people enjoyed an unusual degree of mobility and freedom, working as carpenters, dock workers, or loggers in the pine forests. When the British warship began to bombard Wilmington in February 1776, the fearful white residents were evacuated inland and the town was left almost entirely to its enslaved workforce.

Thomas Peters was a Yoraba man in his thirties who had been imported from Africa fifteen years before. At first he was a laborer on a sugarcane plantation in French Louisiana, and he still carried the marks of whippings and branding inflicted on him for his unsuccessful escapes from a brutal master. He was eventually sold to an immigrant Scot who went to live in Wilmington in 1770. It was here that Peters found a degree of autonomy, dignity, and self-reliance. He was a millwright, probably hired out to one of the timber mills and permitted to find lodging separate from his owner where he could live with his wife, Sally, and their five-year-old daughter, Clairy. This small measure of independence was not enough for Peters, given that he, his wife, and his child were still defined as property and could be disposed of at will. As soon as his Patriot master fled Wilmington in March 1776, Peters took his family aboard a British warship in the Cape Fear River. Taking the same desperate gamble was John Provey, who, like Peters, enjoyed a high degree of autonomy as the valet of a lawyer in Wilmington.[5]

When General Clinton arrived at Cape Fear, he was more than pleased to find about fifty black refugees on board the ships, and he promptly appointed a marine captain as the commanding officer of a specially commissioned black company. As Thomas Peters remembered, he was inducted into a noncombat company called the Black Pioneers, swearing a formal oath that he entered the king's service "without the least compulsion or persuasion" and would "cheerfully obey all such directions as [he] may receive." In return for service, the Black Pioneers were "regularly supplied with provisions and decently clothed," as were their families. The Black Pioneers came from as far afield as South Carolina and even Georgia. They received rations and the same pay as regular soldiers, a sixpence a day. Clinton insisted that all his officers treat the black soldiers with "tenderness and humanity," and he promised that when the rebellion was over they "shall be entitled (as far as depends on me) to their freedom." Peters clearly displayed the qualities that would later make him leader of the black community, since he was made a sergeant and served in that capacity till the end of the war. John Provey, who had been a gentleman's servant rather than a manual worker, was seconded to work for Clinton's secretary.[6]

By July 1776, the British fleet was still off Cape Fear, where it was joined by the exiled governors of South Carolina, North Carolina, Georgia, and Maryland. Morale was at a low ebb after the abject failure of Clinton's ill-judged assault on Charleston in June. With British disasters up and down the Atlantic seaboard, it must have seemed to Isaac Anderson and Thomas Peters that the gamble they took in defecting to the king's men would turn out badly. Their fortune seemed to have reached a nadir when the fleet was joined by the governor of Virginia, with his disheartened refugees. However, two weeks later they arrived at Staten Island, where they were greatly heartened to find that an army of nine thousand troops had come from Nova Scotia under General Howe, as well as another ten thousand Hessian mercenaries from Germany. The British forces were now almost thirty thousand, all primed and ready to take New York from George Washington's Continental army.

The moment had been a long time coming for the governor of New York, William Tyron. For eighteen months he and his secretary, Edmund Fanning, had been trying to maintain royal government on two warships moored just off Sandy Point. Communications with the Loyalist mayor of the city had been managed by employing several black men as couriers. One of the couriers was Fanning's steward, John Thompson, who unobtrusively moved back and forth carrying secret correspondence concerning a plot to trigger a Loyalist uprising by the assassination of General Washington. The plot was discovered by the Committee for the Detection of Conspiracies set up by the Congress. On orders of the committee, the mayor was arrested on June 21, 1776, and a reward of five hundred dollars was offered for the black couriers. Thompson was betrayed by deserting sailors and jailed. When New York was attacked he was taken to New Jersey, where he was kept in chains for several months. During the turmoil of the American withdrawal from New York, Thompson managed to escape, in the company of ten other black men, and get to the British at Staten Island. He never received the handsome payment he had been promised for taking such risks, but he and the other defectors were recruited into a Loyalist regiment Fanning had raised known as the King's American Regiment.[7]

When the British and Hessian armies took control of Manhattan in September 1776 they had with them hundreds of black refugees from Georgia, the Carolinas, and Virginia, all of whom streamed into a city unlike anything they had seen before. New York even managed to impress the Hessian officers with its well-paved streets, rows of substantial brick houses, many fine churches, handsome public buildings, and imposing docks. The size and substance of the city compared more than favorably with any European city these German officers had seen. The key difference was that New York was almost empty of people; the great majority of the population of sixteen thousand had fled, some leaving their slaves behind to fend for themselves. Jacob Duryee hastily vacated his property for the Patriot-controlled state of New Jersey, leaving his enslaved servant, Frank, to look after his interests. Frank looked out for his own interests instead: he married a free woman and negotiated to work with the British on his own terms as a free man, having chosen the name Frank Griffin.[8]

The choice of name was one of the most significant acts for the black people in the British zone of New York. Taking one's own name was a potent gesture of self-emancipation, with much more than symbolic value. In a society where enslaved people were universally known only by a single mocking or infantilizing name, it marked them as chattel as clearly as a brand. Runaway notices commonly observed that fugitives sought would probably change their names, or that they already had more dignified names by which they wished to be known. The mock regal names so commonly bestowed on chattel were dignified by becoming a surname, and first names were commonly formalized from their infantilizing diminutive form. Mary Byrd's serving man Wat became Walter Harris, and Edward Moseley's runaway Jack transformed into John Moseley. More often than not, the new surname would reflect an inheritance from the past life, the usage reflecting the British practice of adding the owner's surname when they entered a runaway's name on a muster. So Patrick Henry's runaway became known as Ralph Henry and George Washington's hostler took the name Harry Washington. Not everyone wanted to carry symbolic markers of their enslaved life, however illustrious their former owners. Mary, one of the survivors from John Willoughby's estate, chose the surname Freeman for her daughter, Patience.

On the heels of the withdrawal of the Continental army from Manhattan, disgruntled Patriots started a fire that swept through the western side of city, reducing about a quarter of the buildings to smoldering rubble. The fire brought disaster, but it also created opportunities. As white artisans had fled the city, enslaved people who had stayed behind, as well as those who arrived with the British army, found themselves in high demand if they had skills. The carpenter Isaac Anderson and the mason William Ashe, who came to New York with the former royal governor of South Carolina, were quickly absorbed into the British effort to reconstruct the damaged city. The civil departments of the army needed all the labor they could find to provide the logistical support necessary for a large army, and each department created a corps of black pioneers. Many of the black recruits of Lord Dunmore's Ethiopian Regiment, including Moseley's runaway Jack, found work with the Wagon Master General's Department, while Nathaniel Snowball, Harry Washington, and Ralph

Henry joined the Royal Artillery Department. Others worked for the Quartermaster General's Department, the Forage and Provision Departments, or for the Commissary.

Only one black company was actually on the military establishment: the Black Pioneers had been created to supply the troops with firewood and carting provisions; to assist in the construction of fortifications and barracks; and to service the army camps. Plenty of black recruits found employment within army regiments as servants to officers. John Provey became valet to the aristocratic Brigadier General Lord Hugh Percy, later the Duke of Northumberland, who was so pleased with his black servant that he took Provey back in England when he quit in 1778. Samuel Burke, the batman of the Brigadier General Montfort Browne, arrived in New York by a most circuitous route. He was originally from Charleston, but some years earlier he had been taken to county Clare, Ireland, as the valet to Browne. In 1774, when his master was appointed governor of the Bahamas, Burke had gone also. He was still with Browne in March 1776 when the governor surrendered the Bahamas to the Patriot navy. Both master and servant were taken hostage and sent to Connecticut, where they were exchanged for Patriot prisoners and repatriated to New York. Once he arrived in the city, Burke threw himself into helping Browne to raise the Prince of Wales American Regiment, which he also joined. Having learned to speak Gaelic during his time in county Clare, Burke proved invaluable in recruiting recent immigrants from Scotland and Ireland.[9]

When General Washington withdrew his Continental army north beyond White Plains, he gave the British control of Manhattan, Staten Island, and Long Island. The British territory was separated from the Patriot-controlled colonies of New Jersey and Connecticut by relatively short stretches of water. At one point on the Hudson River it was possible to wade across to New Jersey. The permeable borders of the British zone facilitated the movement of spies. One was Benjamin Whitecuff, a free man who lived on his father's farm on Long Island. His father and brother had joined the Patriot forces, but he took his chances with the British, finding employment with the Quartermaster General, Sir William Erskine, who decided that a free black man with relatives in the Continental army made an ideal British spy. Whitecuff traveled unobtrusively around New Jersey and back into New York, gathering information about Patriot military activity, "at all times very assiduous and successful in the part he undertook," as he later told the Loyalist Claims Commission in England.[10]

Just as Whitecuff moved easily through the permeable borders of the occupied zone, so too runaways from adjoining colonies were able to slip into the throng of foreign soldiers and Loyalist refugees without attracting scrutiny. Patriot slave owners regularly found that their chattel had slipped away only to reemerge in Manhattan, brazenly "strolling about the town," acting for all the world like independent human beings. Peter Jay wrote to his son John Jay, who was at that time president of the Continental Congress, about two youths, the personal property of John Jay and his brother Frederick, who had run off from the family farm in northern New York in 1777. Peter Jay believed they were then sold to British officers, but in fact they were employed by civil departments in New York and eventually evacuated from the city carrying certificates of freedom.[11]

Runaways who came into the city found employment simply by asserting that they were free; their labor was quickly absorbed by the voracious British war effort. Many more people claimed to be free than had papers to prove it, but inside the British lines few cared to make a distinction. After June 1779, any pretense was no longer necessary. The commandant of New York declared: "All Negroes that fly from the enemy's country are free—No person whatever can claim a right to them —Whoever sells them shall be prosecuted with the utmost severity." While some company commanders feared being overwhelmed with black indigents, especially women and children, the British accommodated everyone, regardless of age or gender. Only occasionally did they remonstrate with "idle" black men, threatening expulsion if they did not work. Because of the shortage of white workers, there was plenty of employment.[12]

Black artisans worked on rebuilding projects and in the naval yards; black teamsters hauled provisions and collected firewood; black nurses and orderlies staffed the hospitals; black laundresses and needlewomen did the washing and sewing; black pilots guided the ships safely in and out of the port; black fiddlers and banjo players provided entertainment for balls and tavern entertainment; black jockeys rode the horses at the races; black cooks, servants, and valets ensured the comfort of the elite. A whole range of opportunities hitherto denied was opened to black people. In almost all cases they were paid for their services, and they could be paid well if they had skills in demand, as carpenters and pilots did. They were also provisioned, for the most part, and they were not required to pay taxes. For these reasons alone, the British zone was a magnet to runaways. During the period of British occupation, the number of absconding slaves from New York and its neighboring colonies exploded.[13]

Persistent British incursions into the seaports in eastern Connecticut provided opportunities for more black defections, like the raid on Danbury in April 1777, where Samuel Burke was badly wounded. A black recruit who was probably scooped up in one of these raids was John Randall. He provided no account of how he came over to the British, only that he came originally from New Haven and was born about 1764. Randall was not a recorded surname in New Haven at the time, so he may have been from New London, possibly enslaved to a Captain John Randall of Stonington. This would make him one of several enslaved people from Stonington who ran to the British. Randall must have enlisted in a British regiment, because more than twenty years later, on the other side of the world in the British colony of New South Wales, he was accepted into a military unit formed from army veterans. His age and his noted ability to play the flute and tambour point to Randall's being recruited as a drummer. Perhaps he was a deserter. In eastern Connecticut nearly 10 percent of the men in the Continental army for whom an enlistment bounty was paid were enslaved substitutes for their white owners, and an additional 5 percent were identified as free blacks. These recruits had distinctive names such as Cato, Scipio, Gad, and Prince, to which the recruiting officer usually added the surname Negro. A number of these black recruits made the decision to run to the British, shedding the demeaning name along with the uniform.[14]

John Twine freely admitted to being a deserter from the Continental army. He was wagoner in the Virginia regiment commanded by General Washington's cousin, and a part of the demoralized army that was with Washington when he crossed the icy Delaware River in late December of

1776. After the war was over, when Twine was seeking compensation in England, he claimed to be the son of free parents in Petersburg, Virginia. He said that he had "lived with a Mr. Bradley who kept a tavern" before being impressed into the Continental army. A more plausible tale is that he was enslaved to the tavern keeper and was put in the army as his master's substitute. In giving his reasons for running away, Twine explained that he was poorly clothed and badly used by the Patriots and he heard that there was "better usage in the British Army." Sometime after the battle of Trenton, early in 1777, Twine deserted to the British and was taken into the Volunteers of Ireland, a company largely made up of men of Irish descent, many of them deserters.[15]

Twine was one of many black recruits among the hundreds of runaways who sought refuge with the British during the ten-month Philadelphia campaign in 1777, when the British actively sought desertions from both the Continental army and the American navy. Dick was an enterprising runaway who came on board the British warship HMS *Roebuck* in the Delaware River and was employed by the captain as a courier and possibly a spy, carrying a pass that certified, "Dick a free Negro is able to pass by water unmolested." After he left with the British in 1778, Dick transformed himself into Richard Weaver and somehow managed to get himself and his wife, Lucy, to England. Eighteen-year-old Nathaniel Wansey ran 360 miles from Newcastle, on the western frontier of Pennsylvania, to join the British in occupied Philadelphia, and he was still with them on their difficult retreat through New Jersey in June 1778. Benjamin Whitecuff provided invaluable intelligence about Washington's movements to aid the retreat, and it was most unfortunate that he was caught by Patriot forces at Danbury and instantly hanged. He would have died but for a miraculous intervention of a British officer who cut him down just before he strangled.[16]

Black refugees from Philadelphia arriving in New York were joined by a large contingent of runaways from the Portsmouth and Norfolk area of Virginia, consisting of 256 men, 135 women, and 127 children who had gone aboard the British fleet when it was making punitive raids in the Lower Chesapeake in May 1779. Edmund Pendleton claimed that the British had taken away three times that many and that they had stolen these people in snatch and grab raids in order to sell them in the West

Indies. The evidence, however, suggests a series of premeditated and well-organized escapes by interconnected family groups. The majority would have been of little use to the British, being disabled men, elderly women, small children, and adolescents. It was nonsensical for the British to have taken as plunder such a large number of elderly and disabled people, as well as small children and nursing mothers. Nor did it make sense for sailors to have gone from plantation to plantation seeking out the kinfolk to ensure that those they took were members of large extended families.[17]

James Jackson, who ran from distant Mecklenberg County, was taken on board, with his wife and his two children, his friend Frank Patrick, and Patrick's parents, each one of whom was enslaved to different people in the town of Norfolk. More than a hundred people ran off from plantations in Norfolk County, demonstrating a complex demographic profile with connections of kin and marriage across numerous plantations. On Crane Island, near Norfolk, more than sixty ran off together from four or five plantations, and several of them had ties of marriage or kinship with another large group that fled from the plantation of Willis Wilkinson in adjoining Nansemond County. One of the threads that appears to have bound people in this group was an attachment to the charismatic Methodist preacher Moses, who had defected to Dunmore three years before; many of them were among his congregation in New York. Luke and Mingo Jordan, who ran from different plantations in Isle of Wight and Nansemond counties, were his assistant exhorters, who later became preachers themselves.[18]

With the British army concentrated in New York, along with the tens of thousands of Loyalist refugees, conditions of life in the British zone were basic. Every necessity was in short supply, especially shelter. Anyone with a decent house in Manhattan might expect to have it taken for the army's use. Samuel Burke had acquired a nice house with some fine pieces of furniture as a consequence of his marriage to the free black widow, Hannah, but he was not able enjoy this luxury for long. The quartermaster general requisitioned the property for a hospital, promising to recompense the owners when the war was over. Five years later, when Burke was destitute in London, he was still trying to get financial restitution for his wife's seized property.[19]

Between Broadway and the Hudson River the burned-out neighborhood was not rebuilt and the charred ruins were used to support rough dwellings created from canvas and found materials. For the most part, the black recruits were crammed into these unsanitary makeshift shelters. Those formally on the payroll, such as people employed in civil branches of the army and the Black Pioneers, were lucky enough to be provided with housing. John Moseley, who was employed by the Wagon Master General's Department, lived in "Negro barracks" across the East River near the wagon yard in Brooklyn. Harry Washington, Ralph Henry, and the Snowball family lived with the rest of their company in the Royal Artillery Department in similar barracks, created out of four row houses in lower Manhattan. They were provided with weekly rations, as well as a lamp and a pint of oil for each room. That runaway slaves should occupy even these meager lodgings infuriated some white Loyalists. A complaint to that effect was registered by one, who recorded his disgust that available houses were not rented to deserving whites and were instead "occupied by dirty, idle, thieving, Negroes invited into the lines." Worse still, he bemoaned that these "wretches" were supplied with "rations of all kinds, equally with the Kings troops." Presumably, another cause for complaint was the fact that runaways working for the British were also paid.[20]

Whether they lived in barracks or in the canvas town of the burned-out district, the black recruits formed communities. Although they came from different colonies and various life experiences, they were bound together by a struggle to survive and memories that reached back to an African past. Music was the rhythmic center of traditional African life and in the multiethnic slave communities of America traditional musical forms were reinvented to express a common experience of enslavement. To the accompaniment of the fiddle, banjo, gourds, bells, and the insistent drumming of feet and hands, improvised song and dance found resonance with people from disparate places, allowing them to share the experience of work, exile, and yearning, as well as their hope for the future.

Storytelling held a central place in a community of displaced and entirely illiterate people. In the repertoire of stories were many variations on the exploits of the trickster, transposed from older African tales, as well as new stories thrown up by the turmoil of revolution. Tales of black heroes, like the New Jersey runaway Titus, made thrilling listening for the thousands toiling at menial tasks behind the British lines. Titus made his break from enslavement in November 1775 and somehow managed to get himself attached to the British invasion force in August the following year. By 1779 he was transformed into "Colonel Tye," commander of the Black Brigade, an armed unit that occasionally operated in tandem with the Queen's Rangers. The usual modus operandi of the Black Brigade was banditry and reprisal, in company with some white men from an encampment of Loyalist refugees on Sandy Hook known as "cow boys." In a daring guerrilla raid into New Jersey in June 1780, Colonel Tye captured the captain of the Monmouth militia with twelve men, spiked the four-pound cannon, and stole the artillery horses. In a spectacular raid on the home of the militia leader Josiah Huddy a few months later, Tye received a small flesh wound that led to tetanus and agonizing death. His audacity and heroism remained vivid in black storytelling.[21]

Tye was not the only black recruit to hold the honorific title of colonel, and neither was his Black Brigade the only quasi-military outfit that was rationed, clothed, and sometimes paid by the army. A motley crew known as the Loyal Refugee Volunteers, created by the New Jersey Loyalist Tom Ward, was partly composed of black runaways. One particular unit of black recruits, known as "Ward's Blacks," was stationed at Bergen Point on Staten Island. Formed originally to cut firewood for the garrison, Ward's Blacks increasingly operated as an armed guerrilla force, making raids on the New Jersey shore under the command of their own elected "colonel." When they successfully fought off an attack on their blockhouse by a thousand soldiers of the Continental army led by General Wayne, Ward's Blacks became instant celebrities in New York and a source of stories to sustain and inspire the black community.[22]

Of all the stories told and retold within the community of runaways, perhaps the most pivotal was that of Moses leading the Israelites out of enslavement in Egypt. A significant narrator of this potent story of deliverance from bondage was the prophetically named black preacher who had led his flock from Virginia in 1776. A self-appointed Methodist preacher, the blind and crippled Moses had brilliantly adapted the Wesleyan emphasis on oral communication and spontaneous religious response to create a form of religious expression that could coexist with older African infusions such as conjuring, divination, and sorcery. Moses positioned himself within the fold of the Wesleyan tradition, even though his form of worship was so tainted with "enthusiasm"—a pejorative term referring to extravagant emotional responses, speaking in tongues, visions, spirit-possessed delusions, and trances—that he would not have met with John Wesley's approval. Completely illiterate, Moses appealed to visions to reveal the will of God and divine the sure road to eternal salvation, finding resonance with the African practice of ecstatic soul possession. His highly emotional delivery blended personal experience with renditions of Old Testament stories in the familiar form of call-and-response. A white visitor to one of his meetings was so affected by the intensity of Moses's preaching that he "felt frequently distressed for him . . . his feelings were so exquisite and he worked himself up to such a pitch that I was fearful . . . something would happen to him." His ecstatic preaching had an electrifying effect on his listeners, who might at any time be seized by the spirit. Harry Washington and Isaac Anderson were among his many converts.[23]

Methodists were nominally within the fold of the established Anglican church, so Moses's congregation would also have turned to the clergy of Trinity Church, who had been baptizing black people since the turn of the century, and the Society for the Propagation of the Gospel, which was associated with Trinity. Trinity's proselytizing mission continued unabated during the war; even though the church was a blackened ruin they found other premises to remain an important resource for black runaways in New York wishing to be baptized, or learn to read, or, most important, to have partnerships legitimized by marriage. Mary, who had run away from the Willoughby plantation in Virginia in 1776, may have had a previous relationship with Caesar Perth from Norfolk, who arrived in 1779, but it was in New York that they were able to formally marry and she took the name Mary Perth. Isaac Anderson married a young woman named Sarah, a runaway from Charleston like himself, who came to New York with General Clinton in 1780. A young woman named Miney, who had seized her opportunity to follow the British army on its retreat from Philadelphia in 1778, married Ralph

Henry in New York, and by the time they were evacuated they had a daughter to whom they gave the name Molly Henry.[24]

Love and marriage, music and dancing, stories and prayers: these were the elements that mitigated the separation from kin and softened the challenging business of staying alive in New York.

CHAPTER 3

MARCHING TO CATASTROPHE

In the winter of 1777 Peter Anderson was doing his best to survive in the Virginia woods. Six months earlier he had escaped from the Williamsburg jail, where he had been awaiting execution for carrying arms in Dunmore's Ethiopian Regiment at the battle of Great Bridge. He managed to get to the Chesapeake, only to find that Lord Dunmore had sailed away without him. Terrified to expose himself by going back to his enslaved wife and child, Anderson hid the woods and hoped that the British would soon return. Surrounded by militia and armed slave patrols, he could muster little assistance from the enslaved community, and had scant intelligence about the progress of the war. Throughout the summer, when the forest cover was dense and there was plenty of game, he managed well enough, but now that winter laid the woods bare he was desperately vulnerable. He must have been mightily relieved in January 1777 when British warships again entered the mouth of the James River, as part of a naval blockade of Chesapeake Bay. This time he was able to slip past the slave patrols to be taken on board one of the British ships.[1]

Anderson may well have been with the British fleet that landed 3,500 British troops on the Georgia Coast a few miles below Savannah in December 1778. The commander, Lieutenant-Colonel Archibald Campbell, was keen to have black recruits to work as spies and guides, as well as pioneers for his forces. Scipio Handley, who had also managed a fortuitous escape from execution in Charleston, was certainly with the invasion force. Campbell's men were meant to wait to join forces with troops that were marching from East Florida under General Augustin Prevost, but Campbell decided to attack when intelligence from a black guide, previously enslaved to the exiled royal governor, revealed Savannah's defenses to be severely undermanned. The same guide led Campbell along a hidden path through the swamp that protected the rear of Patriot forces for a surprise attack. In the chaos that followed the rout of the Patriots, white Georgians fled, often leaving their slaves behind, many of whom sought protection from the British. Campbell was able to allocate these recruits as logistical support. A whole company of Black Pioneers was commanded by a South Carolina Loyalist, Angus Campbell, and two or three Black Pioneers were attached to each company of soldiers.[2]

During the subsequent siege of Savannah by French and American forces, 620 black recruits were listed on the British payroll, though many others who were not on the payroll worked as occasional laborers and foragers. The women served as cooks, nurses, laundresses, and servants. In his report of the successful defense of Savannah, General Prevost singled out the contribution of the black recruits, reporting, "They certainly did wonders in the working way and in fighting they really shewed no bad countenence." Scipio Handley's contribution was to make grapeshot in the armory and carry it out to the redoubts. At the height of the siege, he was badly wounded by musket ball in his leg; the wound turned gangrenous and the leg was very nearly amputated. Although his leg eventually healed, Handley was left unfit for further active duty. He continued on the British military establishment till he was evacuated to England in a shipment of wounded soldiers.[3]

David George did not work directly for the British in Savannah; he ran a butcher's stall and his wife did the laundry for the senior British officers. In a detailed account that he gave of his life (much later, when he lived in Sierra Leone), George told how he was born in Virginia about 1740 and when he was nineteen ran away from an exceptionally brutal master. Pursued by his vengeful owner, he had traveled deep into the Georgia backcountry to the territory of the Creek Nation on the Ogeechee River north of Augusta. For several years he lived as a slave among the Creek and then the Natchez, until he was eventually sold to a Scottish trader named George Galphin, who took George to be his personal servant in about 1770. Galphin, who George found to be very kind, ran a large trading post on the river at Silver Bluff. He was a key political figure in the backcountry; in 1775 he was appointed commissioner of Indian Affairs for the Southern District. Galphin had many slaves, some of whom, like Galphin himself, had intermarried with the Creek. At Silver Bluff, George married Phillis, who was herself part Indian, and they had several children. About 1773, George first came in contact with a black man who had been converted to the Baptist faith in the person of "Brother George Liele," who was originally enslaved to Henry Sharpe, the deacon at the Buckhead Creek Church. The white congregation of the church had ordained Liele and Sharpe had freed him to become an itinerant preacher. George knew Liele from his boyhood in Virginia and was so impressed with Liele's Baptist preaching that he persuaded Galphin to allow a local white Baptist preacher to hold a meeting in the mill at Silver Bluff "to hear what the Lord had done" for his people. The next day, George and his wife were among eight people baptized in the mill stream. Two years later, George and Liele established the first black Baptist church at Silver Bluff, with George also ordained as a preacher.

Acutely conscious of his inability to read the scripture, George painfully set about teaching himself. At the trading post lived at least six of Galphin's mixed-race children, and he employed a white teacher to run a school for them. "I used to go to the little children to teach me a, b, c," George recalled. Every night, he would practice what the children told him: "Then I would go to them, again, and ask them if it was right." He worked at it so hard that he found himself reading in his dreams. "I think I learned in my sleep, as readily as when I was awake," he wrote, "and I can now read the Bible, so that what I have in my heart, I can see again in the Scriptures." George was a charismatic preacher and in three years he increased the size of the congregation at Silver Bluff to thirty.[4]

Galphin had been actively encouraging the local Creek Indians to side with the Patriots since 1775, so when Campbell took the town of Augusta early in 1779 he fled from Silver Bluff. David George, his wife, and children were part of a contingent of ninety of Galphin's abandoned slaves who gave themselves up to the British. Campbell first sought to use them to induce Galphin to give them information, and when this tactic yielded some useful intelligence, Campbell decided to send the ninety to Savannah, "to be preserved for Mr Golphin [sic] in case he continued to act the same friendly part toward us." George remembered being kept in prison for about a month until they were liberated by the intervention of Campbell's subordinate officer, Lieutenant-Colonel

Thomas Brown. This man was a Georgia Loyalist who knew the Silver Bluff area well and was familiar with George and his church.[5]

The patronage of Colonel Brown opened doors for George; he was permitted to travel back and forth between the lines as a vendor of provisions to the British outposts established between Savannah and the Savannah River. For a while his partner in this business was his old friend Brother Liele, and they combined the work with itinerant preaching. Together they also established another black Baptist church that incorporated much of their original congregation from Silver Bluff. Unhappily, contact with the British army also brought trauma to the George family. When the siege began they were nearly killed by a cannonball crashing into the stable where they lived. George removed his family to Yamacrow but he carried disaster with them, having already become infected with smallpox. He lay on the brink of death for weeks, but by the time the siege was over he had recovered enough to return to Savannah, where he was issued with a military pass that certified him to be "a free Negro" and "a good subject to King George." With the help of his black congregation he set up a profitable business as a butcher.[6]

Once the British had secured Savannah as a beachhead in the southern colonies, the British commander in chief, General Clinton, decided to mount a full-scale campaign in the South, beginning in South Carolina. Just before the invasion, Clinton published a proclamation on June 30, 1779, calculated to stimulate a wave of slave defections. He promised that no slave who sought refuge would be sold, and that anyone who came over to the British would enjoy "full security to follow within these lines, any occupation which he shall think proper." The effect of Clinton's proclamation was as dramatic as Dunmore's had been, but across a much larger canvas. As a key British officer observed with satisfaction: "Their property we need not seek, it flies to us and famine follows."[7]

The invasion force for South Carolina came mainly from New York. In that large contingent was Harry Washington, as a corporal in a corps of about sixty Black Pioneers with the Royal Artillery Department. Samuel Burke, having recovered his wounds, returned to his native Charleston as a soldier in the Prince of Wales American Regiment. His wife, Hannah, deprived of her house in New York, was forced to accompany him. John Twine came as a soldier in the Volunteers of Ireland.

Part of the force came north from Savannah, including a large company of Black Pioneers under Captain Angus Campbell comprising 186 men, 96 women, and 74 children. Peter Anderson, who had been plucked from his precarious existence in the Virginia woods, was probably part of this unit.[8]

Once they landed in South Carolina, the invading army had no difficulty recruiting laborers, foragers, and nurses from the enslaved population as they prepared to besiege Charleston. From these new defectors, another five hundred were employed by the Engineering Corps to build fortifications. On March 4 a senior British officer requested five hundred blankets and hats for "clothing Negroes." Those who knew the terrain and were willing to act as spies and guides found an enthusiastic welcome. Thomas Johnson was recruited by the notorious Colonel Banastre Tarleton to guide his British Legion on a night march to the strategic crossroads of Monck's Corner on April 14, 1780. He was very lucky to have escaped capture by the Patriots, who had beheaded a fellow black guide and stuck his head on a stake as a warning to runaways. Johnson later claimed to be a free man impressed into service by Tarleton, yet he went on to display great loyalty to his commander. Johnson, his wife, and two children stayed with Tarleton till the bitter end, when the whole family was evacuated to Nova Scotia with the British Legion.[9]

The siege of Charleston began on March 31 and lasted till May 8. After the city fell, runaways poured into the British lines, drawn by the lure of paid work. Cato Perkins, an enslaved man of about forty, was a carpenter and was readily incorporated into a British occupying force desperate for skilled labor. Jack Gordon, a tailor in his late thirties, insisted that he had been given his freedom on the fall of the city. Tailors were in demand to attend to regimental uniforms, so the British authorities were only too happy to take his word for it, as long as he was prepared to work for them. Boston King was a young man in his early twenties who came into Charleston from about forty miles away, where he had been an enslaved carpenter apprenticed to a builder who beat him so savagely that he was temporarily crippled. As King explained in the account of his life he gave in Sierra Leone, his intention had not been to run away when he borrowed a horse in order to visit his parents. The owner of the horse "was a very bad man, and knew not how shew mercy"; when his return was delayed, King knew he was in for another terrible beating. It was then that he decided to go Charleston and throw himself "into the hands of the English." As a skilled artisan, King was received very eagerly. He had also been trained as a valet and groom, so quickly found himself deployed as a batman to a captain of a Loyalist regiment. He recalled his time with the British military as a source of profound pleasure, for all the rigors of military discipline. Of his time with the British army he said, "I began to feel the happiness, liberty, of which I knew nothing before, altho' I was grieved at first, to be obliged to leave my friends, and among strangers."[10]

In May 1781, General Clinton, who was satisfied that South Carolina was returned to the Crown, sailed back to British headquarters with part of his army, leaving Lord Cornwallis in charge of Charleston. Cato Perkins and Jack Gordon were among some five hundred black recruits who accompanied Clinton to New York. A month later Cornwallis decided to march part of his army north, leaving a small British garrison at Charleston. Harry Washington stayed behind as a corporal with the Royal Artillery Department, as did Peter Anderson, in some capacity. Boston King was only too pleased to accompany his captain on the march north. The keen enjoyment that King took in life in the army may have been shared by other black recruits marching north with Cornwallis, although for them the pleasure they took in being free men was tempered by violent trauma. Thomas Johnson took part with Tarleton's British Legion in a bloody encounter with Patriot troops at Waxhaw in May, said to result in a massacre of Patriot forces that triggered brutal reprisals throughout South Carolina. Two months later, Samuel Burke, who was with the Prince of Wales American Regiment, together with John Twine of the Volunteers of Ireland, were engaged in savage fighting at Hanging Rock, just south of Camden, where Burke was credited with killing five Patriot militia. In the melee, the Prince of Wales Regiment was cut to ribbons and Burke was so badly wounded that he expected to die. Twine survived that bloody encounter only to be grievously wounded in the leg in the subsequent battle at Camden. Both men were returned to Charleston to recuperate.

Boston King was spared the bloody terror of those battles when his military career was almost curtailed by an outbreak of smallpox among the black recruits. King was among the afflicted men quarantined by army surgeons a mile away from the main encampment, "lest the soldiers should be infected, and disabled from marching." He endured a terrible time, lying unattended among the dying, without food or water, until a soldier in his regiment bought him food and assistance. Once the disease had run its awful course, wagons were sent to collect the survivors, who numbered only about twenty-five, according to King. They were allowed a period of recuperation in a makeshift hospital before they rejoined the army. It was there that King discovered the soldier who had saved his life, who was seriously wounded at the battle of Camden. He remained behind to nurse the soldier while Cornwallis moved on to North Carolina, and he continued at the Camden garrison as guide and courier for the remaining British forces.[11]

Everywhere Cornwallis's army went, smallpox went too. As he marched through North Carolina, slaveholders lost as much property to smallpox as to defections. Yet this was only one of the infections on the rampage through the British army; typhus and typhoid fever, transmitted by lice in unwashed clothing and stale bed straw, together with dysentery from water contaminated by sewage, killed eight times as many as battle wounds. Even in such a sickly state, the British army on the move presented an awesome sight. Serried ranks of soldiers in smart red uniforms moving in solemn step to the fife and drum, long silk banners fluttering above their heads, made a brilliant spectacle that belied the sordid and unhealthy reality. Enslaved people who had for years been anticipating a force of liberation saw Cornwallis's army, crippled by disease and doomed to disaster though it was, as a harbinger of jubilee. "Upon the approach of any detachment of the Kings troops," Banastre Tarleton observed, "all the negroes, men, women and children . . . quitted the plantations and followed the army." The massive number of runaways in the army's train constituted a small army in itself, albeit one without any tents or blankets and without the disciplined routines that enforced at least a modicum of sanitary practice among the soldiers.[12]

As Cornwallis marched through North Carolina toward Virginia, so General Benedict Arnold was establishing British control of the Lower Chesapeake. Arnold entered Virginia at the beginning of 1781, making his first call at the huge Byrd plantation at Westover on the James River.

The fact that the widow of William Byrd III was his wife's cousin ensured a civil welcome for the turncoat general, even though Arnold was viewed with almost universal distaste by Loyalist and Patriot alike. His duplicity in switching sides was of no consequence to the enslaved servant Wat, who saw in Arnold's army the promise of an independent life. When Mary Byrd loaned her favorite to Arnold to act as a guide, she fully expected that her property would be returned. Wat saw the relationship quite differently. He never came back to Westover, preferring the precarious freedom as a guide for Arnold, and later for Cornwallis, to indulgent enslavement to Mrs. Byrd, even though he had left a wife and children there. At the end of the war, when he was living as a free man in New York with the name Walter Harris, he showed himself indifferent to Mary Byrd's handsome inducements to return.[13]

From Westover, a detachment of Arnold's troops made a foray into Richmond, the town that now served as the seat of government, arriving with an impressive fanfare of drums on January 5, 1781. The governor at the time was Thomas Jefferson, who made his escape by a hair's breadth, galloping away from the town, having already sent his wife and his daughters to safety with several of his most trusted male slaves. According to Isaac, one of the domestic slaves Jefferson left behind, "In ten minutes not a white man was to be seen in Richmond." Isaac was only five years old at the time, but he could already play the drum. His skill must have caught the attention of the British officers, who took Isaac with them when they left to make a sweep of the surrounding area. Returning to Richmond the next day, they again called at Jefferson's house, probably to help themselves to his excellent wine cellar. Isaac's mother was hugely distressed that they intended to take her little boy and leave her. "She was cryin' and hollerin'," Isaac recalled. The commanding officer's response was to take all seven of the women and children at Jefferson's house. Isaac's reminiscences of this episode in his early life were confused, his memory was faulty on several points, but his account of being taken by Arnold's troops is utterly convincing.[14]

Jefferson's close friend James Madison was one of Virginia's delegates to Congress in Philadelphia, where he maintained a lively correspondence with fellow Virginians to keep abreast of developments. His father wrote to tell him that his neighbors around Richmond had lost "some 40 others 30, every one a considerable part of their slaves." Another of Madison's correspondents provided further intelligence that the British had been to Benjamin Harrison's house and "carried away all his valuable Negroes." Although the letter implied that Harrison's slaves had been stolen from him, the evidence suggested voluntary flight. Madison's informant admitted as much by adding that the only real injury the British could inflict was "receiving the Negroes who may run away and join them."[15]

By the time Arnold moved back to Westover, people from around Richmond were besieging the militia for flags of truce so they could recover their property. In response to a request from the militia commander, Arnold indicated that he would return "such Negroes, horses etc," if certain conditions were met. Jefferson sternly refused any conditions that would "discriminate between several species of property"; it should be all or nothing, he insisted. Arnold moved to secure Portsmouth as a naval base with close to three hundred runaways in tow, including seven of Jefferson's slaves. That the British were utilizing vast numbers of fugitive chattel deeply affronted Edmund Pendleton, who reported to Madison that they were "being kept at hard labour upon a short allowance, so as to perish daily." His jaundiced view was not supported by Isaac, who remembered being treated "mighty well" by the British, and given "plenty of fresh meat and wheat bread."[16]

In late March, the British warship HMS *Savage* cruised up the Potomac River, dropping anchor near the plantation belonging to Robert Carter, where, over a period of nine days between March 30 and April 8, thirty-two enslaved people disregarded the personal appeal that Carter had previously made and "put themselves under the care and direction of some officers in the service of Geo: the third king of Great Britain." Curiously, there is no mention of these defecting slaves in the log of the *Savage*. However, farther up the Potomac, when the *Savage* anchored off Mount Vernon on April 12, the log recorded taking on board thirteen "black refugees." Another five refugees were taken from the shore a little north of Mount Vernon on April 15. These eighteen "black refugees" seem to have comprised sixteen enslaved workers of General Washington and another two people enslaved to Lund Washington.[17]

According to an undated list Lund compiled, probably for a claim against the British made in 1783, these people were extremely valuable property, with highly developed skills, who had been with General Washington for many years. They were all single adults, and their desire to escape from the care of the general may have been accelerated by the knowledge that Washington was desperately in need of money and determined to sell off slaves "provided husband and wife, children and parents [were] not separated." Washington had scruples about forcibly selling his slaves, yet he was increasingly keen to "get quit of the Negroes" in as a humane way as Lund could devise. In January 1779, Lund received a hefty sum of cash on the general's account for the sale of six men and three women, having previously explained to the general that two of these women had reacted with incapacitating terror at being wrenched away from their community at Mt. Vernon. While no more people had been sold, Washington was merely biding his time to see "when the tide of depreciation is at an end," having instructed Lund "to ascertain the highest prices Negroes sell in different parts of the country —where, and in what manner it would be best to sell them." No doubt the men and women who sought refuge with the British knew that being sold to persons unknown was a likely prospect.[18]

How Lund explained the loss of so much valuable property to the enemy remains a mystery; the letter to his cousin cannot be found. For his part, Washington was concerned for his loss, but his greater concern was that Lund had supplied the British ship with refreshments in an attempt to prevent the house being burned. In this furious letter to Lund, Washington implied that the British had stolen his property, even though his friend the Marquis de Lafayette had told him quite bluntly, "When the enemy came to your house many Negroes deserted to them." Even as Washington spoke of plantations along the Potomac being "stripped of their Negroes and moveable property," he knew his slaves had left him of their own volition, just as his white indentured servants had done. In his response to the young Frenchman, Washington also chose to apply the verb "deserted" in the place of "taken." Perhaps he remembered what Lund had told him at the time of Dunmore's proclamation: "There is not a man of them, but woud leave us, if they believe'd they could make there escape. . . . Liberty is sweet."[19]

Those sixteen "refugees" may not have been the only chattel of

General Washington to desert in the spring of 1781. A month later, the county of New Kent was hard hit by slave defections to Arnold's army, many of them boys and youths recruited as drummers. Perhaps these recruitments included a boy named Caesar, who subsequently disappeared from the list of taxable slaves on Washington's New Kent estate. The plantation Washington had established in the Great Dismal Swamp was raided on July 21 by soldiers from Cornwallis's army, who took the draft steers, fifty head of cattle, two hundred barrels of corn, all the work implements, and more than half of the enslaved workforce—twenty-one men, one woman, and five children. Another likely runaway was the unnamed slave of Washington valued at sixty-nine pounds who was executed by the Commonwealth of Virginia in 1781. Washington himself never made specific reference to defections to his enemy from any of his estates; doubtless it was a source of acute embarrassment as well as heavy financial loss.[20]

At the end of spring 1781, Cornwallis joined forces with Arnold in Virginia. By the time the two armies merged, the health problems that bedeviled Cornwallis's troops had taken a toll on the army at Portsmouth, where many of the black recruits had been affected by a deadly outbreak of what was called "camp fever," probably typhus. One of Madison's correspondents was able to inform him that in the British encampment at Portsmouth "a fever raged among the Negroes wch. swept off a great number of them." Cornwallis's army added smallpox to the deadly cauldron of infection. Even well-publicized epidemics did nothing to halt the slave exodus. Word was out that the British fed their laborers good rations and paid them wages—not the kind of treatment that enslaved people had ever experienced, even under the paternalistic regime of Jefferson and his circle. Little wonder they continued to take their chances in the disease-ridden British camps.[21]

Despite the sorry state of his soldiers—many reduced to wearing cowhide tied on their feet for shoes—Cornwallis immediately determined to attack the army of the Marquis de Lafayette, encamped near Richmond. Having dislodged Lafayette's forces, Cornwallis continued to pursue them up the James River valley, without managing to engage. Johann Ewald, a senior Hessian officer with the army, was appalled at the size of the army entourage, with thousands of black "followers of the flag." He claimed that every soldier "had his Negro, who carried his provisions," while the officers had "three or four Negroes, as well as one or two Negresses for cook and maid." Instead of a disciplined military force, Ewald thought, Cornwallis's army and its motley entourage resembled "a wandering Arabian or Tartar horde." Every place this variegated horde passed "was eaten clean, like an acre invaded by a swarm of locusts." This ravaging caravan was essential to Cornwallis in order to supply his army. His black recruits proved indispensable, foraging for the hungry forces, driving off livestock, and stripping the fields and storage cellars. They also procured much-needed horses, which they rode bareback in the army's train. In the James River valley alone they took some eight hundred horses, much to the despair of General Lafayette. "Nothing but a treaty of alliance with the Negroes can find us dragoon horses," he moaned to Washington, "and it is by this means the enemy have so formidable a Cavalry."[22]

In early June, Cornwallis set up his headquarters at Elk Hill, one of Thomas Jefferson's plantations on the James River in Goochland County. When he left ten days later, twenty-three people enslaved to Jefferson, including an old woman and sixteen young children, went with him. These defections had the hallmarks of well-planned, premeditated action. People ran from three different plantations: Elk Hill in Goochland County, Willis Creek in Cumberland County, and Monticello, fifty miles to the west in Albemarle County. Soon after, Jefferson recorded the names of the twenty-three in his farm book, noting how they had "fled to the enemy" or "joined the enemy" or simply "run away." Seven years later, however, when Jefferson was in Paris, the story he told was that Cornwallis "carried off also about 30 slaves: had this been to give them freedom he would have done right, but it was to consign them to inevitable death from the small pox and putrid fever then raging in his camp." Jefferson's memory was seriously faulty or he was being wildly disingenuous, since only fifteen of his runaways were known to have died. Moreover, he could only have arrived at the figure of thirty if he had included the seven domestics who went with Arnold's army from Richmond to Portsmouth. All of these people were returned to him the summer of 1781.[23]

Isaac remembered that the others from Richmond were repatriated to Jefferson as a result of intervention by the American commander in chief. "General Washington brought all Mr. Jefferson's folks . . . back to Richmond with him and sent word to Mr. Jefferson to send down to Richmond for his servants," Isaac recalled. "Old Master sent down two wagons right away." General Washington could not have been involved, as he was not in Virginia at that time, but General Lafayette, who also featured in Isaac's reminiscence, may have intervened on Jefferson's behalf. Among the thousand or so runaways who had congregated in Portsmouth at that time were many women with small children, or men too enfeebled for the labor that Cornwallis required. He agreed that those who could be spared and were willing to return could be repatriated to the Virginia gentry that had been besieging him with requests for their property. Isaac thought this happened after Cornwallis's surrender, but his description of the transfer to Monticello suggests that it happened in July, just before Cornwallis moved the bulk of his forces to the York River to fortify the towns of Little York (later known as Yorktown) and Gloucester as the British base for the southern campaign. Jefferson himself never made any reference to his domestic servants' leaving, or their returning, even though they were the enslaved people most intimately involved with his family and for whom he had a high regard. The meticulous entries in the farm book and his memorandum books are silent about their absence over a six-month period. Perhaps he could not face the awful possibility that they had deserted him.[24]

Jefferson had not inoculated his enslaved workers, so Isaac and his group were lucky to have been at the garrison in Portsmouth, where there was a regime of inoculation in place. Contact with the British army camped at Elk Hill proved to be personally devastating for the enslaved community and financially ruinous for Jefferson. Five of the workers left at the Elk Hill plantation died from smallpox soon after Cornwallis departed. As his army marched eastward, the disease spread rapidly among the fresh black recruits. Pursuing American soldiers reported finding a trail of discarded bodies in the army's wake, "infecting the air about with intolerable stench and great danger." Very probably, the majority of Jefferson's runaways died before they even reached Portsmouth. Jefferson's notes in his farm book grimly recorded their fate, which was, in many ways, indicative of the disaster that would overwhelm Cornwallis within a few months.[25]

By August 1781, Cornwallis was employing several thousand black runaways to assist in fortifying Yorktown and Gloucester. All able-bodied men, white and black, were required to construct a series of re-doubts, but even with all hands Cornwallis was short of labor. Neither could he obtain more black recruits from Portsmouth. Calamity was carried into that garrison in late July when "above 700 Negroes [came] down the river in the small pox." The commander at Portsmouth, Charles O'Hara, reported that they could spare only fifty healthy work-ers, "with hundreds of wretched Negroes dying by scores every day." Forced to concentrate his resources in one place, Cornwallis ordered the evacuation of Portsmouth, which created a terrible dilemma about what to do with the many sick and dying. "[It] is shocking to think about the state of those Negroes," Cornwallis wrote to O'Hara, "but we cannot bring a number of sick and useless ones to this place; some flour must be left for them and some person of the country appointed to take charge of them to prevent their perishing." Faced with about a thousand sick runaways, O'Hara was greatly distressed by this directive. To abandon "these unfortunate beings, to disease, to famine, and what is worse than either, to the resentment of their enraged masters . . . ought not be done, if it is possibly avoided, or in as small a degree as the case will admit," he begged. Cornwallis remained adamant: those with smallpox must not come to Yorktown to use up rapidly diminishing food supplies and spread infection among the healthy. When Portsmouth was evacuated, O'Hara took about four hundred runaways to Yorktown, leaving many more contaminated with smallpox with provisions for fifteen days, which, he judged, was the time it would take to "either kill or cure the greatest number of them."[26]

The influx of people from Portsmouth put a terrible strain on the scant supplies available at Yorktown, where the troops had become weakened by the hard labor of building fortifications and an inadequate diet of "putrid ships meat and wormy biscuits." In early September, bloodletting by the surgeons revealed that everyone's blood was pink, a sure sign of anemia. Before long almost a quarter of the troops were ill with typhoid fever. There was no possibility of getting any fresh food supplies. To compound the health problems, the horror Cornwallis had sought to avoid at Yorktown erupted in a smallpox epidemic among the white Loyalist refugees and black recruits, by which time the British were hemmed in by a powerful French and American force, blockaded by the French fleet and facing a combined army of nearly 16,000, with only 3,500 men fit for duty.[27]

Once the forty-one siege cannons opened fire on October 9, the night sky above Yorktown became a brilliant spectacle, with the fiery tails of dozens of cannonballs streaking through the darkness. Behind the battered defenses terrified civilians huddled under the cliff face at the edge of the river, seeking shelter from the rain of cannon fire, while Cornwallis was forced to move his headquarters into a cave. The place was a scene of carnage, with ships sunk in the river, houses on fire, piles of mutilated bodies, and scattered body parts. Hundreds were dead. There was no food. A forage party had been able to locate only burned corn. Although General Clinton had promised to send an army and the navy to relieve him, Cornwallis despaired of any assistance from his unreliable commander in chief. Even a partial retreat was unlikely to succeed. St. George Tucker, an officer in the French-American camp, found a British journal washed ashore, which read, "Our provisions are now almost exhausted and our ammunition totally."[28]

On October 14, 1781, Cornwallis ordered the horses to be slaughtered and dragged into the river, where their bloated carcasses drifted back with the tide, bumping against the shattered hulks of British ships. Having already sent out of Yorktown those sick with smallpox, he now expelled a large group of runaways from the hospital on the opposite shore at Gloucester, with what pitiful rations could be found. Ewald, who was stationed at Gloucester, thought this a "harsh act" toward black recruits who had served them well, but then the Hessian officer still expected that Cornwallis would somehow succeed at Yorktown. His lordship was not so sanguine; he knew he had no options but to send those people out to fend for themselves. Early on the morning of October 15, Cornwallis sent a message in cipher to General Clinton: "My situation now becomes very critical ... the safety of the place is therefore so precarious I cannot recommend that the fleet and army should run great risque in endeavouring to save us." When a desperate attempt to retreat across the river to Gloucester on the night of October 16 was ruined by a freak storm, Cornwallis could no longer delay the inevitable capitulation.[29]

The booming of cannon, the roar of fire, the screams of pain, the

stench of death, and the sight of terrified runaways disfigured by smallpox being expelled from the garrison must have made an indelible impression on Thomas Johnson and Walter Harris, the black guides who
managed to survive the horror. Isaac Jefferson was almost certainly not
at Yorktown; he must have heard about the siege from a survivor who
returned to Monticello. The story made such a profound impact on the
small boy that in his old age his recall of events was so vivid that he believed he had been there. The punishing bombardment from siege cannon sounded "like heaven and earth was come together," Isaac said, and
after the booming of the cannon came the pitiful cries of men in agony.[30]

At dawn on October 17 a frightful cannon assault blasted Yorktown.
There was no answering fire; the British ammunition was exhausted.
At ten o'clock that morning, a drummer boy appeared on the ramparts
of Yorktown, beating a tattoo that could barely be heard over the pounding cannon, and accompanied by an officer holding aloft a white hand-
kerchief. He was blindfolded and escorted to the Patriot headquarters,
where he presented Washington with Cornwallis's request for twenty-
four hours' cessation of hostilities so the commanders might agree upon
terms of surrender. Washington saw no need to be indulgent. He gave
Cornwallis two hours to "surrender himself and his forces prisoner,"
after which "time would be allowed to settle the terms." That night an
uncanny silence fell on Yorktown as the siege cannons shut down. The
only reminder of the horror of the siege was a trail of fireworks from two
meteors that shot across the starlit sky. At dawn, pipers from the British camp signaled the surrender. After an eerie few minutes the band
of a French regiment struck up to send a reply from Washington's
camp. When the sun rose and the cannon smoke cleared, the besieging
army could see for the first time the full disaster at Yorktown. "How vain
the hope of such a place," the shocked St. George Tucker wrote in his
journal.[31]

No one will ever know just how many runaways fled Yorktown before
the fateful day on October 19 when the humiliated British army marched
out to a solemn drumbeat, dressed in smart new uniforms but with their
colors furled and the drums covered with black handkerchiefs. In asking
for time to discuss terms, Cornwallis fully expected to negotiate with
Washington to take his army back to England. In the face of Washing-

ton's stern intransigence, all he could hope for was "good treatment during their captivity." He could ask nothing for thousands of fugitive slaves who had joined him; they would have to look out for themselves as best they could. Reports from the French-American camp spoke of seeing "herds of Negroes" in the woods, and on entering Yorktown the victors found the place littered with the "sick and dying in every stage of small pox." After such a long and brutal war, Cornwallis's hope of decent treatment was in vain. The postsurrender environment was savage, with no compassion on offer. Within the battered garrison the wounded and sick "died like flies," Ewald reported, because they were left without medicine or food. Amputated arms and legs lying on the bloodied ground were eaten by the dogs. "All hearts had turned to stone," Ewald sorrowfully recalled. "There was neither consolation nor money to be found and everyone was left to his own fate."[32]

Cornwallis was known to have four or five thousand black recruits at Yorktown and Portsmouth. Smallpox killed about 60 percent of those that caught the disease, but in this case some were inoculated against it, so perhaps half the runaways were spared, though wounds and typhus also took a huge toll. Maybe two thousand survived. It is impossible to establish what happened to them. A proportion of the survivors, perhaps half, must have been forced back into slavery. At the time of surrender, members of the Continental army competed with the French forces to lay claim to people who had come out of Yorktown. In late October, Washington had to issue orders to regulate what was becoming a free-for-all, especially for the French. Many runaways would have known that France was not a slave society and so attached themselves to the French army, as they had to the British, to avoid reenslavement. "We gained a veritable harvest of domestics," one happy French officer revealed.[33]

The articles of capitulation stipulated that Americans could recover their property from Yorktown, and to facilitate this Washington gave orders that all captured runaways were to be given over to a designated officer until claimed. Advertisements were placed in southern newspapers. Numerous slave owners reported that they were able recover all or part of the property that they had lost, from Portsmouth and from Yorktown. Washington himself was able to recover two of the young women who had run off from Mount Vernon, although the rest of his runaway slaves eluded him. Washington had prudently inoculated his slaves at Mount Vernon and at the plantation at New Kent, thereby giving them a good chance of surviving Yorktown. Most of the runaways from Mount Vernon avoided capture and escaped northward to Philadelphia, while others were taken to New York.[34]

Jefferson employed an agent to recover five survivors from Yorktown and return them to Elk Hill and Monticello. Perhaps Jefferson thought these people had been infected by their exposure to freedom as much as their exposure to smallpox and were no longer fit members of his enslaved family. Robin was sold almost immediately after he returned to Monticello in January 1782, while Will, who presumably told Isaac about the horrors of Yorktown, was sold in 1790. Nat and Judy were returned to Elk Hill and were subsequently sold at auction on January 31, 1785, while the surviving child, Isabel, was given to Jefferson's sister in 1786. When he claimed they were dead as the result of British perfidy, Jefferson suppressed the knowledge that they were sold off or given away on his own instruction. There were also three people for whom Jefferson could not account, but he did not believe them dead, because he made no note concerning their fate in the farm book; neither did he lodge a claim for the loss of them in January 1783. Perhaps he had hopes for their "salvage."[35]

Numbers of runaways from Yorktown were subject to "salvage" in the city of Philadelphia, undoubtedly having gone with the French army, knowing that Pennsylvania was in the process of emancipating its slaves. They may not have known that the legislation to abolish slavery enacted in Philadelphia in 1780 made exception for the property of members of Congress and other officials. In July 1782 Governor Harrison requested the Virginia delegates to Congress to use their influence so that fugitive slaves with the French could be reclaimed when the army was in Philadelphia. James Madison, as a Virginia delegate to Congress, sought to recover the runaway slave of Edmund Pendleton's nephew, who was known to be with the French army, and another Virginia delegate to Congress tracked down the chattel of St. George Tucker, who had escaped north with the French. The exception to the law also worked for George Washington, whose agent in Philadelphia was able to salvage four valuable men, as well as his overseer, who was the most valuable of all. There were others of Washington's runaways who made it to safety behind the British lines in New York. Almost certainly they went by British ship.[36]

The articles of capitulation at Yorktown insisted that nearly nine thousand soldiers and sailors were kept in Virginia as prisoners of war but permitted the Royal Navy to take paroled British and Hessian officers to New York. The warship HMS *Bonetta* was also allowed to sail immediately for New York with Cornwallis's dispatches and any officers he chose to send. From the moment the surrender was complete, guards were placed along the shore to stop runaways getting out to the ship, although it was feared that many were already hidden on board. The governor of Virginia wrote to Cornwallis, "Negroes are attempting to make their escape by getting aboard the *Bonetta* . . . [where] they will endeavour to lie concealed from your Lordship till the vessel sails." Washington too was deeply suspicious about the *Bonetta*, but he had given his word that the ship could sail without examination, so he had to grimly accept that runaways concealed aboard would evade capture, even though some were likely to be his own property.[37]

Whatever answer Cornwallis gave the governor, he was perfectly well aware of the runaways on board the *Bonetta*, as they were there at his direction. Thomas Johnson, the guide with Tarleton's British Legion, was on board with his wife and children, having made himself especially obnoxious to the Patriots for his part in the defeat at Moncks Corner in South Carolina. At the surrender, one of Washington's generals had made a specific request for Johnson, and had Cornwallis not hidden him aboard the *Bonetta* he would have had a similar fate to the black guide who was beheaded. Another man on the *Bonetta* who ran the same risk as Johnson was Mrs. Byrd's serving man, Wat. They knew they were lucky to be getting out, but from the grim despair of the officers they could guess that the British would never return to Virginia and that their past life was irrevocably lost. What kind of life lay ahead they could not possibly know.[38]

CHAPTER 4

FLEEING THE
FOUNDING FATHERS

The shocking news from Yorktown that Cornwallis had lost the campaign for the South came as a terrible blow to runaways sheltering behind the British lines in New York. Now there was no way they could be reunited with family left behind in the southern colonies except to return as fugitive slaves and face the awful consequences. Boston King already had intimation that the South would be lost when, six months earlier, his garrison in South Carolina was overrun by Patriot forces. King secured a berth on a British privateer that took him to New York, where he joined an anxious mass of Loyalist refugees flooding into the British zone, desperate to escape retribution now that the Patriots had caught the scent of victory. King found that it was not easy to eke out a living among this crush of people. He was a carpenter, but he had no tools; he went into service only to find that his employers had no capacity to pay him; the odd jobs about the city were insufficient to support him once he had married Violet, a runaway from North Carolina. In desperation, he took the dangerous job of a river pilot. One fateful day he was swept out to sea, where he lingered for eight days on the brink of starvation until he was captured by a Patriot vessel. He was taken to New Jersey and sold into slavery as a prize.[1]

About the same time as King found himself enslaved once again, the British government granted independence to the American colonies and opened negotiations for peace. The man charged with negotiating the changed circumstances was Sir Guy Carleton, who arrived in New York in May 1782, having been appointed commander in chief. When he had accepted the post, he had not calculated that within a month there would be a complete reversal of policy. His job, it transpired, was to supervise a wholesale evacuation of British forces from the independent United States. It was "not a matter of choice," he advised the commander in Charleston, General Leslie, "but a deplorable necessity in consequence of an unsuccessful war." The British garrisons in the South would be first to go, Leslie was told.[2]

In Georgia, the savage internecine warfare in the backcountry had turned in favor of the Patriots, leaving Savannah isolated and vulnerable. For the black Baptist preacher David George, life was becoming increasingly fraught. His fellow preacher, George Liele, was taken into custody when his former master died and the heirs disputed the manumission. Although Liele was released after the intervention of a British officer, this unpleasant turn of events made David George nervous. Using the profit from his butcher's stall in Savannah, he took his family to Charleston. He left not a moment too soon.[3]

Carleton ordered the evacuation of Savannah in May, though it was not until July that sufficient shipping was available to take Loyalist refugees, the Loyalist regiments, and some Hessian regiments to the British colony of East Florida. Officials and regular army regiments went either to Jamaica or New York. Acutely conscious of the shortage of transportation, General Leslie instructed civil departments not to evacuate runaways who had worked for them during the occupation; likewise, he tried to restrain his officers from taking their black servants. No one paid him much heed. Close bonds over the previous five or six years proved hard to sunder. Numerous runaways accompanied the evacuated army to New York and East Florida. The redoubtable Scipio Handley, who had escaped hanging in Charleston and survived gangrene in his leg after the siege of Savannah, was evacuated to England with the wounded and discharged men.[4]

David George avoided the traumatic evacuation of Savannah by moving north to Charleston. It gained him only a small amount of time, as Charleston was also scheduled for evacuation. In undertaking an unanticipated evacuation of his army, plus thousands of Loyalist refugees, Leslie had to grapple yet again with the thorny question of the runaways. Confronted with a catastrophic defeat, Leslie could not be expected to be responsible for the runaway slaves who had gambled with their future in taking refuge with the king's men. The gamble was lost. All he needed to do was leave them behind, as the new governor of South Carolina, John Mathews, demanded. Mathews threatened that South

Carolina would default on its massive British debts if any runaways were taken. At the same time, there were powerful contrary forces at work on Leslie. Every time he walked abroad, he confronted the anxious, expectant faces of people who had taken monumental risks in their alliance with the British and were not prepared to passively submit to reenslavement. In such an emotionally charged environment, Leslie found the expedient of leaving the runaways behind morally unsustainable, especially since it was demanded by a colonial upstart who failed to show him proper deference. A contest with Governor Mathews over the fate of runaways permitted this humiliated British general a show of moral superiority. Weighing up the situation, Leslie advised his commander in chief, "Those who have voluntarily come in under the faith of our protection, cannot in justice be abandoned to the merciless resentment of their former masters." Carleton was of the same mind. "Such that have been promised their freedom, to have it," he instructed.[5]

Throughout November until the final evacuation on December 14, 1782, hundreds of runaways queued to be interviewed by the board Leslie had established to determine who could be permitted to leave. Slave owners, keen to retrieve their property, tried desperately to coax them away. "I used every argument I was master of to get them to return," one South Carolina planter wrote, but such arguments had no good effect. Harry Washington had no difficulty proving his eligibility for a certificate of freedom, as he had been working for the Royal Artillery Department since 1776. As in Savannah, civil departments were unwilling to rend the long association that had been fostered with runaways. "Every department and every officer," General Leslie testily observed to Carleton, "wishes to include his slave in the number to be bought off— they pretend them to be spys, or guides, and of course obnoxious, or under promises of freedom." The board also cleared David George, who chose to go to Nova Scotia on November 19, 1782, delighted to find that people passed by the board received their passage for nothing. Patriots later bitterly complained to Carleton that the board had declared obnoxious "almost every Negro, man, woman and child, that was worth carrying away." Loyalists were also disgruntled, withdrawing from the board in protest at so many runaways being given certificates of freedom.[6]

Harry Washington left Charleston in the final evacuation, on the very largest fleet that took the Royal Artillery Department, as well as British, German, and Loyalist regiments, to New York. Another large fleet took discharged and wounded soldiers to England. John Twine, the deserter from Virginia who had been wounded in the thigh at Camden, was still with Lord Rawdon's Volunteers of Ireland. As luck had it, this provincial regiment had been transferred to the regular military establishment, possibly because it was largely made up of American deserters. So, Twine and his wife, Hannah, were put aboard a second fleet destined for Spithead, England, as was Samuel Burke, who had been grievously wounded at Hanging Rock and was also traveling with his wife, Hannah. Another in the fleet for England was the resourceful Peter Anderson, still alive after his miraculous escape from jail in Virginia. Some runaways chose to stay in Charleston rather than face uncertain exile; having been paid wages by the British, some were able to buy their freedom. Others had no choice at all. Left behind were many of the black laborers employed in the final evacuation who had been taken from sequestered estates and were not deemed eligible for certificates of freedom.[7]

No record was kept of how many runaways were evacuated from Charleston. John Cruden, who was the officer in charge of the sequestered estates, estimated that the board cleared "upward of 300," a very conservative estimate that did not include some 200 who had previously been sent to Nova Scotia and East Florida, more than 40 who went to Jamaica with the army, or 250 newly recruited soldiers who were sent to St. Lucia in the Windward Islands with their families. Sailors with the Royal Navy also left without being cleared by the board. Scattered evidence of embarkation and arrivals in the British archives suggests that between 7,000 and 8,000 blacks left Charleston. The great majority of these were people enslaved to departing Loyalists, with about 15 percent, some 1,500 people, going as free people in one capacity or another, be it indentured servant, cook, soldier, seaman, or free settler.[8]

At the same time that Charleston was being evacuated, a provisional peace treaty was being hammered out between the British and the Americans in Paris. The day the treaty was signed, November 29, 1782, a hastily written amendment was scribbled in the margin of Article Seven, to prohibit "carrying away any Negroes or other property of the Ameri-

can Inhabitants." According to John Adams, one of the American negotiators, the clause was inserted at the insistence of Henry Laurens, who
had joined the negotiating team on the very last day, when the commissioners were finalizing the business at the house of the chief British
negotiator, Richard Oswald. In view of Laurens's fleeting connection
with the peace process, it was remarkable that Oswald accepted the last-
minute change without dispute. Up to that point the contentious issue
had been fishing rights. None of the three other American negotiators
had thought it necessary to include a clause about runaways, and John
Jay later admitted that he was surprised the British had agreed.[9]

Oswald's acquiescence to this hasty inclusion owed more to friendship and his financial entanglements in South Carolina than to diplomatic pressure. Laurens considered Oswald as his "very worthy friend."
When Laurens was captured at sea and imprisoned in the Tower of London, it was Oswald who furnished the bail for his release in 1782. Before
the war, Oswald owned a slave factory on Bance Island, in the mouth of
the Sierra Leone River in West Africa, with Laurens acting as agent for
his slave cargo in Charleston. After the war, Oswald intended to become
a plantation owner in South Carolina, transferring slaves he owned in
East Florida onto land owned by Laurens and which Laurens was in the
process of transferring to Oswald's name. Laurens's close friend John
Lewis Gervais was deeply in debt to the British negotiator for the many
slaves he had purchased on credit. He was also the Carolinian who lost
the largest number of enslaved people to the British. When Laurens
wrote to Gervais to remind him of his debt, he was careful to stress how
much gratitude was owed "our dear friend Mr Oswald."[10]

By the time news of a treaty with a prohibition on "carrying away any
Negroes" reached America, David George and his family were safely beyond reach of the treaty provisions in Halifax, Nova Scotia, as were those
en route to England. Harry Washington, who had been transferred to
New York, was in a very vulnerable position, as were the four thousand
black allies behind the British lines. As Boston King recalled, the news
"diffused universal joy among all parties; except us, who had escaped
from slavery and taken refuge in the English army." Promises of freedom
made by successive British commanders had been contingent on the
British winning the war and retaining control of the colonies. Now that

the British government had conceded the American colonies and signed a treaty that prohibited them from taking runaways out of America, those promises could not be considered binding. Unless the black allies behind the British lines had papers of emancipation, as very few did, they might expect to be returned to enslavement in perpetuity, for themselves, their children, and their children's children.

Boston King knew better than most that however difficult a life of freedom, it could never be willingly exchanged for the apparent security of enslavement. When he found himself again a slave in New Jersey, King was agreeably surprised at his good treatment, which was in sharp contrast to the brutal exploitation he had endured in South Carolina. Enslaved people in the northern colonies, he observed, had "as good victuals as many of the English; for they have meat once a day, and milk for breakfast and supper." Better yet, "the masters send their slaves to school at night, that they may learn to read the Scriptures," which was, King felt, "a privilege indeed." But, however comfortable and well nourished he was, he said, "These enjoyments could not satisfy me without liberty." He had seen the cruel punishment meted out to a runaway captured by the Patriots who escaped. The boy was brought back "tied . . . to the tail of a horse," then confined with his feet and hands in the stocks. This was a terrifying sight for King as he contemplated his own escape, yet he was compelled to make a break for freedom. On his walks about he had noticed a river crossing where one could wade across at low tide, although there were guards posted to prevent the escape of prisoners and slaves. Praying that the Lord would deliver him, King slipped past distracted guards just after midnight and crossed the river. He made his way to Staten Island, where a British officer gave him a pass to rejoin his family in Manhattan.[11]

King returned to a city in turmoil and the black community consumed with dread. The terms of the peace treaty had just become known, and rumors that the British would be obliged to abandon thousands of black refugees filled them "with inexpressible anguish and terror." Some runaways, fearing the worst, were prepared to negotiate a return to their past owners, so long as there was no retribution. It was under these terms that Frank Griffin agreed to go to New Jersey with his former master, on the condition that Duryee would employ Griffin's emancipated wife, Dinah, for wages. Still uneasy about the deal he had struck, Griffin judiciously requested that the British mayor provide a pass to allow him to reenter the city.[12]

By March 1783, Patriot slave owners came into the city freely, mingling with Loyalists in the streets of Manhattan. According to a Hessian officer, "Almost five thousand persons have come into this city to take possession again of their former property." His figure may have been exaggerated, but there can be no doubt that a great many slave owners gained entry into the British zone to recover their property. Some, like the mistress of Westover, were prepared to offer generous inducements to runaways. Mrs. Byrd promised Walter Harris that she would overlook his blatant disloyalty and offered a "handsome" reward if he would return to Westover and bring her other runaways with him. His family was most anxious to see him, she told Harris, and he could "rely on the best usage." Her offer fell on deaf ears. Instead of returning to Virginia, Harris got a berth on a ship bound for England.[13]

This attachment to personal liberty was not something Patriots appreciated in their chattel. A slave agent employed by a Virginia delegate to Congress reported that the runaways in New York were "vastly altered for the worse." He thought that the experience of freedom had so devalued the property that he would "scarcely accept one of them as a gift." His view did nothing to diminish the determination of slave owners to reclaim their property. Boston King was in paroxysms of fear at the sight of "our old masters coming from Virginia, North Carolina, and other parts, and seizing upon their slaves in the streets of New York, or even dragging them out of their beds." Without warning, runaways could find themselves knocked on the head, bound hand and foot, and kidnapped and taken back to the place they had fled.[14]

Frank Griffin found that reenslavement in New Jersey was unacceptable, and he used his pass to return to New York. His putative master did not take no for an answer, however. He was arrested in the act of kidnapping Griffin, having tied a rope around his neck and dragged him on board a sloop. Two weeks later, Frank Griffin, his wife, and their baby daughter were evacuated to Nova Scotia. Griffin's liberator was an armed runaway known as Colonel Cuff, who may have belonged to Ward's Blacks, where the honorific of "Colonel" was bestowed on those in positions of authority. If so, Colonel Cuff's intervention was part of a pattern of retributive action against slave owners by members of that unit. A year before, eight members of Ward's Blacks were on trial for the murder of a slave owner whom they had summarily executed as he was returning to New Jersey from New York. According to evidence given at the trial, this was no random act of violence. The executed man claimed ownership of one of the accused, and his business in New York was to sell that man's enslaved wife. Evidence at the trial suggested that Major Ward was complicit in the execution and had supplied the intelligence about the movements of the victim. Ward explained that his black recruits were allowed to carry arms and go on patrols "usually under command of some white person," and that murder was out of character for these men, who were always well disciplined and well behaved. He was exonerated. Six of the accused were found guilty and sentenced to death. Carleton must have had some sympathy for the condemned in this case, as he commuted their death sentences and sent them to the Caribbean as soldiers.[15]

Though few runaways behind the British lines were prepared to take such violent action, they still refused to submit to reenslavement passively. After having experienced years of freedom, they were horrified at the prospect of being turned over to their former masters. They vehemently refused "to be delivered in so unwarrantable a manner," so a Hessian officer noted in his diary. "They insist on their rights under the proclamation." It was an anguishing time for Boston King, fresh from his encounter with slavery in New Jersey, who recalled, "We lost our appetite for food, and sleep departed from our eyes." Day and night they pressed their case with the British authorities to make good the promises of freedom and remove them from the reach of their vengeful masters. Fortunately the British commander in chief lent a willing ear to their pleas. Carleton found the handover of the American colonies a repugnant duty that he undertook with as much dignity as he could summon; he steadfastly refused to renege on a debt of honor with regard to the proclamations of his predecessors. He was simply not prepared to meet the terms of Article Seven of the peace treaty. From the moment the terms became known, in late March 1783, Carleton asserted his own interpretation of the words "Negroes and other property of the American inhabitants."[16]

As soon as the spring thaw began, he sent to Nova Scotia a fleet carrying some five thousand refugees, including an unknown number of runaways. By the time the fleet had sailed, he was assaulted by a cacophony of protest from state governors, delegates in Congress, and slave-owning individuals. "They mean to make a clamour about the evacuation of New York," he told the secretary of state in England. Carleton instructed his officers that any black allies that had been within the British lines for a year or more were to be issued with a certificate of freedom. He then appointed commissioners from both the British and American forces to supervise the embarkation to ensure that no one without evidence of free status was allowed to depart.[17]

John Willoughby, whose entire slave estate had run to Lord Dunmore, was greatly alarmed by this flagrant violation of the treaty, and he and other prominent Virginians petitioned Congress to stop the embarkation runaways. The governor of Virginia, Benjamin Harrison, went one better; he complained directly to George Washington, who wrote back, "I have but little expectation that many will be recovered; several of my own are with the enemy, but I scarce ever bestowed a thought on them; they have so many doors through which they can escape from New York." Washington bestowed more thought on his own runaways than his letter to Harrison implied. He was keen to have his property returned, just as those who escaped to Philadelphia had been. In early May 1783, Lund Washington requested help for a friend going to New York to look for his runaway slaves "and any of the General's" who needed assistance from someone who knew "the proper mode" of recapturing runaways behind the British lines. Such a person was the army contractor Daniel Parker, whom the general had already asked to keep an eye out for his lost property. "I am unable to give you their descriptions; their names being so easily changed, will be fruitless to give you," he told Parker. "If by chance you should come at the knowledge of any of them, I will be much obliged by your securing them so I may obtain them again." He also forwarded a list of Harrison's runaways, together with those of his cousin, Lund.[18]

The choice of Parker was strategic. The army contractor had done personal errands for Washington in the past; on this matter he was uniquely positioned to help. Only a week before Washington wrote to ask this favor of the army contractor, Carleton had chosen Parker to be one of the American commissioners appointed to inspect all embarkations and report any infraction of the treaty. In his capacity as American commissioner, Parker inspected all but two of the ships in the evacuation fleet that sailed on April 27, 1783. In his capacity as his general's slave catcher, Parker proved impotent. His signature was on the bottom of a list of the names of 382 men, 230 women, and 48 children who were able to demonstrate to the satisfaction of the British inspectors that they were leaving America as free people or, in a few instances, were the property of departing Loyalists. One of those on the list allowed to leave on the ship *Polly* bound for Nova Scotia was Deborah, a twenty-year-old runaway from Washington's Mount Vernon estate, traveling with her husband, Harry Squash (Quash), said to be the property of a white Loyalist, though she was registered as free.

The certificates of freedom were signed by Brigadier General Samuel Birch, commandant of the New York garrison, and typically stated that the bearer had "reported to the British lines in consequence of the proclamations of Sir William Howe and Sir Henry Clinton" and therefore had permission to "go to Nova Scotia or anywhere else he may think proper." Even with all the best intentions, the process of issuing certificates to thousands of runaways who had first to be interrogated about their personal history was chaotic and time consuming. The terror and apprehension that Boston King witnessed drove many to take their chances in embarking for Nova Scotia before they received certificates. The majority of people who sailed in the fleet on April 28 did not carry General Birch's certificate. They traveled under the protection of departing Loyalists and offered the commissioners various explanations as to their status. The story given by Jack Gordon, who was embarked on the *Polly*, was that his master had given him freedom at the siege of Charleston, though he had no papers to prove it. Isaac Anderson, embarked on the *Baker and Atlee*, claimed to have been born free in Charleston, and his wife, Sarah, explained that her master in Charleston had died five years earlier. For Anderson's old Charleston friend William Ashe, on the *Providence* with his wife, Mary, and their daughter, it was enough that he and his family had been with the British for eight years.[19]

A week after the fleet left for Nova Scotia, Carleton and his en-

tourage sailed up the Hudson River to Orangetown for a conference
with General Washington to discuss the evacuation. As the victorious
commander, Washington opened the meeting by reiterating the resolution of Congress regarding "the delivery of all Negroes and other property." In response, the defeated Carleton indicated that in his desire for
a speedy evacuation he had already sent off some six thousand refugees,
including "a number of Negroes." Presumably Washington knew this;
Daniel Parker would have informed him that the fleet that sailed in late
April took hundreds of runaways, including a woman Washington
claimed as his own property. If Washington did know, he was at pains
not let it show. Observers from both sides noted the general's consternation as he remonstrated with Carleton that the action was against the express stipulation of the treaty. Calmly, Carleton offered an unapologetic
explanation, saying that in his interpretation, the term *property* meant
property owned by Americans at the time the treaty was signed, so did
not include those who had responded to British proclamations years before. Never would the British government have agreed "to reduce themselves to the necessity of violating their faith to the Negroes," he told
Washington. Warming to his subject, he further insisted, "Delivering up
Negroes to their former masters ... would be a dishonourable violation
of the public faith." In the unlikely event that the British government
put a different construction on the treaty, he promised compensation
would be paid to the owners, and to this end he had directed "a register
be kept of all the Negroes who were sent off." Protesting as he was bound
to do, Washington understood the depth of feeling behind the words
"dishonourable violation of the public faith." By the time the meeting
came to its inconclusive end, he had privately conceded defeat.[20]

That night, Washington sat at his desk and wrote to the governor
of Virginia: "The slaves which have absconded from their masters will
never be restored to them." Whatever his private feelings on the matter,
Washington was determined to follow through on his instructions from
Congress to prevent the removal of runaways. In a second letter he reiterated his position to Carleton, in expectation of a meeting at dinner
the following night. Carleton did not attend the expensive meal that
Washington had provided, pleading illness. Having taken to his bed
with fever, Carleton had a brief private meeting with Washington in his

cabin. His written response arrived a week later. "I had no reason to think the embarkation or any circumstances attending it could have been a matter of surprise to Your Excellency," Carleton wrote in icy prose. "The Negroes in question, I have already said, I found free when I arrived at New York, I had therefore no right, as I thought, to prevent their going to any part of the world they thought proper." Should Washington fail to comprehend his intransigence on this point, he added a thinly veiled warning: "I must confess the mere supposition that the King's minister could deliberately stipulate in a treaty, an engagement to be guilty of the notorious breach of public faith towards people of any complexion, seems to denote a less friendly disposition than I would wish, and, I think, less friendly than we might expect." Washington was right to have conceded that the case for Article Seven was lost.[21]

The delegates to Congress from Virginia and South Carolina were incensed. James Madison sent the news to Thomas Jefferson, describing Carleton's interpretation of the treaty as "a palpable and scandalous misconstruction." There was little the delegates could do by way of retaliation, for fear that any action would reignite hostilities. Congress was so impoverished and so weak that no enemy need be afraid of insulting them, a delegate from South Carolina fumed. The best the delegates could do was to remonstrate. Carleton remained unperturbed, forwarding the protests from Congress to the secretary of state, with similar resolutions from the governors of New York and New Jersey. Among the letters that Carleton dutifully sent to England was one from American commissioners appointed to inspect the embarkations, who protested that seventy-three out of one hundred people they had inspected were American property, yet they had all been permitted to leave. Carleton's confidence in his action was borne out when he received the opinion of the secretary of state that the evacuation of runaways was "certainly an act of justice due to them from us" that could in no way be deemed an infraction of the treaty.[22]

By July, the number of embarkations increased dramatically. Boston King recalled, "Each of us received a certificate . . . which dispelled all our fears, and filled us with joy and gratitude." Boston King and his wife, Violet, were on *L'Abondance,* which sailed on July 31 with another four hundred men, women and children. Many of the adults were part of the large Methodist congregation, including Nathaniel Snowball and his family and Mary, the runaway from John Willoughby, with her husband, Caesar Perth, her daughter, Patience, and three orphan children. The blind preacher and his wife were embarked on the accompanying ship, *Clinton*, along with his fellow preacher Luke Jordan and his family. Also on board that ship were more than two hundred black evacuees, including James Jackson and Frank Patrick from Norfolk. This was another occasion when Daniel Parker's exertions yielded General Washington no benefit. Harry Washington was part of the exodus on July 31, taking leave of America on *L'Abondance*, without so much as a backward glance.[23]

The frustration experienced by Parker and his fellow American commissioners boiled over in a series of letters sent to General Washington in which they indicated that although thousands had been sent off they had been able to retrieve only seven. The outgoing transports that they were permitted to inspect contained only a fraction of those departing, they complained, because they were not allowed to inspect the Royal Navy, or military transports, or the many merchant vessels leaving the port. Black seamen, who made up about 10 percent of the Royal Navy and its accompanying fleet of privateers, simply sailed away. John Thompson, onetime courier for the governor of New York, was one of thousands of black seamen from America discharged from the Royal Navy in Portsmouth in 1783 and 1784. Plenty of military officers took their black servants away with them without suffering any scrutiny from the commissioners. Runaways were still on the musters of regiments when they left. John Randall from Connecticut was probably with the Sixty third Regiment of Foot when it was demobilized in Manchester. Thomas Johnson, the black guide from South Carolina, and his wife and children were relocated to Nova Scotia with Tarleton's British Legion.[24]

As the pace of evacuations quickened, all available vessels were pressed into service to take refugees to Nova Scotia, Jamaica, the Bahamas, and England. The American commissioners continued the fruitless task of supervising embarkations until the end of October, when the inspections were finally abandoned. Subsequently, General Washington was to characterize the whole exercise as "little more than a farce."[25]

It was not a farce for the few people the American commissioners did manage to remove from the ships. There was inevitable heartbreak when cases were disputed, usually the wives and children of runaways who had not come into the British lines within the stipulated twelve months and so were deemed to remain the "the property of American subjects." A board established to adjudicate ruled that one man who had been with the British for six years could not take his children to Nova Scotia because the children were too young to have been able to respond to a proclamation. They were returned to their former master. In another case, a man who joined a Loyalist regiment in 1776 was unable to claim freedom for his wife and three children because they stayed outside the British lines during the war. Such stories of grief and forced separation were duplicated every Wednesday when the board met at a Manhattan tavern. A woman from Virginia successfully petitioned Carleton directly to have her unfavorable decision reversed, but she was unable to save her daughter, who was illegally sent back to Virginia. She stayed on in New York desperately trying to recover her child until the very last evacuation on November 23, 1783.[26]

The ruling that children were not capable of responding to a proclamation meant that many orphans among the runaways in New York were likely to be reclaimed as property, unless they were young enough to have been born within the British lines. Unaccompanied children and youths who were under the age of fifteen on outgoing transports were usually listed as the property of departing Loyalists, even though few produced papers to prove ownership. In some cases, the relationship between adult and child was more equivocal. Caesar, a "stout fellow" with an age estimated at fourteen, was embarked on the *Minerva* for Spithead, England, in August 1783 in the company of a Yorkshireman named John Watson, who claimed that "he had brought him up." There was no suggestion that Caesar was enslaved to Watson, so the ambiguous explanation was probably offered to deflect suspicion that the youth was a runaway. In a similar vein Mary and Caesar Perth took with them to Nova Scotia several orphans from John Willoughby's plantation as part of their family.[27]

The process of removing thirty thousand troops and as many Loyalist refugees put considerable strain on the logistical resources in New

York. The Black Pioneers, with Thomas Peters still as sergeant, were not permitted to leave for Nova Scotia until October, when all the British Hessian and Loyalist regiments had been evacuated. Nearly all black workers on the musters of the Royal Artillery Department and the Wagon Master General's Department were kept on the job right up to final embarkation and were among the very last to go on November 23, 1783, when the final vestiges of the British army departed to join the evacuation fleet waiting off Staten Island.

It was a war-weary General Washington who finally laid claim to all of the United States of America on November 25, 1783. His satisfaction at victory was somewhat diminished by the magnitude of the Loyalist defection, by which as many as sixty thousand Americans took their leave. Just how many fugitive slaves had also gone he had no way of knowing, but he was correct to assume that it was greater than the three thousand listed in the documentation British commissioners later sent to Congress. Taking into account the people who had left from the southern ports, as well as from Boston and other northern ports, plus those in the army and navy, the number of runaways who had left America as free people must have been close to nine thousand.

An unknown number of the black allies of the British who found freedom in the revolutionary period chose to stay. Washington was well aware that runaways had "many doors" through which they could escape within the newly created United States, recognizing the extreme difficulty of recovering people whose names could be so readily changed and whose physical appearance could no longer be recalled after years of absence. His friend Governor Harrison, aggrieved that he had "lost thirty of his finest slaves," believed that many had stayed on in New York. Harrison appealed to New York's governor to give his "kind assistance for the recovery of them," although the governor proved as ineffectual a slave catcher as was Daniel Parker. Washington chose not to further pursue his own runaways, even though six from Mount Vernon were never accounted for. These were young men with skilled trades who could readily have found a niche for themselves as artisans in the cities of New York, Philadelphia, Baltimore, or Boston. It is highly possibly that they, together with thousands like them, successfully forged a free life in the new republic.[28]

With the city finally in his hands, General Washington led his army on a victory march through Manhattan streets packed with jubilant Patriots who had flooded back into the city, their hats and bonnets adorned with ribbon cockades or sprigs of laurel. A week later, a spectacular display of fireworks was staged to celebrate his victory. Roars of approval from the boisterous crowds probably wafted out to Staten Island, where the final British fleet lay waiting for a fair wind to take them to Nova Scotia. On board the *Danger* was Patrick Henry's runaway Ralph Henry, with his wife, Miney, and their four-year-old child, Molly, who would have seen Washington's triumphal fireworks light up the clear night sky. Also watching from the *Concord* on that still, cold night was Daniel Payne, who had been enslaved on Washington's Mount Vernon plantation only three years before. That Daniel had survived the war and was now leaving America as a free man was his own particular triumph.[29]

PART II

CHAPTER 5

STARVING IN THE
STREETS OF LONDON

London was the greatest city in the world in 1783, home to more than 750,000 souls. The crush of humanity in its congested streets, with the cacophony of hawkers' cries, church bells, horses' hooves, wagon wheels, organ grinders, animal calls, and a general hubbub of voices, presented bewildered newcomers with a violent assault on the senses. The greatest city in the world was also the most odiferous, its air polluted with coal dust and reeking with the stench from untreated human waste, rotting rubbish, slaughterhouses, and tanneries. There were days when the city was completely enveloped in a dark, suffocating miasma of fog mixed with coal ash. Animals left to decompose in the streets leached into the puddles of urine and stagnant water, and even a discarded human corpse might be found among the decaying detritus. This was quite unlike any place in America.

Samuel Burke arrived in this teeming and fraught metropolis in August 1783, accompanied by his wife, Hannah. From the relative security as a free black couple with their own home in New York, the Burkes were reduced to utter penury in this strange new environment, neither of them possessing the physical capacity to work for a living. Both of them had been evacuated from Charleston in a bad way. Burke had been so severely injured during the battle at Hanging Rock in 1780 that he nearly died. Hannah had endured the appalling conditions that were the lot of followers of the flag for six years. Together they had been evacuated from Charleston to Spithead toward the end of 1782 as part of a contingent of wounded and discharged veterans that also included John Twine, his wife, Hannah, and their child. Their transport ship was captured by the French, who were still at war with England, and they were imprisoned in France until the formal cessation of hostilities.

Arriving in London with little money and no prospects, the black refugees like Burke and Twine converged on the noisy and evil-smelling concentration of derelict tenements in places such as the Minories, Wapping, St. Katherine's by the Tower, Whitechapel, Spitalfields, Shadwell, Limehouse, Ratcliffe Highway, Stepney, and Mile End New Town, all in the East End of the city. Here they competed with poor Londoners for space in lodging houses where, for sixpence a night, they could sleep head to toe with light-fingered strangers on vermin-infested straw pallets. Those with less than sixpence might take turn about with prostitutes and their tricks, or make do with a nest of loose straw beside the stinking privy. During the day, they jostled with one another in a labyrinth of narrow streets and laneways, dodging the wagons and hackney coaches, carrying slops, running errands, cajoling, begging, or picking pockets. There was plenty of entertainment to be found. London's noisy, serpentine streets were a theater of curiosity, where every form of human oddity was on display, along with a menagerie of performing animals. The theater of cruelty was no less evident, with public executions a regular feature on Tower Hill, with lesser felons flogged through the streets. Oblivion was never hard to find; one could get blind drunk on gin or rough cider for just a few pence.

In Goodmans Fields, an area close to the London docks, between the Tower and Whitechapel, Burke and his wife rented space in the lodging house of John Williams and Thomas Watkins. At least a dozen other black refugees were also in residence, including John Thompson, courier for the governor of New York, who was recently discharged from a British warship at Portsmouth. It was probably the white landlords who alerted the black lodgers to the Loyalist Claims Commission, established by Parliament to enquire into claims for losses in the war and for the confiscation of property. Burke, Thompson, and four others submitted a joint petition to the Loyalist Claims Commission written by Thompson's previous employer, Colonel Edmund Fanning, asking for relief from destitution. As this petition plaintively declared, the cessation of war that had brought "hope of ease and plenty to most" had rendered them "unemployed, unprotected and homeless objects of poverty, want and wretchedness." Couched in the appropriate language of submission, the petition nonetheless expressed indignation that these black veterans had "not had any reward, recompense or emolument whatever for such services . . . loss and sufferings."[1]

For their part, the commissioners were not impressed with these ragged black men and were inclined to regard them either as dupes or opportunists. The commissioners quickly perceived the claims to be a scam operated by the landlords Williams and Watkins on behalf of the black refugees who lodged with them. Almost every petition that was submitted by a black claimant in September 1783 came with identical documentation to validate the loss of property, written and signed by these two men. "The case of many of these black men is an absolute imposition," the commissioners stated in response to one such application; "many of them pretend to have the same quantity of land which is written and valued and certified by John Williams and Thomas Watkins who have an interest in representing a falsity to us." It was the opinion of the commissioners that if any money were awarded to the black claimants, "probably these men [were] to have a considerable charge of it." Nevertheless, the commissioners believed Colonel Fanning's recommendation to be genuine, and on the strength of his word alone they agreed to grant some financial compensation.[2]

John Thompson had been Fanning's steward in New York and had acted as courier in 1775 between the Loyalist mayor of New York and the royal governor in New York when the governor had been forced to take refuge on a warship. After the British occupied New York, Thompson was recruited into the Royal Navy, where he was wounded and discharged as unfit. To him the commissioners awarded ten pounds, but they gave no credence to his story about a house he claimed to own on Long Island, probably because the certificate to validate the claim was signed by Thomas Watkins and was identical to a one submitted by a black claimant from Rhode Island. Three others on the same petition were granted five pounds apiece. Burke was better favored, as he had not relied on his shifty landlords; he had a supporting letter from a captain of the Prince of Wales American Regiment and another from Brigadier General Browne. Having listened to Burke's testimony and read his testimonials, the commissioners agreed he could have twenty pounds, which they meant to be "in full for all his losses."[3]

Whatever Burke did with his twenty pounds—maybe it was spent caring for his ailing wife or swallowed up by unscrupulous landlords—within two months it was gone. In November, at which time he claimed his wife was dead and he was working as a flower seller for the piti-

ful sum of a penny a day, he made another appeal. This time he specifi-
cally requested compensation for the loss of the house and furniture at
5 Dutch Street, New York, owned by his late wife, which had been requisitioned by the barrack master in 1779. In truth Hannah Burke was
not dead; three years later she was baptized in Stepney. Not that the dis-
crepancy mattered. There was no corroborating evidence of the house
ownership, the papers having been lost in the siege of Charleston, so the
commissioners declined to provide any further compensation.[4]

John Twine, whose experience mirrored that of Burke in many ways,
applied to the commission in his own hand in November 1783. By virtue
of his attachment to the British, he told the commissioners, he had lost
land and a small house in America "and dare not return again to that
country." In a strange new environment, with a wife to maintain (no
mention of the child, who may have died), he was unable to get work and
found himself "reduced to great poverty." Even though Twine said he
had recently been baptized and understood the nature of the oath he had
taken, the commissioners did not think he was telling the truth. They
decided that he had been a slave emancipated by the war and that was
reward enough. It was a common response from the commissioners,
who looked upon the black claimants as largely undeserving of compensation, as they believed nearly all of them were slaves who had had the
good fortune to be emancipated by the British. It was the same story for
Richard Weaver, who had worked for the captain of HMS *Roebuck* in
Philadelphia. Weaver had been in England for four years when he applied in November 1783 for money to assist him to take his wife and children to Nova Scotia. Although Weaver said that he "work[ed] for his
daily bread," the commissioners treated his claim with utter disdain.[5]

That black claimants like Twine and Weaver were given short shrift
by the Loyalist Claims Commission was not entirely due to the class and
racial bias of the commissioners. The earliest black applicant was Walter
Harris, the runaway from Westover, who petitioned for temporary relief
in June 1783, backed up by "a very handsome certificate from Lord Cornwallis of his attachment and fidelity to the British cause." He was readily granted ten pounds. However, the documentation the commission
required, such as written proof of property losses and certificates of status, was rarely provided by the black claimants; when it was, the com-

missioners had reason to be very suspicious. It was the rash of fraudulent cases in September 1783 that damaged the credibility of the subsequent applications. Anyone without supporting testimonials from illustrious British officials had poor prospects before the commission, even when they did not lodge with Williams and Watkins. One-third of the black claimants were left empty-handed. Somewhat grudgingly, the commissioners allowed twenty-six of the black claimants temporary relief payments of between five and twenty pounds.[6]

Scipio Handley, the free fishmonger from Charleston who had escaped the hangman and then been so grievously wounded in the siege of Savannah, was the sole claimant to receive compensation for property loss. He got only twenty pounds. Benjamin Whitecuff, the spy originally from New York, had a remarkable story to tell. Having escaped hanging in New Jersey in 1778, he was then sent to Virginia, presumably to work as a spy, when his ship was captured by the French and taken to Grenada. Condemned to be executed yet again, this time he was sent to Boston to be hanged but was intercepted by a British privateer and taken to the island of Tortola, in the middle of the Caribbean. From Tortola he caught a ship to England, where he joined the Royal Navy. He served at the siege of Gibraltar, which lasted from 1779 to 1782, before he was finally discharged in England at the conclusion of the war with Spain. For his pain and suffering Whitecuff was awarded ten pounds.[7]

Four claimants were awarded lifetime pensions. The largest pension of eighteen pounds a year went to Shadrack Furman, who provided the commissioners with an astonishing tale of woe. He had already tried for compensation in Nova Scotia, and having failed in that arena, he had traveled with his wife to London "with the hopes of meeting some of the officers who had known the services rendered by petitioner to the British Army." Unable to find officers to vouch for him, Furman threw himself on the commission's mercy, pointing out that he and his wife, "from a comfortable situation in life," were reduced to "the lowest ebb of poverty and distress." Furman's troubles had begun in 1781, when Benedict Arnold invaded Virginia. Furman had provided the army with accommodation and supplies, and, as a consequence, enraged Patriots burned his house and crops. His petition detailed how he was tortured for information, then tied to a post and given five hundred lashes, finally being left for dead, blinded in both eyes, with one leg nearly severed by an ax and "so much impaired from the wounds in his head received from them, that he is sometimes bereft of reason." Blind, crippled, friendless, and impoverished, Furman was reduced to playing the fiddle in London's streets, "entirely depending on the charity of the public" to provide for himself and his wife.[8]

Whatever various circumstance deposited black refugees in England, within a year or so of arrival almost all were out of work and living by their wits on the crowded London streets. The distant world to which they had been carried, with or without their consent, proved to be an alien and uncongenial environment. It was a desperate predicament to be unemployed in England at a time when the labor force was swamped with demobilized sailors and soldiers. The black refugees from America who flooded into the city had no support networks on which they could draw, and their predicament was worsened by the fact that they did not fit easily into the framework of the existing Poor Laws. A pauper was required to return to his "parish of settlement" before being entitled to receive relief. The Scots and Irish were sent back to their country of birth, yet it was neither practical nor desirable to return refugees to America. Instead, poor blacks were "unfeelingly driven from place to place by parish officers," according to one observer. Even the resourceful Peter Anderson, who had managed to keep himself alive for months in the woods of Virginia, was unable to find the wherewithal to survive in the crowded streets of London. His plaintive plea to the Loyalist Claims Commission echoed the plight of most of his fellow refugees. "I endeavoured to get work but cannot," Anderson told the commissioners. "I am really starvin about the streets, having nobody to give me a morsel of bread and dare not go home to my own country again."[9]

Anderson's account of his capture by the Patriots in Virginia and his subsequent escape to join the British forces on their way to Charleston was dismissed by the commissioners as "a very incredible story... the sort of thing which would have pretty strong proof to support but he not only gives no proof but admits he cannot therefore we pay no credit to the story." When Anderson returned with a letter from Lord Dunmore to vouch for his "incredible story," he was awarded ten pounds. He was lucky that he could locate the Earl of Dunmore. The choleric response of the commissioners to the application of John Provey gave the flavor of their general view of claims without such illustrious testimonials. Provey, from North Carolina, had been brought to England in 1778 as a servant to the Duke of Northumberland. As supporting documentation he tendered a letter from the private secretary of Sir Henry Clinton, for whom he had worked, which was judged to be not worth a penny of compensation. According to the commissioners, Provey's claim was utterly unfounded. "Instead of suffering by the war, he gained by it for he is in a much better country where he may with industry get his bread," the commissioners declared, "where he can never more be a slave, for notwithstanding he pretends to have been born free we cannot easily give credit to it being the common tale of them."[10]

The problem was that there was no work by which Provey could earn his bread in London in 1783. Of the forty-five black claimants, only a few indicated that they had paid employment. Those like Provey, who had come to England as servants to officers and then lost their employment when the officers resigned their commissions, were in dire straits. Massive demobilization of hundreds of thousands of veterans had created fierce competition for unskilled employment, and black refugees from America, with work experience confined to plantation slavery and support services for the war effort, had few saleable skills. The story told by Anderson of "starvin about the streets" was the experience of the great majority of black claimants. Like Shadrack Furman with his fiddle, many black refugees found themselves "depending on the charity of the public" to survive.[11]

Contemporary estimates of the number of people in this marginal, impoverished community were wildly unreliable. In 1772, Edward Long gave an estimate of three thousand for the black community in England, which he quickly revised upward to fifteen thousand to correspond with the figure cited during the Somerset case. This famous legal case focused on the rights of James Somerset, a slave who had escaped from his master in London 1771 but was recaptured and forced aboard a ship to Jamaica. With help from the prominent humanitarian and antislavery campaigner Granville Sharp, Somerset obtained a writ of habeas corpus to prevent his forcible removal to Jamaica. In what became a high-profile court case, Chief Justice Lord Mansfield ruled that no master ever could take a slave out of the country to be sold abroad. This decision effectively meant that slavery, while still technically legal, had become impractical in England. The lobby for the West India slave trade, of which Long was the chief spokesperson, inflated the number of slaves in England because they wanted to frighten the English into believing they could be swamped by idle and indigent blacks freed from slavery. By 1788 this figure had been further inflated by another West India lobbyist to forty thousand.[12]

Greater London was undoubtedly the site of the highest concentration of the black diaspora in the 1780s, and the black population in that city was around ten thousand. London parish records indicate a concentration in certain parts of the East End, including Stepney, the Minories, Wapping, Shadwell, Limehouse, and Deptford. Most of the parishes in these areas registered that between 1 and 3 percent of baptisms were of people identified as black, mostly adults, while in a small parish like the Minories the proportion jumped to 16 percent. Black baptisms were also a feature in Marylebone, a huge parish in the fashionable west of London, where black servants were employed and where there was also a very large workhouse.[13]

Some members of this community were enslaved. In the late eighteenth century the slaves in England were almost always domestic servants brought to England from the Caribbean and America, or imported direct from Africa by wealthy English families. A decade after the Somerset judgment, people who had once been slave servants could be found living independently in the poorest parishes of London. Between 1775 and 1782 the number of black servants baptized in Marylebone declined, while at the same time baptisms of black adults became a feature of parishes such as Wapping and Stepney. Many of these people had escaped from domestic slavery, or been manumitted, or simply turned out of doors by owners who realized that their property had lost saleable value. Those who remained in service may have been technically slaves, working for no wages, since Mansfield had ruled only that slaves could not be shipped out of England, not that they were entitled to be paid for their service.[14]

No one knew just how many slave servants there were in the 1780s, as the line between employment and enslavement was so blurred. Famous black servants, such as Francis Barber who worked for Samuel Johnson, were certainly free, while others were just as certainly enslaved. Evidence of black servants can be found in criminal indictments of the period. The man identified as the "bellwether" of the mob that forced its way into Newgate Gaol and liberated the prisoners during the Gordon Riots in June 1780 was a black servant who was brought to England from America in 1774. Another prominent rioter was a black servant of a lawyer in Westminster. The status of these two as enslaved or free was not established in their trial records.[15]

The ambiguous status of servant or slave was also an issue in the case of the young man known only as Caesar, who was convicted at the Kent Assizes in March 1786 of stealing four shillings and four pence. His ubiquitous slave name and the absence of a surname strongly implied that he was household chattel. In one of the court records he was described as a servant, although this could be an error, since at his indictment Caesar was described as a laborer, the usual description for a male with no specific employment. The most plausible interpretation is that he had recently been a slave servant and was now unemployed. Caesar's trial record provided no indication of his origin. Most probably he was either an enslaved person brought to England by a refugee Loyalist, or a runaway who came as part of the final British evacuation, maybe as a servant.[15]

Caesar was one of the most common names for a male slave in America. There were more than a dozen men of that name listed in the Book of Negroes during the evacuation from New York in 1783. Only one was evacuated to England, one Caesar, who embarked for Spithead in the service of John Watson. The age given for Caesar at embarkation in New York was said to be fourteen, which was probably the guesswork of the commissioners. The estimated ages in the Book of Negroes were wildly unreliable, so the "stout fellow" said to be fourteen years old in August 1783 could have been older and may have been the same person who was sentenced at the Kent Assizes three years later, when his age was estimated to be twenty-two.[17]

At the time of his trial, Caesar lived in the parish of St. Paul, Deptford, an impoverished maritime district of London with a rapidly expanding black population. Even before the American War, maritime districts in London had had a noticeable black community, largely consisting of seamen. In the years following the Somerset decision in 1772, word was carried from port to port in the Atlantic that slavery was untenable in Britain and that enslaved people who reached England could not be returned against their will. Ironically, the vehicle for freedom was often a slave ship. African American and African Caribbean men, often runaway slaves, joined ships heading for England, taking the place of the large number of European seamen who had deserted. One of these was sixteen-year-old James Williams, who said he had been on an errand to deliver letters from the captain of a West Indian ship when he was tried at the Old Bailey for the theft of clothing and shoes. African seamen also formed part of the maritime communities of Deptford, especially the Kru from Sierra Leone and the Fante sailors from the Gold Coast, who were employed as sailors, interpreters, cooks, sentinels, and stewards on slaving vessels.[18]

Also among the motley crew at Deptford were black mariners from the Royal Navy. Brutal and coercive though service in His Majesty's Navy was, it had appeal for men of the African diaspora. As well as the lure of prize money and pensions, the navy provided a measure of protection against man stealers and slave owners, as British authorities would generally refuse to surrender slaves working aboard their ships. The most famous black man of the age, antislavery campaigner Gustavus Vassa (known to us by his pen name, Olaudah Equiano), served on board a British warship during the Seven Years' War. Numerous black men serving in the British fleet began to appear in the London baptism registers during the American War. In the period immediately after the war, as thousands of African American seamen recruited during the war were discharged, the number of black baptisms increased dramatically, with the two Deptford parishes registering a tenfold increase. John Williams had been recently baptized in Deptford when he came before the Kent Assizes in 1784, charged with stealing a cask of wine, two silver spoons, a greatcoat, and twenty shillings.[19]

Most of those in the black maritime community were homeless men in desperate circumstances, waiting on their wages and prize money. Whatever their loyalties, they had not freely chosen England as their destination. As one discharged seaman lamented to the Loyalist Claims

Commission, he had little say in the dramatic life changes that had up-rooted him from America and deposited him in England: "I got nothing to help me and my wife after leaving what little I had behind me." Yet another runaway from Boston who was newly discharged from the navy told the Loyalist Claims Commission that wages for his previous service had not been paid because "when he went to Broad Street to receive [his wages] they told him it had been paid to some persons who had forged his name."[20]

The commissioners dismissed this claim as "incredible," yet the same story was true for Amos Anderson, a black seaman from HMS *Loyalist* who had come from New York in November 1783. Anderson was able to identify the imposter as a fellow black seaman. The culprit, who gave the name John Shore, was indicted for the crime at the Old Bailey in April 1784. The captain of the *Loyalist* gave evidence that he knew the accused man very well, saying, "He came on board as John Moseley." All the in-dications point to the accused being John Moseley, the runaway from Virginia, who was listed in the Book of Negroes as bound for Nova Sco-tia on the *Elijah* in October 1783. Moseley never took the voyage to Nova Scotia; subsequent musters in the various settlements there included no record of him. Moseley worked near the dockyards in New York for many years and would know crew on the *Loyalist*. It would have been easy for him to have left the *Elijah* and signed on to the *Loyalist* when the ship left New York to return to England. The captain testified that Amos Anderson and John Moseley had applied together for the certif-icates to claim their wages after the ship arrived in England at the end of November 1783. Shortly after this visit, Anderson was shanghaied and taken to the West Indies to be sold. Moseley returned to the *Loyalist* in late December to get a certificate for Anderson's wages for an earlier voyage between Charleston and New York, in 1780. Explaining that Anderson was sick in Wapping, Moseley induced the captain to sign the certificate to say that Anderson had not deserted. He was then able to claim Anderson's wage, perhaps rationalizing that the money would never be claimed and that he had desperate need of it. Unhappily for Moseley, Anderson escaped from his reenslavement and got a berth on a ship from Rhode Island. He was back in England in March 1784 and quickly established that his friend had defrauded him. Even though

Moseley had changed his name, he still lived in Wapping, where Anderson tracked him down and was able to make an arrest.[21]

Because black refugees from America came to England as seamen or officers' servants or soldiers, the cohort was almost exclusively male, in contrast to those who went to Nova Scotia, nearly half of whom were women. The addition of thousands of male refugees from America made for a dramatic gender imbalance within the black community in London, which was already dominated by seamen from Africa and the West Indies. In parishes such as Stepney and Wapping there were four black men for every woman. In Deptford, the ratio was sixteen to one. Those few women among the influx of black refugees usually came with a male partner. Samuel Burke, John Twine, and Richard Weaver brought their wives from America, but they were not typical.

A common complaint of those who applied to the Loyalist Claims Commission was that they had been forced to leave their wives and families behind and they lacked the wherewithal to be reunited with them. Peter Anderson guessed his enslaved wife and three children were still somewhere in Virginia. Walter Harris knew his wife and children were still at the Byrd plantation of Westover in Virginia, and he was resolved to return to them. At least, that was what he told the Loyalist Claims Commission in his second application in 1785, which was also supported "in the strongest terms" by Lord Cornwallis. Harris asked for money for his passage to join his family in America and was granted an additional twenty-five pounds. Two years later Harris was still in England, making plans to emigrate to Africa.[22]

About a quarter of the black claimants to the Loyalist Claims Commission indicated that they had married in England, and the implication was that their wives were white Englishwomen. John Provey's wife, Ann, was white, as was Benjamin Whitecuff's wife, Sarah, and John Thompson's wife, Ann. Parish records and other sources reveal no stigma attached to black men in the late eighteenth century, at least among the poor, as evidenced by the high level of interracial marriage. It took a rabid apologist for slavery such as Edward Long to see the prevalence of mixed racial marriages as objectionable. It was the fault of degraded lower-class women, he said, who were "remarkably fond of the blacks, for reasons too brutal to mention." What Long most feared was that within a few generations miscegenation would "spread so extensively, as even to reach the middle, and then the higher orders of the people, till . . . every family catches infection from it." Long's racist invective pinpointed a key issue for people of the African diaspora in late-eighteenth-century England: they were unlikely to perpetuate themselves as a distinct community. Whereas Long saw the influx of black men contaminating English blood so that eventually everyone would be the same corrupted type, others understood that black people would be completely assimilated into the dominant racial group. As a friend of Samuel Johnson observed, all this racial mixing was preparation for "the moment when we shall all be made one fold under one shepherd."[23]

Not everyone was as sanguine as Dr. Johnson and his circle about the large numbers of indigent black men making their appearance in the streets of London. The West India interests were quick to draw attention to the hopeless plight of those who had escaped the paternalistic benefits of slavery, issuing dire warnings of the threat to the property of white Londoners, despite that the war's end had reduced many times more white men and women to crime or beggary. The very harsh winter of 1784–85 was particularly cruel for an indigent black community struggling to survive on whatever they could beg or steal. Poor Law restrictions were relaxed in some parishes such as Marylebone and Wapping to allow starving black people access to food and shelter. It was too little, too late. In December 1784 three young black men died in a workhouse in Wapping.

CHAPTER 6

BOUND FOR AUSTRALIA'S
FATAL SHORE

In May 1782, a black sailor named John Martin was caught red-handed with a bundle of clothes just as he was about to exit a London house. His trial at the Old Bailey was perfunctory. The owner of the house told the judge and jury how he had apprehended Martin with four overcoats, several waistcoats, and a pair of breeches, all of which he valued at sixty-eight shillings. No statement was recorded in Martin's defense. For Justice Buller and the Middlesex jury this was a clear-cut matter: larceny over the value of forty shillings was a capital offense.

Under the draconian sentencing regime of the day, death was the penalty for some two hundred crimes, and public hangings were a common feature of life in London. As the numbers of men and women facing execution spiraled upward, the legal fraternity became increasingly squeamish about their city being festooned with gibbeted corpses. The next best deterrent, a sentence of transportation beyond the seas, was liberally applied to reprieve about half the number of felons sentenced to the gallows. In addition, transportation was now given as the initial sentence instead of being reserved for a conditional pardon. As luck would have it, Martin was sentenced to seven years' transportation rather than the gallows. Transportation to where, exactly, no one could even hazard a guess.[1]

One of the many disagreeable aspects of the revolt of the American colonies was the abrupt end to the traffic in convicts that had seen up to fifty thousand transported to the American colonies as indentured labor. It had been a lucrative business for tobacco merchants like Duncan Campbell, who contracted to transport the convicts on his outbound ships and sell them into indenture for seven years in the colonies of Maryland and Virginia, after which they would return to England with a cargo of tobacco. For Campbell, the war had been an economic disaster. It also had disastrous consequences for Britain's inadequate jails. Courts continued to give out sentences of transportation to America, as if nothing had changed. Every kind of institution of incarceration filled with felons waiting to be sent off. Stopgaps were employed to try to ameliorate the desperate situation in the country's prisons, which were never meant to serve as long-term penitentiaries. In 1776, it was agreed that the hulks of decommissioned warships could be used for convicts awaiting transportation. Duncan Campbell, who had diversified his business interests, contracted to accommodate about 450 convicts on two hulk ships, *Censor* and *Justinian,* moored in the Thames off Woolwich, where the felons were put to work raising sand and gravel from the bed of the river. This measure was introduced for only two years, after which time it was expected that "the usual mode of transportation might again be adopted." Six years later, the hulks were still in the Thames, where they continued to alarm Londoners as the source of runaway felons and contagious diseases.[2]

Two hulks made little difference to the overcrowded and parlous state of the prisons. When John Martin was sentenced, he joined thousands already slated for transportation who were struggling for survival in fetid and disease-ridden jails. Eighteenth-century prisons were run on a private enterprise basis. The prison governor and the turnkeys made their money by selling accommodation, procuring sexual favors, dispensing gin, accepting bribes, and charging admission fees to a curious public. Most notorious was London's Newgate, an overcrowded, stinking cesspit that had been the focus of incendiary fury in the Gordon Riots. By the time Martin was received into Newgate, the prison had been rebuilt, but it was no less foul than before the rioters burned it down. Its population had almost doubled without the jail's being increased in size. Little had changed since the prison reformer John Howard condemned Newgate in 1777. Poor prisoners like Martin were held in disgusting conditions in the common wards. There were no beds and no bedding, no proper sanitary arrangements, no medical attention, and next to no food, except for the prison issue of a three-halfpenny loaf supplemented by charitable donations and a weekly ration of dubious meat. For clothing, food, and bedding a prisoner had to depend on bribes offered to the turnkeys by the visitors who streamed into the jail. Without any work or exercise, the sole distractions for the prisoners were sex, drinking, and gambling, all of which were rife inside Newgate.[3]

During the day, the prison thronged with families, curious strangers, hawkers, prostitutes, and accomplices. Wives managed to hide and stay overnight with their imprisoned husbands, pets were kept, spirits flowed freely (as long as one could pay), and sexual activity of all persuasions was openly indulged. With its rudimentary sleeping arrangements and unsanitary conditions, Newgate was little worse than the poor sections of London, the only real difference being that it was so densely crowded and so closely confined. When John Howard revisited the new jail in 1783, he was shocked to find that the stench of the prison still overwhelmed him, as it had six years earlier, and that sanitary conditions continued to breed epidemic disease. He warned that without more care, the prisoners would be in great danger of a deadly outbreak of "jail fever" (typhus), which could readily spread to the rest of the London population. Although Newgate had an infirmary, doctors could not be induced to enter it. The sick and dying were left untended. The only time the keeper of Newgate paid any attention was when a burial was required. As John Martin was a stranger in England, without a family to provide the bare necessities of life such as food and bedding, he was condemned to a squalid existence that must have been utterly soul-destroying.[4]

Late in October 1782, Martin received a reprieve from the foul environment of Newgate when he was selected to go aboard the *Den Keyser* at Portsmouth. This ship had been chartered to take forty men and women to west coast of Africa. Earlier that year, another 350 convicts who had been reprieved on the condition that they become soldiers were formed into two independent companies and landed at the slave trading fort of Cape Coast Castle. Supposedly, they were to defend Britain's slave trade interests against attack by the Dutch, who had joined the alliance against England. Having been starved and brutalized by their corrupt and murderous commander, these soldier-felons created havoc at Cape Coast Castle. According to the governor of the castle, "From the very day these convicts landed, their thoughts were turned upon rapine and plunder." In a trice they picked the locks on the company storehouse and broke into the market stalls of the local Africans. Muskets and ammunition issued to them for an attack on the nearby Dutch settlement were sold to the Africans in exchange for brandy, and thirty convicts deserted to the Dutch and used their weapons to assist in the Dutch defense. Twenty-five men who were embarked on a ship to go down the coast to relieve another fort overpowered the crew and sailed away. Those who remained at Cape Coast were perpetually drunk. By the time the *Den Keyser* was ready to sail from England, only some thirty of the soldier–felons were left alive at Cape Coast. The African Company, whose interests they were meant to protect, lodged vigorous protest against receiving any more convicts, so only fifteen of those on the *Den Keyser* were to be taken to Cape Coast Castle; the rest were to be taken to Goree and dumped there.[5]

Martin was seriously ill when he embarked on board the *Den Keyser* on November 1. If he was anticipating a future of freedom and possibly a return to a long-lost homeland, he was to be disappointed. Too sick to make the voyage, Martin was returned to jail. Those who did make the journey, including the two black men convicted in the Gordon Riots, had every reason to wish themselves back to the horrid confines of Newgate. They were landed without any provisions and no direction as to what was expected of them. The exasperated governor at Cape Coast Castle had no provisions to spare and ordered that they must look out for themselves or starve. He was not without sympathy but was at a loss for what to do for people "landed naked and diseased upon the sandy shore; . . . under the scorching heat of the sun without the means of support or the least relief afforded them." He was especially shocked by the state of the women, whose fate was "to be common prostitutes among the blacks," and arranged for them to be taken to the town. Three of the youngest and fittest male convicts landed at Goree did eventually manage to get back to England, where they were promptly arrested and re-tried for returning unlawfully from transportation, another hanging offense. Soon they were back in Newgate with Martin. Once more, these three were reserved as beneficiaries of the king's mercy and once more were sentenced to transportation to Africa.[6]

Sending convicts to Africa made economic sense. Slave ships from English ports usually went empty to the coast of Africa, so it would be advantageous if they could be stocked with a profitable cargo of convicts, just as previously ships bound for America had carried convicts and returned with tobacco. Since 1776, however, legislation had made it impossible for a contractor to trade in convicts: they could no long sell convict labor, and neither could they transact with a convict to buy out servitude. Nevertheless, there was still money to be made. Anthony Calvert, of the slave-trading company Camden, Calvert, and King, was keen to be involved. The stumbling block was the refusal of the African Company to take any more convicts into its slave forts after the debacle at Cape Coast in 1782.

Despite the African Company's vehement opposition, the Home Office received unexpected support for an African solution from a previous governor at Cape Coast Castle, John Roberts, who put forward a radical plan to deport the country's accumulating felons. Recognizing that "the government must get rid of them some how or another," Roberts suggested that convicts should be sentenced to a life of hard labor on plantations established adjacent to Cape Coast Castle. "There is not an island in the West Indies produces better cotton than we every day see growing spontaneously in Africa," he enthused. Land could be purchased cheaply from the free Africans who lived around the castle, and gangs of convicts could be set to clearing the ground for the cotton, under the supervision of drivers with whips. Essential to his scheme was the construction of a penal fortress with twenty strong-locked chambers, each holding ten men under the surveillance of a driver armed with a musket. As well, there must be some authority invested with judicial power to hang any who tried to desert or shirk their work. "No doubt many of them would soon die after they got there," he allowed, if not from fever then from hard labor in the African sun. Still, he reasoned, "This set of people are now got so numerous that it seems absolutely necessary for humanity to give way in some measure."[7]

Roberts's utterly outlandish plan appears to have been taken seriously by the undersecretary of the Home Office, Evan Nepean. At the very time that Nepean was digesting Roberts's plan to turn convicts into plantation slaves at Cape Coast, he was arranging with Camden, Calvert, and King to transport convicts to Cape Coast on the slave ship *Recovery*, then lying in the Thames. Arrangements were made with the Treasury to have convicts taken to Gravesend, where the *Recovery* was tendered with provisions for 150 convicts. However, when the secretary of state for the Home Office, Lord Sydney, proposed the plan to the committee of the African Company, they would not have a bar of it, insisting that more convicts "would endanger their settlements." Nepean was left holding a contract with Camden, Calvert, and King. Anthony Calvert was a member of the Committee of the African Company, so more pressure was applied until the committee gave a little ground. On January 13, 1785, some twenty-two convicts were loaded into the *Recovery* and shipped to Cape Coast Castle. It is not known what happened to all of them; mostly they died.[8]

Nepean then turned his attention to Lemaine Island, about four hundred miles up the Gambia River, which he thought capable of sustaining a settlement of some four thousand convicts. The idea of convict settlement in the Gambia River was first mooted by John Roberts years earlier but revived by Nepean's friend James Bradley, chief clerk to the newly formed India Board. Bradley had approached his two brothers about a business venture in Lemaine in late 1784, and subsequently informed Nepean that a convict settlement could be organized and managed as a family enterprise. On January 5, 1785, Nepean authorized Richard Bradley to go to Gambia to negotiate for the purchase of the island from its indigenous owners. At the same time the slave traders Camden, Calvert, and King indicated that they were keen to tender for the transport contract. In January, officials of the city of London were personally briefed by Lord Sydney that convicts would soon be sent to Africa. The judiciary swung into action to facilitate the process with sessions at the Old Bailey converting sentences to transportation to Africa.[9]

It was apparent from the draft proposal that Lord Sydney sent to the Treasury in February that convicts sent were not to be set to establishing cotton plantations on Lemaine. Instead, they would be left to their own devices while provided with building materials, agricultural tools, and seeds, to create some kind of a self-governing, self-sustaining society. An agent on an offshore vessel would prevent their interfering with any slave-trading interests. The person appointed in this role was Anthony Calvert, the slave trader with the contract to transport the convicts, who had not the slightest interest in their welfare. On March 19, Duncan Campbell was able to inform the Treasury that he had secured the hulk *Ceres* "for a temporary reception of convicts under sentence of transportation to Africa" and that he had set about getting it ready. It was the government's intention to delay the voyage until the end of August or early September, after the rainy season had passed, and to concentrate the designated convicts on the *Ceres*. Campbell, well aware how eagerly prison governors across the country would embrace the offer of accommodation, advised the captain of the *Ceres* that felons "will be forced upon us as quick as we can take them." He also warned that as soon as the convicts discovered they were bound for Africa, there would be mutiny.[10]

Lord Sydney's determination that transportation would be resumed was a great relief to provincial officials who were in despair at the state of the country's prisons and the escalating rate of criminal convictions. A magistrate from the county of Lancaster reported to the House of Commons that the Manchester prison was so dreadfully overcrowded that it was a serious financial burden. Manchester was beset with unemployment as a result of the demobilization around that city of four or five regiments, including the Fourth, Forty-seventh, and Sixty-third regiments from America. This influx of idle men, suddenly cut loose from military discipline and without any paid employment, inevitably led to an increase in larceny and other crime. The city had no way of recouping the cost of incarcerating all these felons, the magistrate explained, because they were "so closely ironed" that they could not be put to work. Some convicts had been confined for three or four years waiting for transportation, and still more were anticipated.[11]

One of the closely ironed felons in the Manchester jail was John Randall, age twenty-one, from Connecticut. He had recently come from America as part of a regiment that had been demobilized and that "lay about town." Very likely, he had been a drummer with the Sixty-third Regiment of Foot. On April 14, 1785, Randall was found guilty of stealing a watch chain, in the company of another black man. Both were sentenced to transportation to Africa and sent immediately to join the *Ceres*.[12]

John Moseley had been in the condemned cells in Newgate for nearly a year, waiting to be hanged for defrauding his friend, when he reappeared at the Old Bailey on March 3, 1785, to have his death sentence reprieved in favor of transportation to Africa. He must have been happy to be the subject of His Majesty's prerogative of mercy, but a sentence of transportation to Africa meant a separation as profound as death. While languishing in vile Newgate, Moseley had managed to maintain a relationship with his wife or with a female inmate. There was no barrier to sexual intimacy in Newgate, and conception was a highly desirable outcome. For women prisoners in Newgate, being in a condition to "plead the belly" was significant in the manipulation of mercy. A "mulatto" baby of three months named Jane Moseley was baptized in St. Marylebone in November 1785. The child was almost certainly taken into Thomas Coram's foundling home of that parish, which took in infants from Newgate.[13]

John Moseley and John Martin were among a hundred convicts from Newgate transferred to the *Ceres* in April 1785. Convicts were selected for the *Ceres*, the House of Commons was told, because they were judged to be "of the most desperate and dangerous disposition, deserving for the sake of the public example of the greatest severity." From Winchester, a little north of Portsmouth, Janel Gordon was sent to the *Ceres;* he had been sentenced to transportation for stealing clothing. When Gordon was put aboard he was judged to be around fifty, the appropriate age range for the runaway from South Carolina called Jack Gordon listed in the Book of Negroes as embarked for Nova Scotia but who had failed to arrive.[14]

Duncan Campbell's mode of incarceration was more efficient and more humane than that of the keeper of Newgate. It was also much better regimented. The opportunity for intimate interaction was much more limited on the *Ceres,* if for no other reason than the cumbersome business of getting aboard a ship moored in the Thames. Nevertheless, families and friends hired lighters to take them to the hulks to bring money and clothing, as well as food to supplement the ration based on the naval allowance of bread, potatoes, pease soup, oatmeal, and small quantities of bullock head or beef. Though the food allowance was more substantial than in Newgate, the hulk diet was conducive to scurvy and other illnesses, compounded by damp, confined living arrangements. Between July and December 1785, sixty men died on the *Ceres.* John Moseley was mistakenly reported to have been among the deceased. He must have been misidentified as another black man, possibly John Randall's companion from Manchester. Moseley was still recorded on the *Ceres* a year later.[15]

All the convicted black men in London, with the exception of the youngest—John Williams, age sixteen, and James Williams, age seventeen—had been put aboard the *Ceres* for Africa, regardless of the severity of their sentence. The black convicts awaiting transportation to almost certain death represented 6 percent of the men on the *Ceres*, in contrast to the prison population, where black felons constituted less than 1 percent. Perhaps they had been considered most likely to survive abandonment in Africa, although few observers had any doubts that the place would make short work of one and all of those assembled on the *Ceres*. As Edmund Burke sardonically observed at the same time Moseley received his conditional pardon, a death sentence that had been commuted to transportation to Africa was nothing less than a "singularly horrid" death sentence "after a mock display of mercy." Gambia was "the capital seat of plague, pestilence and famine," Burke told the House of Commons, where "the gates of Hell were open day and night to receive the victims of the law."[16]

Burke was one of the members of the House of Commons who had raised the alarm about the Lemaine Island proposal and persuaded Parliament to establish a committee to investigate it in April 1785. One after another, experts told the committee that Africa was a place of disease and death. An army surgeon who had spent some years in Senegal said that two-thirds of the army had died within a year of being sent there. Another who had lived on the west coast told the tale of three hundred men who had been sent by the French up the Gambia River to work the gold mines. Only three had returned. Convicts sent to the Gambia River would "either die from disease or at the hands of the natives," he stated flatly. The disastrous 1782 venture was still fresh in the memory of many witnesses, not just for the appalling mortality rate but also for the riotous and undisciplined behavior of the convicts that had caused problems with the Africans and destabilized the slave trade. Finally, the committee heard the most damning evidence from Henry Smeathman, a botanist who had lived four years in Sierra Leone and married the daughters of two African chiefs. He reckoned that even if the convicts were landed "in the most healthy part of the country," half would be dead within a month and "only two at the most would be alive after six months."[17]

Evidence of that kind killed the Lemaine Island proposal. Under Secretary Nepean was more than a little disgruntled that "from the mistaken humanity of some and the affected tenderness of others" the plan had been shelved. He still had some cause for optimism, though, as the committee had put forward another African possibility. The committee took the view that the only practical place in Africa for transporting criminals would be one with no previous European contamination, "between twenty and thirty degrees of south latitude." They suggested that a naval sloop, HMS *Nautilus,* be sent to examine Das Voltas Bay, in present-day Namibia. This region was seen to have many advantages. It had mineral deposits, the soil was fertile, and the animals were plentiful. Convicts could be carried there on outward-bound slave ships that could then continue up the coast on their normal business. Encouraged that Africa had not been ruled out, the Treasury drafted an order on May 13, 1776, appointing Africa as the place to dispatch "sundry convicts under sentence to be transported to parts beyond the seas, still to be conveyed on transports," to which was attached a list of names that was drawn up while the committee was still sitting.[18]

Although Lord Sydney remained committed to the African solution, he allowed himself to consider an even more radical proposition to create a convict settlement at Botany Bay, an impossibly remote place thirteen thousand miles away, on the coast of the isolated southern continent that the explorer James Cook had named New South Wales. This spot was recommended by a refugee Loyalist from New York, James Matra, who had been a midshipman on Cook's voyage of discovery. It was after Matra's evacuation from America, with his prospects for advancement growing dimmer by the day, that he began to promote New South Wales as a wonderful new site for imperial enterprise where Loyalists could be settled. At Lord Sydney's prompting, he incorporated convicts into his scheme, not as plantation slaves but as free yeoman farmers, to be provided with a small grant of land and the tools for its cultivation. Matra made three separate appearances before the parliamentary committee to explain his scheme. Neither Sydney nor the members of the House of Commons were much impressed. The obvious drawback was the absence of any established trading enterprise that could easily incorporate convict transportation. No ships were outbound for remote New South Wales that would return with valuable cargo.[19]

Lord Sydney had not entirely jettisoned Matra's scheme. In January 1786, Under Secretary Nepean made a tentative request of Duncan Campbell for a costing of the transport of some six hundred convicts to Botany Bay, as well as feeding and clothing them for a year and equipping them with farming tools. Campbell told Nepean that the journey would take fifteen months. Given that the ships would come back empty, the cost of carrying each convict would be more than fifty pounds, he calculated, although the cost could be defrayed somewhat if the ships were to call at China on their return. With that monstrous expense in mind, Nepean's gaze remained firmly fixed on Africa. In June 1786 he was making arrangements with Camden, Calvert, and King to ship a thousand convicts, of whom 150 were to be women, to Das Voltas Bay.[20]

A month later, the sloop *Nautilus* returned with the news that the Das Voltas region was "sandy and barren and from other causes unfit for settlement." This was unwelcome news. There were by now about 1,300 convicted felons incarcerated on five separate hulks, and the government was more than anxious to be rid of them. As Lord Sydney acknowledged, it was imperative to solve the problem of the "crowded jails and infectious distempers that may break out." With that matter in the forefront of his mind, Sydney continued, "His Majesty thought to fix on Botany Bay" as the destination for his unwanted felons. Shedding his previous objections, Sydney now expounded on the "fertility and salubrity" of this place where hardly a soul had ever ventured, drawing on the evidence of Joseph Banks that its climate was healthy and the land fertile enough to produce "any kind of grain," while cattle could be grazed on "as fine meadow as was ever seen." Sydney was especially enthusiastic about Botany Bay's location, so far away from England that it was "hardly possible for people to return without permission." Having sung the praises of this Elysium of the Antipodes, Sydney requested that the Treasury provide shipping to transport about eight hundred convicts to its far distant shore. Unhappily, the troublesome Lord George Gordon had gotten wind of the idea to send convicts to New South Wales and wrote a letter to himself, which he passed off as a petition from prisoners in Newgate, to which he responded by visiting the supposed petitioners and warning them to "preserve their lives and liberties and prevent banishment to Botany Bay." The government was determined that the hero of the London mob was going to be permitted to scuttle this latest plan. Gordon and the printer of the petition were convicted of libel and of inciting mutiny against sentences of transportation.[21]

The slave-trading firm of Camden, Calvert, and King showed no interest in transporting convicts to this remote corner of the world. The successful tender came from a prominent Royal Navy contractor who was paid about £54,000 to provide and provision six transports and three store ships. Prudently, he had organized with the East India Company that three ships would stop at China on their return to buy tea, thereby making the voyage more economical. With the transport ships secured, the Treasury set about making them safe to hold prisoners. The *Alexander,* moored at Woolwich, required reinforced hatches with "bars and strong bolts," as well as a supply of "security handcuffs." Once these had been organized, transfers from the *Ceres* began. John Randall, John Martin, and Janel Gordon were transferred to the transport ship *Alexander* on January 6, 1787, along with Caesar, who had been placed on the *Ceres* the previous March.[22]

These black convicts had spent the past few years in appalling incarceration, contemplating a life of labor in slave forts on the coast of Africa: a hideous prospect for men who had emancipated themselves from slavery. Botany Bay, at least, was not an outpost of slavery. Captain Arthur Phillip, the naval officer who was placed in charge of the expedition, made it clear that the laws of England would regulate the settlement at Botany Bay and that one law in particular would come into effect from the moment their feet touched the ground: "There can be no slavery in a free land and consequently no slaves."[23]

A wit in the *London Evening Post* pictured the forlorn procession of convicts in clanking chains as on their way to an earthly paradise:

> *They go to an Island to take special charge,*
> *Much warmer than Britain, and ten times as large:*
> *No customs house duty, no freightage to pay,*
> *And tax free they'll live when in Botany Bay.*

However idyllic the popular perception of their final destination, none of the 184 who were put aboard the *Alexander*, black or white, could have taken any pleasure from his changed circumstances. They were in a pitiful condition. Some were so sick "they were unable to help themselves," complained Captain Phillip. John Moseley must have been too ill to be moved. He had to wait another two months before he was transferred from the *Ceres*, by which time the ships for Botany Bay were in Portsmouth. He was sent by wagon, chained by the neck and ankles to other prisoners, under guard to join the *Scarborough*. Transferred from the other hulks to the *Scarborough* were the black youths James Williams and John Williams.[24]

By the end of March, 582 male convicts and 193 female convicts, with 18 children, plus 212 marines to guard them, were congregated at Spithead, where two navy vessels joined the fleet of transports, in readiness for an immediate departure. Innumerable delays meant that the convicts endured up to four months at Spithead, ironed together on the transports, with scant opportunity for exercise or fresh air. Conditions were not much better on the hulks. Four men bolted together shared a space of seven feet by six feet, with so little headroom that they needed to bend almost double in order to stand. Between the decks where the convicts were stowed it was perpetually dark, since lanterns were forbidden for fear of fire. Initially there were no medical supplies on board. Phillip remonstrated to Nepean about the difficulty he had to "prevent the most fatal illnesses amongst men so closely confined." Inevitably, in the cramped conditions, with the sick and the healthy handcuffed together, disease broke out in the fleet. It was concentrated on the *Alexander*, where most of the black convicts were held. Eleven convicts had died by early April. The fearful rumor in Portsmouth was that there was "malignant disease" on the fleet, but the surgeon general for the fleet disagreed. He went belowdecks on the *Alexander* to find that the sick men's complaints were "neither malignant nor dangerous." Some had a cold, others were chronically debilitated, mentally and physically, from the effect of long incarceration, and others dressed only in rags were incapacitated by the piercing cold. He ordered warm clothes and made sure the convicts' rations would be supplemented with fresh meat and vegetables. The master of the *Alexander* was instructed to bring the men up on deck to take some clean air. Another five convicts died before the fleet sailed, even though the ship was scoured and fumigated. All the black convicts survived to make the momentous journey.[25]

Despite the "slight contagion" on the *Alexander*, the convicts were "in high spirits," according to Watkin Tench, an ebullient marine officer with an inquisitive eye. He felt that they shared with him "an ardent wish for the hour of departure." It came at first light on May 13, 1787, when all eleven ships of the fleet weighed anchor and set a course for Tenerife, their sails filling with a brisk easterly breeze.[26]

CHAPTER 7

RELIEF FOR LONDON'S BLACK POOR

When Benjamin Whitecuff from New York was baptized in the parish of St. Nicholas, Deptford, on February 25, 1783, he was taking the first step toward his marriage to Sarah, a white Londoner. He had just been discharged from the Royal Navy, so he could offer Sarah the prize money and wages due him. In addition, he had a naval pension of four pounds a year and was granted ten pounds from the Loyalist Claims Commission as compensation for his losses that resulted from his spying for the British. Sarah brought a small annuity of ten pounds to the marriage. This was no fortune, and work was scarce. Whitecuff set himself up in his old profession as a saddler and chair maker, but within a few years he and his wife were feeling the pinch of desperate poverty. Whitecuff was one of the more fortunate black refugees in London; others were literally starving in the streets.[1]

The plight of indigent black people in London became a matter of public concern on January 5, 1786, when the *Public Advertiser* reported that a gentleman had authorized a baker in the city to give out quarter loaves of bread to "every black in distress." That same gentleman was taking subscriptions to assist this purpose. Five days later he met at a coffeehouse with several other gentlemen—all prominent men and known philanthropists, including the chairman and a director of the Bank of England—to form the Committee for the Relief of the Black Poor. The driving force was Jonas Hanway, a man already famous for his philanthropic concern for the poor. Hanway first thought that the subjects for charity were lascar seamen from the East India ships, but after surveying the people who had applied, the committee discovered that the overwhelming majority were refugees from America, at least half of them sailors. This understanding of the problem gave an additional impetus to their philanthropic concern. As one correspondent to the *Public*

Advertiser pointed out on January 19, 1786, these black refugees had a special claim on British justice, as they had "served Britain . . . fought under her colours, and after having quitted the service of their American masters, depend[ed] on the promise of protection held out to them by British Governors and Commanders." Such loyal allies could not be left to "perish by famine and cold, in the sight of that people for whom they [had] hazarded their lives, and even (many of them) spilt their blood," the writer continued, because they were "unfriended and unknown." Another correspondent went so far as to suggest that Lord Cornwallis should "exert himself to make relief permanent to the poor remains of his sacrifice in Virginia."[2]

The direct appeal to Cornwallis was not so very far-fetched. In facilitating the flight of enslaved African Americans, British generals such as Cornwallis, Leslie, and Carleton understood that their actions could serve as a kind of moral redemption from the ignominy of defeat. They had nothing to gain in protecting and evacuating their black allies; by not repatriating runaways to their former owners they opened themselves to charges of duplicity and dishonor. On the other side of the ledger they accumulated moral capital just when national self-regard was at a particularly low ebb. So it was that, a decade later, Prime Minister William Pitt could instruct the United States emissary John Adams that the evacuation of runaway slaves was a moral decision, taken according to the dictates of the law of humanity, which constituted a higher authority than the dictates of a treaty that his government had signed. In its steadfast refusal to abide by the conditions of the Treaty of Paris, the British government provided the Americans with a rationale for resisting the repayment of prewar debts amounting to a staggering five million pounds.[3]

That matter surfaced in a meeting between hulk contractor and tobacco merchant Duncan Campbell and Thomas Jefferson in London in April 1786. Campbell met with Jefferson in his capacity as the chairman of the organization of British merchants to whom Jefferson personally, and the state of Virginia collectively, owed a great deal of money. In explaining the impossibility of paying, Jefferson referred Campbell to the British violations of the Treaty of Paris, especially "withdrawing American property contrary to express stipulation." A few days earlier, when dealing with one of his personal creditors, Jefferson had emphasized the stumbling block was that "a great number of slaves were brought away contrary to stipulation." Explaining his own incapacity to meet his debts, Jefferson made the disingenuous claim, "Ld. Cornwallis's army took off 30 of my slaves." Nine months later he excused defaulting on another British debt in much the same terms, asserting that Cornwallis had carried off thirty of his slaves: "The useless and barbarous injury he did me in that instance was more than would have paid your debt, principal and interest." Several times he was to repeat this claim of thirty stolen slaves, even though he had lost eighteen at most. He estimated that the slave loss to Virginia in one year alone was thirty thousand, a number he seemed to have derived from adding zeros to his own spurious total.[4]

That material benefit might be sacrificed for moral satisfaction indicated a significant shift in British thinking that had been taking place ever since Lord Mansfield had made his ambiguous judgment in the Somerset case that slaves in England had the rights of Englishmen. His decision led intellectuals in Britain to an intensified self-scrutiny about the imperial enterprise, in which complicity in slavery was seen to have sullied the moral character of the nation. As tension with the American colonies mounted, these men began to articulate views about slavery that would distinguish the British from the slave-owning American colonists. It was during the war with America that Granville Sharp, the champion of Somerset, put forward the view that the slave trade was a national disgrace and the emblem of imperial tyranny, which undermined the nation's claim to integrity. The notion that slavery was an institution inconsistent with British law and repugnant to British sensibility was increasingly voiced as an index of national virtue, especially in the face of ignominious defeat. Sharp went so far as to suggest that the disastrous war was a form of divine punishment for Britain's complicity in the slave trade.[5]

It was at the close of the war that the black Londoner Gustavus Vassa (now known by his pen name, Olaudah Equiano) provided Sharp with a powerfully emblematic case that he used to great effect to stimulate public unease about this repugnant trade. Vassa informed Sharp that in 1781 the captain of the slave ship *Zong* had thrown 132 chained Africans into the Atlantic Ocean in order to claim insurance for lost cargo. A dispute over the insurance had been heard by Lord Mansfield, who had found in favor of the owners of the *Zong*, ruling that they were to be compensated for the loss of their human cargo just as for any other property. Sharp responded with a very public attempt to have the ship's captain and crew prosecuted for murder. Although Sharp failed in that attempt, he did succeed in making an indelible impression on the public imagination of the brutal inhumanity of this British mercantile enterprise. In the wake of an unpopular and ultimately disastrous war, benevolence toward runaway slaves had a critical role to play in maintaining national pride and integrity. Since the impoverished blacks of London were the closest many people might come to victims of the abhorrent trade in slaves, the ready response to their plight should be understood as an aspect of incipient abolitionism in English society.[6]

By April 1786, the Committee for the Relief of the Black Poor had raised close to nine hundred pounds. Donors included the Duchess of Devonshire, the Countess of Salisbury, the Countess of Essex, the Marchioness of Buckingham, and the leader of the government, William Pitt. William Wilberforce and Granville Sharp, who were to achieve prominence the following year as leaders of the London Abolition Society, were among the subscribers to the appeal, while the largest single donation came from the most vocal source of antislavery opinion, the Society of Friends. The committee hired a room in the White Raven in Mile End and another at the Yorkshire Stingo on Lisson Green in Marylebone, which they kept open for several hours each day to distribute relief. Through newspapers and word of mouth, impoverished blacks were directed to apply at these places to get broth, a piece of meat, and a two-penny loaf. In the first few months more than two hundred people were served each day, many of them very ill.

To extend their philanthropy, the committee also established a hospital on Warren Street, which took in some fifty people suffering from various fevers, venereal disease, rheumatism, consumption, inflammation of the breast, and terrible ulcerations. It was apparent that illness was often a consequence of poor black people having to pawn their shoes, shirts, and jackets and being exposed to the elements without warmth or shelter. People were given straw and blankets, and sometimes they were provided with lodging. A few sailors were outfitted and sent to sea, and three people were given passage back to the West Indies. One woman was sent back to America.[7]

As news of the Committee for the Relief of the Black Poor spread, the number of needy attending at the White Raven and the Yorkshire Stingo rose dramatically. It soon became apparent that short-term relief was no answer to the entrenched problem of poverty among London's black community; the fundamental cause was chronic unemployment. Finding jobs for a few black seamen had no impact on the thousands of black refugees who arrived after 1783, when unemployment had already reduced many whites to beggary. Once it was understood that many of the black refugees were unhappy at finding themselves in a destination they had not chosen, the idea took root that the committee's task was to relocate the black poor to "such a place as may put them in a condition of getting their bread in freedom and comfort." For a venture of this magnitude, government financial support was imperative. The committee sought help from George Rose and Thomas Steele, secretaries of the Board of Treasury, both incipient abolitionists whose sympathy for the committee's work was known.[8]

From the time the Treasury became involved, food relief was replaced by a direct payment of sixpence a day, paid weekly out of Treasury coffers. Although this handout was scarcely enough for subsistence, the provision of financial relief without any work requirement was unique. It was a measure of the particular humanitarian concern that Rose and Steele felt for the black refugees that this system was implemented, as they showed no inclination to provide relief payments to London's many white poor. On July 6, 1786, the House of Commons formally resolved that an address should be presented to the king, requesting funding to send the black poor to a place where they would be able to become independent and self-sufficient.

Casting about for a place to repatriate their impoverished charges, the Committee for the Relief of the Black Poor looked to Nova Scotia. They were apprehensive that the climate in that place was not well suited. Moreover, it had proved uncongenial for black settlers. Not a few of their constituents had already left Nova Scotia for England. Thomas Johnson, one of the black guides smuggled out of Yorktown, was one. He and his family were settled at Port Mouton with the rank and file of the British Legion in October 1783. They found that they were marooned for the winter at a disastrous site exposed to easterly gales, equipped with nothing but prefabricated frames and canvas to ward off the excruciating cold. Using logs they cut on the site, the refugees created a rough settlement that they called Guysborough, after Sir Guy Carleton, and hunkered down to endure five months of bitter winter. Once the imprisoning ice began to thaw, the heads of families held an election at which the great majority voted to dismantle the shelters and move to a less exposed site. Those who remained at Guysborough were devastated by a fire that swept through the settlement in mid-May 1784. By that time, fortunately, Thomas Johnson and his family had already left. That same month, Johnson and his wife, Margaret, were described as paupers in the parish of St. Marylebone, where a daughter, Elizabeth, was baptized. The other children may not have survived the Nova Scotia winter. Presumably the Johnsons were taken into the huge workhouse of St. Marylebone, having just arrived impoverished from Nova Scotia. Two years later they were listed as among the families receiving weekly payments from the Committee for the Relief of the Black Poor, along with Betsy Johnson, their child.[9]

In view of the doubtful prospects for Nova Scotia, a better option looked to be Sierra Leone, on the west coast of Africa. A proposal for a settlement in that place came to the committee through the good offices of Granville Sharp, who introduced the mercurial botanist Henry Smeathman, who had lived in Africa for four years, where he had dreamed of the possibilities of an agricultural settlement on the Sierra Leone River to produce export crops for Atlantic markets. This was the proposal he put before Granville Sharp after failing to sell the idea to a raft of other potential backers, including Benjamin Franklin and the king of Sweden. In order to win over the committee, Smeathman recast his commercial proposal as an opportunity to create a "Province of Freedom," under the protection of the British, to compete with the slave trade, as well as to provide an alternative economic base in Africa where the black refugees could make "a comfortable livelihood and secure relief from their former sufferings." As a beacon of liberty, the colony would gradually absorb its slave-trading neighbors and "change them into subordinate free states" and, by offering "a sanctuary for the oppressed people of colour," would gradually abolish the slave trade. Sharp had not thought to ask Smeathman why, if he was so confident of a settlement on the west coast of Africa, he had given such damning evidence to the House of Commons on the deadly prospects for a penal settlement there.[10]

Sharp's enthusiastic recommendation ensured that the committee embraced Smeathman's plan. A special handbill directed to impoverished black people pointed out, "No place is so fit and proper, as the Grain Coast of Africa; where the necessaries of life may be supplied, by the force of industry and moderate labour, and life rendered very comfortable." Those interested in going to this near paradise were directed to apply to Smeathman at the Office for Free Africans on Cannon Street. While Smeathman looked after the process of recruitment, Sharp undertook to write a plan of government for the proposed settlement. Into this assignment Sharp poured all of his deepest convictions about humanity and justice among people of all races. Here he saw the opportunity to revive the archaic Anglo-Saxon system of frankpledge, which he thought was the only form of government to guarantee authority, order, and liberty. As he envisaged it, the mostly illiterate black people destined for Sierra Leone were as capable of self-government as any people. In his plan, all males over sixteen could vote in the common council, rather like a New England town meeting. Households were grouped in tens, called tithings, each of which would elect a tithingman, and every hundred households would choose a hundredor. Ultimate power was to reside in the common council, allowing for a degree of direct democracy far in advance of what was on offer to Englishmen of the day. Land was the responsibility of the community as a whole, with majority vote to dispose of it. Each person over sixteen, regardless of sex, was entitled to a one-acre town lot and a small farm. Though Sharp sometimes spoke of Sierra Leone as a colony, he believed the "Province of Freedom" to be quite independent, since the settlers could make any laws not inconsistent with Britain's, hold their own courts and assemblies, elect their own leaders, and maintain control of their militia.[11]

In the meantime, the Committee for the Relief of the Black Poor was paying out weekly bounty to as many as seven hundred people at its two relief centers. Although there was an expectation that the payment was linked to the Sierra Leone project, accepting the bounty did not obligate a person to emigrate. Nor was there a requirement that everyone who received the bounty had to be present in person. Consistently, between April and August 1796, "arrears" were paid to those unable to come in person to collect their allowance because of sickness or some other reason. This was how this list of recipients came to include Caesar, who was at the time incarcerated on the *Ceres* hulk in the Thames River, awaiting transportation to Africa. His name was variously given as Thomas Caesar, John Caesar, John Caesar Johnson, and John Caesar Thomas, reflecting the appalling indifference to the accurate use of first names that was so common in the eighteenth century, as well as a predisposition to call any black man either John or Thomas interchangeably. The different variants of his name suggest that the bounty was collected for him by friends, no doubt in the expectation that his being sentenced to transportation to Africa would allow him to go to Sierra Leone. However, the inclusion of incarcerated blacks in the Sierra Leone project was a matter of concern for the committee. In late June they received a petition from "a poor black . . . under confinement . . . who wish[ed] to go to Africa." The committee resolved to try to persuade the relevant authority to let the man "go free in order to join the expedition with his wife and family."[12]

By June 7, 1786, the recruitment of settlers had begun in earnest. Those receiving relief were informed that the payment of the bounty would be conditional upon going to Sierra Leone. Some who had turned up for the bounty on that day said that "they wished for time to consider," while others made it clear that they would be happy to return to their home in America but not to go to Africa. Although no one was refused payment on that or subsequent occasions, the clerk handing out the money was instructed to try to distinguish those who were genuine emigrants from those who intended to take the money and run. Keen to incorporate the black community in the process of recruitment, the committee appointed twelve corporals, men identified as having leadership qualities, to whom they gave responsibility to recruit a company of twelve settlers each. Only one of these corporals, a protégé of Granville Sharp named Elliot Griffiths who had been taught to read and write at

Sharp's expense, was to achieve any prominence in the venture. As preparations advanced, the committee also arranged for two of the white wives of prospective settlers to be trained as midwives.[13]

Thomas Johnson was among those who signed the agreement to go to Sierra Leone. At that stage, Johnson discovered another avenue to economic self-sufficiency that did not require yet another uprooting of his family. In July 1786, Johnson applied to the Loyalist Claims Commission. In his claim he said that he had gone to Nova Scotia with the British Legion and when the company had been disbanded he "went on board the *Rhinoceros* commanded by Capt. Duncan, with whom he came to England." Johnson emphasized that since arriving in England he had "subsisted poorly upon what little he had saved in the Service" and was now a pauper in Marylebone. In his memorial Johnson claimed he was an enslaved man who had been manumitted in South Carolina. At time of the British invasion, he said, he had the use of a house and ten acres of land and stock, as well as an annuity of forty pounds sterling but could not "hazard his life" to return to Charlestown to claim it. Pleading that he had a "wife and child, and another in expectation without any means of subsisting them, having no employment," Johnson asked for "the small sum of twenty pounds to enable him to get into some way of Business." When the commissioners granted his request, Johnson took no further part in the Sierra Leone project.[14]

Benjamin Whitecuff and his wife, Sarah, must have felt that Sierra Leone promised a rosier future than their precarious life in Deptford. They were among the later recipients of the bounty, signing up in October 1786. Other couples who signed on for the venture included John Twine and his wife, Hannah; John Provey, his wife, Ann, and daughter, Lucy; Richard Weaver, his wife, Lucy, and their daughter, Judeah; and John Thompson and his wife, Ann. Hannah Twine and Lucy Weaver were among the few black women in the expedition. Some 70 percent of the women who signed to go to Sierra Leone were white, most of them married to black settlers. Walter Harris was among those who signed up as unattached men.[15]

One prominent black Londoner who remained entirely skeptical of the enterprise was Ottobah Cugoano. He thought it was absurd for the government to create a colony for refugees from slavery at the very same place that "supports its forts and garrisons, to ensnare, merchandize and to carry others into captivity and slavery." He doubted that emancipated slaves would want to go to West Africa , observing, "A burnt child dreads that fire." Cugoano had a valid point. The proposed free settlement was smack in the middle of British slave-trading operations. The slave factory at Bance Island, now owned by the nephews of Richard Oswald, was in the mouth of the Sierra Leone River, just across a small stretch of water from the intended settlement. Indeed, the whole region was saturated with slaving activities. The proximity of the proposed settlement to the slave trade caused unease among the Committee for the Relief of the Black Poor, who had begun to suspect that Smeathman's real intention was "trafficking in men" and his proposal was just a ruse to get into the slave trade. When Smeathman suddenly died in August, the committee members were relieved. Immediately they began to look at an alternative site for settlement, not in Africa.[16]

In making the decision to shift location, the Committee for the Relief of the Black Poor had not taken into account the autonomy of the black emigrants, who were now so committed to Sierra Leone that they could not be persuaded to go elsewhere. A petition to say that "no place would be so agreeable to them as Sierra Leone," which was probably written by Elliot Griffith and signed by all the black corporals, was presented to the committee in August 1786. Furthermore, the black emigrants expressed such confidence in Smeathman that they elected his agent, Joseph Irwin, to replace him as the project leader, even though Irwin had never been to Africa. The black corporals like Griffith were in touch with skeptical observers like Cugoano, and they remained wary of the threat from the slave trade. The corporals were adamant that the black emigrants must be given arms to defend themselves and documents to protect them from the slavers. In response to their representations on this matter, four hundred firearms were allocated and a certificate was printed on parchment that carried the royal coat of arms, to certify that the bearer was a loyal British subject.[17]

The Sierra Leone project was complicated in multiple ways by public awareness that the west coast of Africa had been selected as the site for a penal settlement. Indeed, Lord Sydney's description of the plan to purchase territory in Sierra Leone to settle the black poor, "also furnishing them with tools and implements etc, for the cultivation of the land, as well as provision for their subsistence, until it is supposed they will be able to raise food for their future support," sounded almost the same as the ill-fated Lemaine Island proposal. Just prior to embarkation on the ships for Sierra Leone, Captain Thompson in the *Nautilus* returned to England with a negative report on Das Voltas Bay. Immediately, Thompson was given a new commission to escort the black emigrants on their journey. Just at the same time that they began to shift their meager possessions onto the ships at Gravesend, the projected penal settlement at Botany Bay became a hot item in the London gossip.[18]

Although the Sierra Leone project should have been seen as a completely different concept from a penal settlement at Botany Bay, the two were constantly linked in the press, in the popular imagination, and in government business. Treasury and Naval Board discussions continually switched between the proposed settlements at Sierra Leone and Botany Bay as if they were interchangeable. Government departments concerned with ordering supplies for the two expeditions found it convenient to deal with both in the same letter. The same firm was contracted to supply both expeditions and in at least one case surplus supplies for the black emigrants were transferred to the convict ships.

The entanglement of the expedition to Sierra Leone with the penal settlement at Botany Bay heightened concern among the black poor about friends and relatives in prison or on the hulks. Soon after the Botany Bay penal settlement became public knowledge, an unsigned letter "from the Blacks" to the Committee for the Relief of the Black Poor requested the release of a certain prisoner, stating that they would not go to Africa without him. While deliberating this case, the committee was informed by one of the black corporals that there were five men and one woman incarcerated who also expected to go to Sierra Leone. The members of the committee agreed to secure the release of these people and agreed to write a letter to the sheriff requesting their release. An even more troubling development was a widespread rumor that the Sierra Leone settlement would also be a penal colony, or, worse still, that the black settlers were actually to be sent to Botany Bay. Such persistent misinformation undoubtedly contributed to the reluctance of people to go aboard the ships *Belisarius* and *Atlantic* moored at Gravesend.[19]

By October 1786, about nine hundred people were receiving government support on the presumption that most would leave the country, but few had actually presented themselves to Gravesend for emigration. The Treasury was especially keen to keep down the costs; they had no intention of indefinitely paying the bounty to an escalating number of indigent black people. The Committee for the Relief of the Black Poor was directed that they should pay only those who had actually gone aboard the ships. Yet for all the Treasury's pressure, the bounty continued to be paid, even to those who had not signed the agreement. Thomas Johnson and his wife and daughter continued to collect the bounty, despite having chosen to stay behind. By December, the Treasury decided to take drastic action, informing the committee that they would imprison on vagrancy charges any who had received the bounty and not gone aboard the ships. Once again this was bluster. No such order was ever issued.[20]

In late November there were said to be 105 people living aboard *Belisarius* and 154 on the *Atlantic,* although there was some duplication of names on the lists supplied to the Treasury, so the true figure was somewhat less. Gustavus Vassa, who had returned from a voyage as a steward on an American ship, had been appointed by the Navy Board to be the commissary. Despite his reservations about the lack of advance preparations for securing the settlement in an area surrounded by slave traders, Vassa threw himself wholeheartedly into the project. His job was to manage the food and stores. He was fortunate that he was not required to live on board. For the Provey family living on the *Belisarius,* the experience of shipboard life was much like being confined on a prison hulk. The food was much the same, as both were based on the navy ration, the only difference being the daily rum allowance for the black emigrants, which Granville Sharp chose to blame for disturbances and disagreements that bedeviled the expedition. Winter was approaching. The people on board had little in the way of clothes, having pawned their jackets. The only way to keep warm was to light fires, creating a smoky environment that added respiratory problems to a raft of other health problems. The masters of both ships complained of their charges' "burning fires and candles at all times of night."[21]

By November 29, 1786, the Navy Board ruefully conceded that less than three hundred were on board the ships, with no more expected to embark "unless some means were taken to enforce them." Keeping those already embarked was proving to be a problem. While the ships lay at Gravesend, those on board grew increasingly restless. Anxiety about the expedition somehow came to the attention of Lord George Gordon, who made another of his odd public interventions. The *Public Advertiser* of December 18, 1786, reported that six of the black emigrants had come up to London to implore Gordon to use his influence to stop the ships' sailing until Parliament would resume to consider their being forced to leave the country. This supposed deputation was probably a fictional device, much like the prisoners' petition from Newgate that Gordon was in the process of writing. Nevertheless, there was discontent aboard the ships, and some of the prospective settlers, perhaps encouraged by the well-connected Vassa, could have gone to see the radical lord. The anonymous newspaper report, no doubt written by Gordon himself, gave an outline of the Sierra Leone venture that painted a tyrannical military government presiding over a settlement, just like the one proposed for Botany Bay. Gordon advised the deputation not to go to Sierra Leone, and the newspaper reported that subsequently some four hundred people had quit, leaving only a few paid stooges behind on the two ships.[22]

Vassa was probably behind Gordon's intervention. He was increasingly disturbed by the way the expedition was being handled, particularly by the role of Smeathman's agent, Joseph Irwin. Vassa certainly was the source of a strident campaign against the expedition mounted by the *Morning Herald* in a series of articles between December 29, 1786, and January 4, 1787. These news stories repeated much of what had been published in the *Public Advertiser:* that black people were being transported against their will, having been decoyed aboard the ships, and that they were being held in conditions similar to those on slave ships. The *Morning Herald* also published a letter, said to be signed by twenty of the black emigrants, complaining that Joseph Irwin had failed to supply appropriate provisions and was creaming off supplies to make a profit for himself. Irwin vigorously defended himself against these allegations, and the controversy died away. There was no voluntary exodus of the kind reported; any who left the ships at Gravesend did so in a coffin.[23]

Poor nourishment from a lack of fresh vegetables and a dependence on salted rations, as well as the cramped conditions in winter weather, ensured that fatal illness was a constant companion on the ships. Soon after Vassa took control of the stores, he ordered a completely new set of clothes for all the people on board and had the old ones burned in order to prevent an epidemic of typhus. His precautions were too late. A "malignant fever" had taken hold on the *Belisarius*. By the time the ship sailed for Spithead off Portsmouth, on January 11, 1787, John Provey was dead and so was his daughter, Lucy. Ann Provey survived into 1787, but she too must have died, as she was not part of the final expedition to Sierra Leone. Another death from illness was Benjamin Whitecuff, whose traumatized white widow, Sarah, chose to stay on the ship and make the journey into the unknown. Granville Sharp blamed the rum ration and a steady diet of salted rations for the fifty deaths before the ships left England. Sharp did his best to assist those who survived to make the journey, outlaying about eight hundred pounds to retrieve pawned clothing and valued items belonging to black emigrants before they left. It mattered greatly to him that the "Province of Freedom" should prove a success.[24]

At Spithead the two ships from London made a rendezvous with their naval escort, HMS *Nautilus*, and a third ship, the *Vernon*, joined the fleet a month later. As the ships swung on their anchor at Spithead, those aboard would have been aware that nearby, at Portsmouth, preparations were well under way for another fleet to take felons to Botany Bay. Vassa was instructed to redirect surplus clothing and supplies from the smaller-than-expected Sierra Leone expedition to the nearby Botany Bay fleet. Even at that late stage, the expectation that the black convicts sentenced to transportation would be permitted to join the fleet for Sierra Leone was not entirely extinguished. Any hope that the black convicts would be permitted to join the expedition was dashed when the Sierra Leone ships sailed out into the English Channel on February 23, 1787.[25]

Almost immediately after the ships departed, they were caught in a severe gale that forced them to divert to Plymouth. For three unhappy weeks the ships were at Plymouth, with their captains under orders to "quiet the spirit of disturbance and dissatisfaction" among their passengers. During this time, Gustavus Vassa filed a formal complaint against

Joseph Irwin, charging that he had misappropriated the sugar and tea allowance and failed to provide proper quantities or quality of medicine,
clothing, and bedding. The matter was referred to Captain Thompson
of the *Nautilus*, who agreed that Irwin was dilatory about his responsi-
bilities, with little concern for his charges. However, it was Vassa who
was the source of the most profound problems, in Captain Thompson's
view. Unless "some means [were] taken to quell his spirit of sedition,"
Thompson advised, the expedition would continue to be in trouble.
Vassa was put ashore at Plymouth with at least two other black men
deemed to be troublemakers. John Twine and his wife, Hannah, may
also have been among those who left with Vassa; either that or they both
died during the time the fleet was delayed at Plymouth.[26]

A letter from Vassa to his friend Cugoano, written on the day of his
discharge, appeared in the *Public Advertiser* on April 4, 1787. He denounced the white men in charge of the expedition as "great villains,"
claiming that people had died on the ships for want of supplies to which
they were entitled. "I do not know how this undertaking will end," he
wrote; "I wish I had never been involved in it." The same newspaper
quoted a letter from the protégé of Granville Sharp, Elliot Griffiths,
who wrote that those on the ships were "very sickly" and died "very fast
indeed," the result of doctors who were "very neglectful of the people."
Cugoano had always been distrustful of the enterprise, and he took up
the case, claiming that letters written to him from Plymouth revealed
that the black poor had been "dragged away from London and carried
captives to Plymouth, where they have nothing but slavery before their
eyes." He advised those on board that they "had better swim to shore, if
they can, to preserve their lives and liberties in Britain, than to hazard
themselves at sea with such enemies to their welfare." Those who sailed
to Sierra Leone would have done well to heed his advice.[27]

On May 10, 1787, the ships landed at a place known as Frenchman's
Bay. It was a beautiful harbor on a mountainous peninsula on the southern side of the Sierra Leone River. The 377 people who went ashore cut
a track through the thick vegetation to a vantage point on a nearby hill,
where the British flag was raised. They met no opposition. After many
years of interacting with slave traders, the Koya clan of the Temne had
no fear of Europeans and little curiosity about them. The day after dis-

embarking, Captain Thompson and Joseph Irwin met with the local ruler, known as King Tom, to negotiate the purchase, "at trifling expense," of a tract of land that stretched about ten miles along the Sierra Leone River, which was then assigned to the settlers "to be theirs, their heirs and successors, for ever." In return for the land, Thompson and Irwin handed over "thirteen pieces of Britannia's," as well as 130 gallons of rum, 36 swords, 8 muskets and ammunition, 34 pounds of tobacco, 10 yards of scarlet cloth, and 117 bunches of beads.[28]

Thompson was not to know that the resplendently attired King Tom, who was wearing a colorful assortment of European clothing topped off by a huge hat adorned with lace, was only a subchief of the Koya Temne, with no authority to give permission for a settlement. Thompson was also unaware that the permanent transfer of land the treaty proposed was unknown to the Temne. In previous dealings with Europeans, settlements were allowed on the basis of mutual obligation of landlord and tenant, and Europeans were never given ownership over the land, so King Tom had every reason to believe that this was the agreement he had signed with Thompson. Subsequently, this misunderstanding about the land tenure was to have a disastrous effect.[29]

While the land negotiations were under way, the settlers began the task of clearing the ground and creating temporary shelter with the canvas the Navy Board had supplied. They gave the name of Granville Town to the rude settlement, and they elected Richard Weaver, the runaway from Philadelphia, to be their governor. In his first report to the Lords of the Admiralty, Thompson expressed confidence that all would be well, despite "the licentious spirit that prevail[ed] among the people." By July, Thompson was no longer confident, complaining bitterly, "[The settlers'] obstinacy and laziness, which neither remonstrance, persuasion, or punishment can subdue, do not leave much hopes for their future welfare." On two occasions he had a settler flogged for "misbehaviour."[30]

The delay in sailing had bought the fleet to Sierra Leone at the worst possible time. "We have every reason to expect much sickness, having arrived here at the commencement of the rainy season, the whole of which we shall have to struggle against," Captain Thompson ominously warned in his first report. Struggle they did, in ever diminishing numbers, as more and more were carried off by "fevers, fluxes and bilious complaints." The canvas proved inadequate against the rain. Food became scarce. Joseph Irwin died. In September the *Nautilus* sailed away. On returning to England, Captain Thompson presented the Admiralty with list of settlers, on which he had noted the deaths of 122 people. As for the black settlers who remained alive in Sierra Leone, Captain Thompson entertained no high hopes. Such "a worthless, lawless, vicious, drunken set of people," who could not even be bothered erecting a tent to keep off the rain, were sure to "perish through their own indolence," he concluded. The return of the *Nautilus* also brought painful news to Granville Sharp, for whom the settlement was named. "I am sorry, and very sorry indeed, to inform you, dear Sir," Elliott Griffiths wrote to his old patron, "this country does not agree with us at all; and, without a very sudden change, I do not think there will be one of us left at the end of twelvemonth. . . . It really was a very great pity we ever came to the country."[31]

PART III

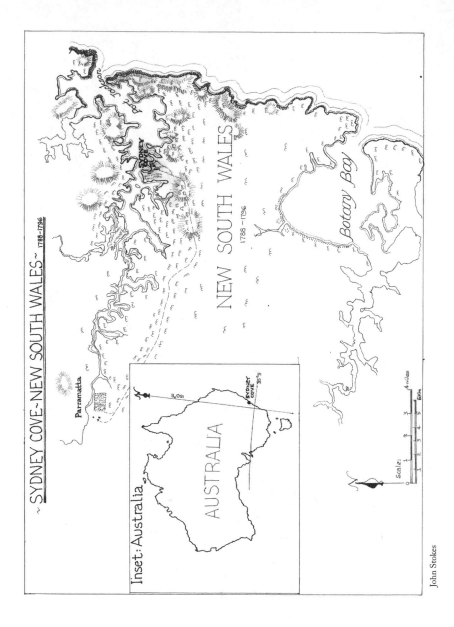

~ SYDNEY COVE ~ NEW SOUTH WALES ~ 1788-1796

NEW SOUTH WALES
1788 - 1796

Botany Bay

Parramatta

SYDNEY COVE

Inset: Australia

AUSTRALIA

150°E

SYDNEY COVE

35°S

Scale:

John Stokes

CHAPTER 8

RECALCITRANT CONVICTS
IN NEW SOUTH WALES

"Heavily in clouds came on the day," wrote Watkin Tench, a young captain of marines, as his ship sailed into Botany Bay on the east coast of Australia on January 20, 1788, after a voyage of nearly nine months. He was quoting, as best he could remember, Joseph Addison's much-admired play *Cato:*[1]

> *And heavily in clouds brings on the day,*
> *The great, the important day, big with the fate*
> *Of Cato and of Rome.*

For the man named for Cato's nemesis, landfall at Botany Bay would not have occasioned lofty sentiments. Caesar had arrived in fierce sunshine on the previous day, as a convict on board the transport *Alexander.* Remarkably, the fleet of convict ships that left Portsmouth in May 1787 had all arrived at their distant destination within two days of each other. Like every man on the transport ships, Caesar must have been desperate to see land, even if the land in question was to be another prison; anything was better than remaining penned up in a ship beset with illness. On the *Alexander,* ten convicts died in the first few months of the voyage. The source of their illness was identified as the ship's bilge water, in which food waste, excrement, vomit, and stale water had fermented to such a degree that the noxious gases it emitted tarnished the officers' metal buttons. When the surgeon removed the bilge hatches "the stench was so powerful that it was scarcely possible to stand over them." Even though the source of the foul miasma was eliminated, the convicts arrived at Botany Bay with their teeth loosened in their jaws, muscles that had turned to pulp, skin that bruised at a touch, and fragile bones that could barely support their body weight. Nearly all those on board the *Alexander,* in common with the sailors and convicts on every other ship, were showing signs of advancing scurvy.[2]

The first to set foot on land at Botany Bay was Captain Arthur Phillip, who arrived two days earlier on the faster escort ship. Phillip and some of his officers were rowed to the north side of the bay, where a group of indigenous men was sighted, calling out to the intruders "in a menacing tone and at the same time brandishing their spears." The Aborigines were entirely naked, their dark skin scarred with raised weals on the chest and upper arms. Each man had his right front tooth knocked out, and several wore a bone through the cartilage of the nose, as well as ornaments of shell in their greased hair. For all their appearance of hostility, the men responded when Phillip made signs indicating he wanted water by directing him to "a very fine stream." Tentative at first, the astonished Aborigines accepted the glass beads and mirrors that Phillip held out to them. They would have been even more astonished to know that this small pale man in his ridiculous uniform held the title of governor in chief and that in putting ashore he had assumed control of the entire region of eastern Australia. More naked Aborigines brandishing spears were seen the following day, calling across the water, *"warra warra,"* which was later translated by the amateur linguist Lieutenant William Dawes to mean "go away."[3]

The strange visitors had no intention of going away. Over the next few days Phillip explored his new domain, with Lieutenant Dawes and several other officers in tow. They found that New South Wales was a place that deceived the eye. At first it appeared as a gentleman's park, with stately trees and grassy meadows, but in reality nothing could have been more alien to the tranquility of pastoral England. Massive tree trunks rose straight up for fifty feet or more before extending contorted limbs to the sky, with drooping, narrow leaves that provided little shade from the remorseless sun. Beneath the trees, the grass was long and coarse. Throughout the day, the officers were tormented by flies crawling into their eyes and ears. As dusk fell, they were ready prey for swarms of mosquitoes. The more closely they looked, the more bewildered they became: Botany Bay in no way resembled the salubrious descriptions offered by Captain Cook.

However disappointed, Phillip determined that a start had to be made to create this latest outpost of empire. Small work parties of convicts from the transport ships were landed each day to cut grass for the livestock and clear a site. Fortunately, the Aboriginal inhabitants proved to be inquisitive rather than hostile. They were especially curious to find a black man among the interlopers attacking the landscape with strange weapons. None of the fleet's many diarists recorded exactly which black convict landed with the initial work party—there were four black convicts aboard the *Scarborough* and five on the *Alexander,* with another two on the *Charlotte*—but it could have been Caesar, who was said to be the strongest convict in the fleet. A watching naval officer thought that the Aborigines were delighted to see a "man of their own complexion," and he thought they expressed puzzlement that the black convict failed to understand their language. This was his fanciful rendering of the unintelligible behavior of indigenous people who had been isolated from contact with other people for tens of thousands of years. Someone from Africa dressed in a convict uniform was certainly different from those with pale faces, but no less alien.[4]

As the governor and his retinue of officers continued to explore their new location, every new day brought greater dissatisfaction. When the straggly trees were cut, the timber was "fit for no purposes of building or anything but the fire." The soil beneath was nothing but black sand. No one could locate the fine meadows of which Captain Cook had boasted. After days of searching they had found only "country low and boggy and no appearance of fresh water," as one disgruntled officer recorded. On January 24, Phillip resolved to move the entire fleet farther north to the place Captain Cook had called Port Jackson, where there was a magnificent harbor large enough to hold the navies of all of Europe. An extremely picturesque cove with a heavily wooded shore promising fertile soil beneath was selected for settlement and named for Lord Sydney. At sunset on January 26, the governor and his party of officers briefly stepped ashore at the cove and hoisted the Union Jack up the ready-made flagstaff. As the flag fluttered limply in the humid air, marines fired several volleys, loyal toasts were drunk, and Phillip took formal possession of the continent in the name of King George III.[5]

First to come ashore at Sydney Cove the next day were the men from the *Scarborough,* with orders to clear the trees to make a site for settlement. Included in this work party were John Moseley, the runaway from Virginia convicted of stealing his shipmate's wages; James Williams, the young black seaman known as Black Jemmy; and another black youth, John Williams, known as Black Jack, who had been caught stealing in Deptford. They must have been relieved to finally find themselves on land, although it would have been cruelly painful after 258 days at sea, lurching about on sea legs with scurvy-softened bones. If it were not difficult enough to hew enormous trees when the earth appeared to be heaving beneath them, the timber was so hard that it blunted the axes and twisted their inadequate crosscut saws. After two days of work in searing heat they had cleared enough ground for most of the fleet to disembark and start pitching tents among the tree stumps. The *Alexander* disgorged its complement, including the black convicts John Martin, John Randall, Janel Gordon (now called Daniel), and Caesar. By the time the fleet had disembarked all of the 546 male convicts, the black men represented only a tiny minority of 2 percent.[6]

A large number of tents were commandeered by the surgeon general to serve as a makeshift hospital for the many men completely debilitated with dysentery and scurvy. "More pitiable objects were perhaps never seen," he lamented. "Not a comfort or a convenience could be got for them." Convicts able to fend for themselves could share tents, if they were lucky, or find a place to sleep under the vast star-studded sky. One of the black convicts made his accommodation in the hollow burned into a massive tree trunk. A handful of the convicts eluded the guards to make a break into the surrounding forest, where the dense tangle of undergrowth promised concealment. Some were never seen again, but two or three staggered back many days later, nearly demented with starvation.[7]

February brought electrical storms of terrifying intensity. After days of torrid temperatures, rainstorms swept in from the ocean accompanied by drumrolls of thunder and jagged shards of lightning that spat in all directions, igniting wildfires and splitting trees from crown to roots. Squalls of rain turned the raw ground on which the convicts and marines slept into a filthy quagmire. On February 6, the 189 convict women were finally put ashore, bringing the full complement of convicts to 732. The women were barely assembled on the land, with no tents pitched, when the settlement was pounded with incessant, drenching rain. While the officers huddled in their tents in terror of being struck by lightning, the convicts, the marines, and the sailors slithered and rolled in the mud, "not in the least regarding the tempest," presenting the shocked officers with a "scene of debauchery and riot" that lasted all night. The governor, sheltering in the commodious canvas house that had been custom built for him in London, resolved that proper order must be established forthwith. Midmorning the following day, everyone was summoned to hear him give the orders.[8]

The bedraggled convicts sat in the mud, encircled by marines, while the officers flanked Governor Phillip as he read out his commission. Turning his attention to the convicts, he told them that any man attempting to get into the women's tents at night would be shot and anyone who stole even "the most trifling article of stock or provisions" would hang. Moreover, all convicted felons needed to understand that they were in New South Wales to work. If they did not work, they should not eat. Their first labor would be to build houses for the officers, next for the marines, and lastly for themselves.[9]

Phillip's words came as a severe shock to his convict audience. Nothing in their sentence implied that they were being transported to years of forced labor. Yet Lord Sydney's instructions to Phillip were very precise on this point: the labor of the convicts was assigned to the governor. In effect, these instructions made Phillip the master of a bonded labor force of more than seven hundred people. Lord Sydney had intended the convicts to go on the land and become self-sufficient farmers, but it was Phillip's view that before any land was allocated, the convicts must serve out their sentences, working as he directed. He did not even know when their terms expired; that paperwork had not accompanied the convict fleet. John Martin had only six months left on his sentence, but the governor was not about to take the word of a thief on the subject, insisting he must receive written proof from England, a process that was bound to take several years.[10]

As for the governor's grim warning about entering the women's tents, there were plenty of men ready to risk it. An unusually prim marine officer complained to his distant wife that a "scene of whoredome" was taking place at the women's camp and that Sydney Cove would more ap-

propriately be named Sodom. He chose to overlook the fact that his
fellow officers got to take first pick of the women, and in due course he
too followed his peers in choosing a mistress from among the convict
women. Second in the pecking order were ordinary marines, and the
male convicts came in a poor third. For those women not spoken for by
the officers, marriage to a convict or marine must have seemed the safest
option. Throughout February, the chaplain presided over numerous
convict weddings. John Randall, the black ex-soldier from Connecticut
convicted of stealing a watch chain in Manchester, was married to Esther Howard, a white London oyster seller, convicted at the Old Bailey
of stealing a watch.[11]

The man appointed judge advocate for the fledgling colony was Marine Captain David Collins. He had no legal training whatsoever, but he
took his job seriously, unperturbed by his ignorance of the law, handing
down vicious punishments to the refractory convicts and wayward
marines who came before him. On February 29 it was the turn of two
black men, Daniel Gordon and Black Jack Williams, to face Collins's
fierce justice, having been accused of the theft of eighteen bottles of wine
from the commissary store. Two white convicts found blind drunk on
the very day the wine went missing had implicated the black convicts
in return for a pardon. Black Jack was sentenced to death and then immediately pardoned, on account of his being "an ignorant black youth."
Middle-aged Gordon was led to the hanging tree between the male and
female camps, where the chaplain said the prayers for his soul and the
noose was fastened around his neck. In that excruciating moment, as the
crowd waited for him to give his final speech, Gordon was dramatically
reprieved by the governor, on the condition of his being exiled to the extreme southern cape of the continent, a sentence that no one could be
expected to survive. The impracticality of carrying out the new sentence
led to a further reprieve; a few days later Gordon was imprisoned on a
rocky outcrop in the middle of the harbor.[12]

Gordon and Williams were widely separated by age and experience.
They had been tried in completely different parts of England, incarcerated in different jails, housed on different hulks, and transported on
different ships. The charge against them for premeditated theft, only a
month after they landed, provides some evidence that the distinctive mi-

nority of black convicts chose to keep their own company. John Martin and John Randall formed a lifelong friendship, and when Randall built a rough hut for his new wife, he invited the black convict Moseley to share it with them.

The huts such as the one Randall built were woefully inadequate for the torrid climate; they were thrown together from soft cabbage palms and chinked with grass and mud, which disintegrated in the torrential rain that lashed the settlement throughout the antipodean summer. To achieve even such rudimentary housing, the heavy work of clearing and building had to be done by convicts still suffering the effects of scurvy, most of them from the urban slums of England and unaccustomed to laboring. The tools supplied were next to useless. Clothing was quickly reduced to tatters, with no possibility of mending because no thread had been supplied. Shoes fell apart in weeks. There were no beasts of burden; the task of carting the huge trees and stones fell on the puny shoulders of the convicts. The black convicts may have had an advantage here, as they were taller and stronger than most. At six feet, both John Randall and Caesar were each a head taller that almost every other man at Sydney Cove. Judge Advocate Collins, another tall man, identified Caesar as "the hardest working convict in the country; his frame was muscular and well calculated to hard labour." Unfortunately, the ration allocation took no account of size or the amount of labor undertaken. With remarkable fairness, Phillip had decreed that, regardless of status, every man would have the same weekly ration: seven pounds of beef, three pints of pease, seven pounds of bread biscuit or flour, and six ounces of butter. Within two months, the protein allocation had been cut by 12 percent. This ration was nowhere near sufficient to sustain someone of Caesar's size at eight to ten hours of backbreaking labor each day. He was always ravenous, Collins observed, "for he could in one day devour the rations for two days."[13]

The governor intended for the meat rations to be supplemented by the local game, an amazing creature that Captain Cook had called kangaroo. When standing erect, this animal was the height of a man. It had a head like a whippet and short, puny forepaws, with powerful hindquarters like an oversize hare, which propelled the animal across the landscape in great bounds. Kangaroos were numerous, but they were also well attuned to any signs of danger and accelerated to an astonishing speed. The cumbersome Brown Bess musket was next to useless in hunting them. The hungry newcomers were rarely able to supplement their meager diet with seafood because the seasonal movements of the fish were a mystery. A few edible herbs and berries were found to make sweet tea and help cure the scurvy, but these did nothing to fill empty stomachs. Within a few months, hunger had begun to determine the pattern of life at Sydney Cove.[14]

On April 30, 1788, Collins's court heard a series of cases concerning the theft of rations. One of those charged was Caesar, who was said to have taken the bread ration from the tent of a fellow convict. Caesar denied the charge, claiming the bread found in his bag was given to him by a marine officer for whom he worked as a servant. Only a fragment of his trial record survives, though almost certainly Caesar was found guilty. The usual sentence for men convicted of petty larceny was between one hundred and three hundred lashes. Caesar was not the only man to be punished that day. One of the officers who heard the cases remarked in his journal the following day, "We had a few trials and plenty of floggings, but I believe the Devil's in them, and can't be flogged out."[15]

To be publicly flogged was a humiliating and emasculating ordeal. It was a calculated invasion of the body designed to reduce the convict to an insensible thing with no will to resist. Stripped naked to the waist, the offender would be tied at ankles and wrists to a vertical triangular frame and beaten with a lash made of nine strands of whipcord, each strand knotted in three places. Each time the flagellator drew back the cat o'nine tails he would run the cords through his fingers to dislodge the bloodied flesh. To ensure that the victim did not die under the lash—a very real possibility for men affected by scurvy—the surgeon was always in attendance, as was Collins himself. The "iron men" who could withstand the cat without screaming before they passed out were admired for their capacity to resist the awesome power of the flagellator. Three hundred lashes was an astonishingly brutal sentence, far in excess of the floggings meted out in the Royal Navy; a body could not endure much more in one session, yet Collins sentenced some convicts to five hundred or six hundred lashes, a sentence that had to be dealt out in stages. At the conclusion of the punishment, or the intervention of the surgeon, the bloodied and insensible body slumped at the triangle was cut down and taken to hospital. When the pulped and lacerated back had healed sufficiently, those sentenced to more lashes were spread-eagled on the triangles for a second dose.[16]

As the number of lashes meted out by Collins's court steadily rose, the bloody ritual of humiliation and intolerable pain became one of the most common features of life in the fledgling settlement. Collins himself admitted that the offenders were often unaware of the rules they were supposed to have transgressed because convicts were unused to living in a society "where their conduct was to be regulated by written orders." This understanding did not temper the severity of Collins's judgments; he had men flogged for the smallest infraction. John Martin was given twenty-five lashes because he lit a fire to warm his flimsy hut. Collins's interpretation of the law made a mockery of the English fantasies that New South Wales would be some sort of paradise. In the face of his "exemplary punishments," convicts were loath to implicate their fellows in any crime. "There was such a tenderness in these people to each other's guilt," Collins bemoaned, "that unless they were detected in the fact, it was generally next to impossible to bring an offense home to them."[17]

Governor Phillip was a humane man, for his time, and he took his prerogative of mercy very seriously, personally considering every sentence and issuing pardons or modifications to the sentence. On the birthday of King George, on June 4, 1788, Phillip was keen to mark the occasion with pardons to any convicts under secondary sentence. This extravagant show of mercy included Daniel Gordon, who was released from his rocky island prison to rejoin convict society at Sydney Cove. On that day, every convict was allowed a pint of grog and mustered around an enormous ceremonial bonfire to give three cheers for King George. Even as they cheered lustily for the king's health, these convicts had no enthusiasm for building a new society in his name. It was a source of dismay to Phillip that his charges displayed no commitment to his project and would not work without brutal compulsion. Before leaving England he had insisted that there would be no slavery in New South Wales, but he could not escape the knowledge that his outpost of empire bore the hallmarks of a slave plantation. The only way a few marine officers could compel the labor of people against their will was the widespread use of violent torture to induce submission born of fear.[18]

Little by little, the straggling camp at Sydney Cove began to take on the look of a permanent town. Bricks made from the local clay were used to construct a courthouse and barracks, while a stone house was built for the governor. Two dirt roads were lined with the wattle and daub huts of the convicts. On a small promontory that jutted into the harbor on the west side of the cove, an observatory was built for Lieutenant William Dawes, who had been instructed by the Board of Longitude to take observations of a comet expected in the southern skies. Dawes was the scientist among the marine officers, a studious and deeply religious young man. As well as his astronomical observations, he also began an ethnographic study of the local Aborigines. Even he was not able to explain why they had become hostile to the white intruders and why they were likely to spear those who ventured beyond the cleared area of settlement.

In December 1788, a convict was found dead among the trees near the edge of the settlement where he had been cutting shingles. At first it was assumed that he must have been killed, even though his body showed no marks of violence. An autopsy showed he had died of malnutrition. It transpired that he had been selling his food rations to buy his return passage to England when his sentence expired. He had no shortage of buyers. Food was the most highly sought-after commodity at Sydney Cove. All the crops that had been sown failed. The gardens produced a few vegetables that helped to ward off the scurvy for those in the hospital but otherwise did little to assuage the hunger.

The local Aboriginal people, while not entirely ill disposed to the newcomers, could provide no assistance. Smallpox had found its way into the indigenous population, probably introduced by Indonesian traders visiting the far northern coast of Australia. Relentlessly traveling south, the disease reached Port Jackson about the same time as the First Fleet. Having never been exposed to smallpox, Aborigines had no immunity and died by the score. All around the harbor, the coves and inlet became polluted with their putrescent bodies. The bewildered Europeans did what little they could to help, though they managed to save only a few people. The British were immune to smallpox; the only victim of the epidemic was a Native American seaman. None of the black convicts succumbed, which shows that either they had been exposed to the disease or they were inoculated against it. Daniel Gordon would have been exposed to smallpox in South Carolina and was probably inoculated against it since the British had instituted a widespread program of inoculation among the black followers of the army. John Moseley had survived the epidemic that decimated Lord Dunmore's Ethiopian Regiment. The sight of the afflicted Aborigines must have awakened unbearable memories for each of them.[19]

The smallpox catastrophe was distressing for everyone at Sydney Cove, but the focus of attention within the settlement remained firmly fixed on food. Driven to backbreaking labor, the convicts grew desperate to assuage their hunger. On April 29, 1789, "Black Jemmy," as eighteen-year-old James Williams was known, was given the shocking sentence of five hundred lashes for helping himself to the tobacco of a marine. Caesar was in court on the same day on a second charge of stealing. Collins felt that flogging had failed to make its mark on this "incorrigibly stubborn black," and instead he extended Caesar's sentence of transportation from seven years to life, shrewdly guessing that Caesar could absorb the blow of the lash on his powerful body but that the prospect of a lifetime of forced servitude would strike terror in his soul. Such vicious sentences were by now commonplace in Collins's court, reflecting his iron determination to cow the convicts into subordination. As a horrified marine private observed, the convicts were "the same as slaves all the time thay are in this country," and in this situation the idea of liberty became an obsession, with the convicts willing "to try all skeemes to obtain it."[20]

Only a fortnight into his extended sentence, Caesar decided that the terrors of the unknown hinterland were less fearsome than a penal system arbitrated by David Collins. Armed with a musket he had taken from a marine, and a cooking pot, he headed into the wilderness. A week later, provisions disappeared from the brickfields a mile west of Sydney and soon after the discarded musket "and a pot still boiling on the fire," was found nearby. Collins was highly gratified when Caesar was captured that same night, less than a month after he had fled. Weakened by hunger, he had offered no resistance. On his reappearance in court, this "wretch" further incensed Collins by expressing complete indifference to his death sentence, claiming that he would "create a laugh before he was turned off, by playing off some trick upon the executioner." The subversive notion of hanging as pantomime gave Collins pause. Hanging Caesar would not "have the proper or intended effect," he decided, as the execution of a "mere animal" could not function as a deterrent. He was sentenced to work in chains on an island in the middle of the harbor where the first vegetable gardens were planted. Caesar was permitted to supplement his rations with the produce he grew.[21]

By this time, John Martin had served nearly twelve months over and above his original sentence, without any respite. Martin heard a woman in a similar predicament had been to see the judge advocate and was told there were "two years provisions for her and she would not starve." Martin spread this intelligence around the settlement. On July 28, 1789, a petition on behalf of Martin and five others whose time had expired was delivered to the judge advocate, requesting that they be "restored the privileges of free men." Collins felt some sympathy for the situation of convicts like Martin, who were "most peculiarly and unpleasantly situated," but until such time as the paperwork arrived from England they would have to continue to work as directed in order to be fed from the store; as no one had the capacity to be independent of the store, "there was little to be gained by them being restored to the rights and privileges of free men." The white convict who wrote the petition sought an interview with the governor to explain how he was told by the lieutenant governor that he would be fed whether he worked or not. Phillip refused to accept that any officer would have made such a confidential statement to a man so inferior in status, and the man was charged with uttering "a gross and scandalous falsehood." John Martin was brave enough to give evidence in support, but when his friend was sentenced to six hundred lashes and then forced to work in chains for nine months, Martin saw the wisdom of accepting his lot with no further complaint.[22]

Two months later, Daniel Gordon was charged with the armed theft of food and clothing. This time Gordon knew he was doomed to be either hanged or flogged to death. When the court met on August 20, 1789, to consider his case, Gordon appeared before it "with an appearance of delirium and wildness," his tongue lolling in his mouth and his eyes rolled back in their sockets, even though he had been in his perfect senses only hours earlier. The surgeon general declared him to be in an unfit state of mind to stand trial and Gordon was taken to hospital.

"Many of his fellow prisoners gave him credit for the ability with which he had acted his part," Collins wryly observed, agreeing that Gordon probably "deserved their applause."[23]

In December 1789, the "incorrigible" Caesar made another bolt for the wilderness, having been released from his chains by his sympathetic marine guards. The man was "insensible alike to punishment and to kindness," Collins fulminated, noting that Caesar had taken a week's provisions as well as the canoe to get to and from the island. Three days later, a marine officer reported that Caesar "paid them a visit in the night and stole a musquet." It was six weeks later that Caesar was brought back to the settlement, horribly lacerated by multiple spear wounds. In the account he gave to Collins's court, Caesar said that he had found the cattle that were lost in the first few months, which he was intending to return to the settlement. He was speared by Aborigines as he attempted to drive the cattle away, he said. Collins was having none of this, declaring the whole story "a fabrication (and not that well contrived) to avoid the lash . . . he was well known to have as small a share of veracity as of honesty." If Caesar's story were true he would have been killed by the Aborigines, whose aim with a spear was unerring, whereas the multiple wounds to the arms and legs indicated that they were merely trying to drive him out of their territory. In an account given on the day of his surrender, Caesar told a different story. He said he had no ammunition and had to get food by frightening the Aborigines away from their cooking fire, "coming suddenly on them swaggering with his musquet." When he lost the gun, he was attacked. There was no mention of cattle in this account. Watkin Tench believed that Caesar had been trying to ingratiate himself with the Aborigines "with a wish to adopt their customs and live with them, but was always repulsed by them . . . and forced to return to us in hunger and wretchedness."[24]

Even the unbending Collins agreed that because of Caesar's ravenous hunger "he was compelled to steal from others, and all his thefts were directed to that purpose." Collins's court was by now overwhelmed with men in the same situation, stealing food because of desperate hunger. No garden was safe from nightly raids on the cabbages and potatoes. The number of lashes awarded had climbed to one thousand, yet, Collins noted with consternation, "so great was either the villainy of the people, or the necessities of the times" that even this excessive response seemed to have no effect. Collins despaired that he could flog men to death and it would make no difference.[25]

Life was not so hard on Norfolk Island, a small uninhabited island Captain Cook had located one thousand miles to the northeast, where a small penal outpost had been established in February 1789. Reports spoke of rich soil that could support luxuriant gardens, as well as plentiful fish and game. In order to alleviate the looming famine at Sydney Cove, Governor Phillip decided to send a large detachment of convicts and two marine companies to Norfolk Island. Among the convicts he chose for relocation was Caesar, now released from the hospital, and Daniel Gordon, who had miraculously recovered his senses. Most of the convicts were carried on the small ship *Supply*, while the stores were on the *Sirius*, the only ship large enough to carry substantial provisions, which was to sail on to China to buy more food. They left on March 5, 1790, sailing into a big swell that had everyone prostrate with seasickness. As a marine officer shakily confided in his diary, the smell of vomit between decks was "a nuff to suffocate one." One week later they arrived at Norfolk Island, where the ships had to maneuver through treacherous surf to unload the convicts, who struggled through the pounding waves to the beach. For the next six days the seas were too rough to allow the stores on the *Sirius* to be landed. On the seventh day, to the horror of those watching on the beach, the *Sirius* ran onto a reef. Two convicts volunteered to swim out to the wreck to throw overboard the rest of the stores and livestock. Once on board, they broke open the spirit casks, got hopelessly drunk, and set fire to the ship. There was now no possibility of securing additional supplies. Slow death by starvation seemed inevitable.[26]

A mass effort salvaged the great majority of the stores from the wreck of the *Sirius*, but even then food supplies would last only a few weeks. The commanding officer persuaded all the convicts to take an oath agreeing to support a plan for survival in which they were divided into small groups of men, women, and children, each group with an area of land to clear and cultivate. The convicts were required to work for the government two or three days a week and the rest of the time work toward supporting themselves on these lots of land. With these incentives Caesar proved once again what a strong and willing worker he was. Within a few months he and a fellow convict had cleared ten acres. Even with that kind of hard work, it was not possible for the island to be self-sufficient in the production of food staples. What saved the Norfolk Islanders from famine was the mass slaughter of petrels that nested on the island every winter. A meticulous daily tally was kept of the number killed; between April and July, 172,184 dead birds were counted.[27]

At Sydney Cove, the food situation deteriorated from critical to life-threatening. On April 1, 1790, the ration was reduced to bare subsistence: 4 pounds of flour, 2.5 pounds of salt pork, and 1.5 pounds of rice a week. Recognizing that no man could work ten hours a day on such meager rations, the governor cut the hours of forced labor to sunrise till one o'clock in the afternoon, giving the convicts the remainder of the day to work in their vegetable gardens, if they could muster the energy. The salted meat, now four years old, would last only till August, and the flour would be exhausted by December. To supplement the miserable ration Phillip chose the best marksmen in the settlement to shoot kangaroo and they were given an additional allowance of flour and salt pork as an incentive. The ex-soldier John Randall was among these chosen few. It was a stroke of luck for Randall and his wife, but also, most likely, for his friends John Martin and John Moseley. As the shooters worked unsupervised, Randall had opportunity to get additional game for himself and his friends, which may explain why none of these three black convicts came to the attention of the judge advocate through this terrible time.

Despair at being abandoned by the British government, combined with desperate hunger, created a pervasive atmosphere of gloom at Sydney Cove. Grim silence descended on the settlement, with each person sunk in fatalistic contemplation of the future, yet all the while "on the tiptoe of expectation" that a ship would any day arrive with supplies. One of the best places to keep a lookout was Dawes's observatory, where on April 5 the sails of ship were seen. It was the *Supply* back from Norfolk Island, bringing the news of the wreck of the *Sirius*. The shock of this disaster was "almost sufficient to have deranged the strongest intellect amongst us," Collins wrote. All eyes now turned toward any distant speck on the horizon in the hope it would be a ship. For the anxious watchers, "some fantastic little cloud . . . deceived impatient imagination into the momentary idea it 'twas a vessel," or else the retort of a musket was thought to be the distant sound of a ship's cannon. No ship came.[28]

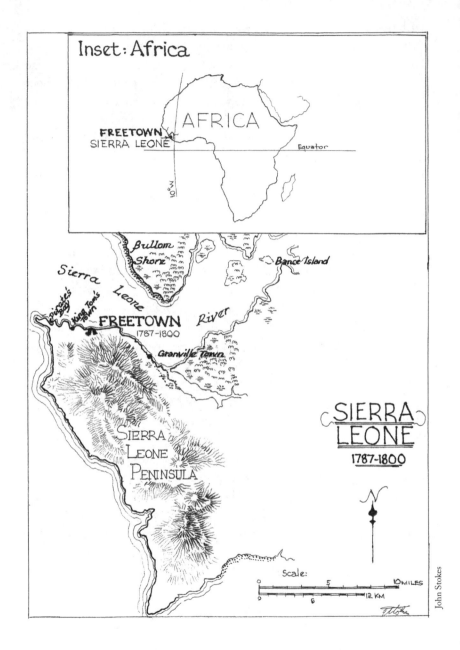

Inset: Africa

AFRICA

FREETOWN
SIERRA LEONE

Equator

10°W

Bullom Shore

Bance Island

Sierra Leone

River

Pirates Bay

King Tom's Town

FREETOWN
1787-1800

Granville Town

SIERRA LEONE PENINSULA

SIERRA LEONE
1787-1800

N

Scale:

0   5   10 MILES

0   6   12 KM

John Stokes

CHAPTER 9

THE PROVINCE OF FREEDOM
IN SIERRA LEONE

In the spring of 1788, the Province of Freedom in Sierra Leone persisted, albeit in terrible hardship. Richard Weaver, the runaway from Philadelphia, was elected governor and chief magistrate soon after arrival. When he fell ill, his position was taken by another black settler, who sold off all the guns and ammunition. In the jaundiced view of the captain of the escort ship, the settlers chose a "chief" every few months and nobody paid that person any heed. Contrary to this opinion, Weaver regained his position as governor and still held the post twelve months later. It was the case, however, that there was no structured form of government to regulate the settlement, such as Granville Sharp had proposed. As Sharp's protégé Elliot Griffith complained, the settlers refused to "be brought to any rule or regulation."[1]

Neither civil nor clerical authority carried weight at Granville Town. Most of the white people sent to assist in the establishment of the Province of Freedom died of fever in the first few months. None of the survivors lingered at Granville Town, promptly seeking alternative employment at the nearby slave factories. The chaplain decamped to Bance Island rather than remain among his anarchic flock, who would provide him neither with a church nor with adequate shelter. He returned to England in March 1788, carrying the news that only about 130 settlers were left in Sierra Leone.

The Committee for the Relief of the Black Poor had been naive to suppose that the settlers would quickly become self-sufficient in Africa. The black emigrants "came too late to plant any rice, or anything else," Richard Weaver complained to Granville Sharp, "for the heavy rain washes out all the ground." Once the rainy season had passed, the seeds sent from England proved to be too old to germinate. Without adequate food supplies, the inexperienced settlers had to barter for food, and their ignorance of local custom led them to give away most of their material goods, including clothes and farming implements. After a year they had no proper shelter and were without the tools or material to build houses. Faced with starvation, many of the settlers took whatever employment they could find. Elliot Griffiths accepted the post as interpreter and teacher for the paramount Koya Temne chief Naimbana, whose daughter he later married; others went to work in the nearby slave depots or took a berth on passing slave ships. It was a cruel irony, but as Weaver explained, the settlers were merely doing what they could to get provision for their support.

Those who continued living at the rudimentary settlement found Sierra Leone a very strange and frightening place, especially after dark. Drums beat throughout the night in the Koya Temne village, less than a mile away, and even this unsettling racket could be drowned out by a sinister concert of whining, whirring insects that found their voice as the dark descended. In the dead of night, leopards emerged from the surrounding forest, looking for prey. The settlers' pet dogs were easy victims for these stealthy hunters. Even more fearsome than the wild beasts were the neighboring slave traders. An entirely destitute people living in a strange place surrounded by slave-trading enterprises, the black settlers at Granville Town were perpetually at risk of being seized as slaves.

Although the settlers were British subjects, they could expect little in the way of protection from the Liverpool slave traders at the nearby Bance Island slave factory. These two white Englishmen regarded their new neighbors as troublesome and offered no protection when the mercurial landlord King Tom decided to settle a dispute by seizing two settlers and selling them to a passing slave ship. A couple of months later, the agents at Bance Island used the very same tactics when five of the male settlers stole some of their provisions. The culprits were given a hasty trial at Bance Island and then sold to a passing French slaver bound for St. Domingo. Richard Weaver made a poignant summation of the settlers' dilemma when he wrote to Sharp, "I think within my own breast that the government did not take the pains to send us here to be made slaves of."[2]

Matters deteriorated further late in 1788, when King Tom died and was succeeded by King Jimmy. The new landlord refused to recognize the treaty his predecessor had signed. Encouraged by the "Liverpool traders," he took a confrontational approach, the settlers complained to Sharp: "[He sent] repeated challenges to our senit [senate], and endeavour[ed] to aggravate us as much as possible . . . leaving us under constant apprehension of all being massacred." Sharp did what he could to respond to the pleas for help from the distraught settlers. Using his own funds, plus a little assistance from the Treasury, he contracted the brig *Myro* to take supplies to Sierra Leone. The *Myro* arrived in August 1788, just in time to deter King Jimmy from forcibly evicting the settlers from Granville Town. Employing Elliot Griffiths as mediator, the captain of the *Myro* negotiated a new treaty with the paramount chief in which the land was ceded to the settlers in return for goods worth eighty-five pounds. Once again, the treaty stated that the Koya Temne would relinquish all claim to the land, only this time the treaty was signed by Naimbana and all four of the local chiefs, including King Jimmy. Richard Weaver and Elliot Griffiths signed on behalf of the black settlers. The land tenure in this treaty was no better understood by the Koya Temne chiefs than in the first.[3]

King Jimmy's aggressive stance was not in the least constrained by this new treaty. By 1789, Richard Weaver was no longer the elected governor and the settler who assumed that role proved impotent in dealing with King Jimmy, who was in constant conflict with the settlers and employed terrifying methods to resolve disputes. Early in 1789, a captured youth was sold as a slave to Gambia, while four other men he seized for debt were sold to a ship on its way to the West Indies. The agents at Bance Island had little sympathy, believing the people at Granville Town to have brought trouble upon their own unruly heads. By the middle of 1789, however, they were prepared to take sides against the aggression of King Jimmy after he captured an American longboat carrying puncheons of rum to Bance Island. He murdered the American sailors, sold the boat to the French depot, and kept the rum for himself. An ungovernable settlement of free blacks was just a nuisance to slave traders; murder and piracy by a local chief threatened the viability of their business.[4]

When the British warship HMS *Pomona* anchored in the bay, both the settlers and the Bance Island agents appealed to its captain to curb

King Jimmy. A party of marines was sent to remonstrate with the chief, with terrible consequences. A spark from a musket discharged by a nervous midshipman set fire to the thatch of a village hut, and within minutes the entire village was ablaze. In the battle that followed, two marines and a settler were killed, as well as about forty of King Jimmy's people. For the next few days, a series of armed skirmishes saw a marine officer and several settlers killed. John Thompson, the man who had once been courier for the governor of New York, was deputized to make contact with Naimbana, the paramount chief, to ask him to negotiate with King Jimmy. Naimbana lived many miles away, and the mission to reach him involved great risk. Thompson was shot dead almost as soon as he set out. The terrified settlers knew that they would be safe from retribution only as long as the *Pomona* stayed at anchor in the bay. In December 1790 when the ship sailed away, King Jimmy gave notice that they had three days to move to a place of safety; then he burned Granville Town to the ground.[5]

Although it would take more than a year for the news of this catastrophe to reach Granville Sharp, the account of events from the captain of the *Pomona* plunged Sharp into despair. Anguished appeals for government assistance to the prime minister for his "poor little ill-thriven swarthy daughter, the unfortunate colony of Sierra Leone" fell on deaf ears. Sharp then turned to his wealthy abolitionist friends, requesting them to form a trading company to provide a stable economic base for his Province of Freedom. Sharp's intention was to elicit subscriptions from men of good faith willing to invest in a trading enterprise in Africa as an alternative to the abhorrent slave trade, as well as a base for spreading Christianity throughout the heathen continent. He recruited the abolitionist parliamentarian William Wilberforce and close associates from the Evangelical Clapham Sect: the banker Henry Thornton, who had succeeded Jonas Hanway as the chairman of the Committee for the Relief of the Black Poor, and Thomas Clarkson, who was the powerhouse behind the campaign for the abolition of slavery.[6]

The incipient Sierra Leone Company had hardly held its first meeting, in February 1792, when the belated news arrived that King Jimmy had destroyed Granville Town. On Thomas Clarkson's advice, the company engaged Alexander Falconbridge, who was once a ship's surgeon in the slave trade and now a vocal opponent of the trade, as their agent to go to Sierra Leone and sort the matter out. Falconbridge left on a slave ship bound for Bance Island, taking with him his new young wife, Anna Maria. He carried a letter from Granville Sharp to "the worthy inhabitants of the territory purchased by the King of Great Britain in Sierra Leone, called the Province of Freedom." Sharp's letter signaled an important change: the black settlers were now regarded as inhabitants of land purchased by the king rather than the owners of land assigned to them and their heirs forever, as both the treaties with the Koya Temne had stated. Sharp explained to the settlers that their future now lay with the company formed by "a number of merchants and gentlemen of the first fortune and credit," and that the land was to be transferred to the company. So long as the settlers behaved, he told them, the directors of the company would provide free lots of land.[7]

The distressed settlers Falconbridge found in Sierra Leone were in no state to take account of these significant changes in their status. They were barely surviving in "an intolerable swamp" on Bob's Island, just up-river from Bance Island, where the Liverpool traders had reluctantly allowed them to shelter. There was no way that they would be permitted to stay. As one of the agents explained to his employer, "It is too near us and they are a set of people we do not like." In particular the slave agents did not like these free black settlers because they mixed with the Africans and gave them "a great many bad notions of white men in general that . . . made them more saucy and troublesome than ever they were before."[8]

Among the forty-six refugees at Bob's Island, Anna Maria Falconbridge was appalled to find seven nearly naked white women who were so "decrepit with disease and so disguised with filth and dirt" that she would never have guessed they were white. Ann, the widow of John Thompson, may have been among them, but Anna Maria did not reveal who exactly these white women were. She lent a willing ear to the lurid story of one of the women that about a hundred prostitutes from London had been made drunk, put aboard the expedition ship, and married to men they had never seen before. When she published the narrative of her visits to Sierra Leone, much was made of this implausible tale. Her horror at the idea of white women married to *"black men . . .* they had never seen before" resonated with voyeuristic titillation.[9]

By April 1791, Alexander Falconbridge had renegotiated a land transfer with Naimbana, in which the Koya Temne were compensated for the assault on King Jimmy's village. In these transactions he was greatly assisted by Elliot Griffiths, now Naimbana's son-in-law. A new settlement was created several miles to the east of the original site, where there was an abandoned village with about seventeen huts ready for occupancy. Falconbridge renamed the new settlement Granville Town and cajoled survivors into forming an armed militia to defend it against any further incursions. The reports he brought back to the company were sufficiently encouraging for the directors to agree to raise £100,000 to develop Sierra Leone as a base for their trading and civilizing enterprise. Subscribers were guaranteed a good return on their investment from money raised through a quit rent on land allocated to new settlers the company would recruit, as well as the cultivation of plantation crops and an extensive trade into the African interior.[10]

The act to incorporate the Sierra Leone Company passed through the House of Commons on June 6, 1791, giving the directors the right to hold the original land grant even though the land was granted to the black poor and their heirs in perpetuity. The directors successfully argued that when the settlers abandoned the land to King Jimmy they lost their claim on it. The directors were also granted the right to make the laws for the governance of the colony. Granville Sharp was forced to accept this "humiliating change" to his original scheme, whereby the settlers were stripped of their right to choose a governor and office bearers, or to exercise control over their affairs. At the same time, he was forced to relinquish the chairmanship to businessman Henry Thornton. Henceforth, the visionary for whom Granville Town was named had next to no influence on its future.[11]

Clearly, if the Sierra Leone Company's beachhead in Africa was to prosper, new settlers would need to be found. No one held hopes for the sixty or so gritty survivors resettled at Granville Town, whom Alexander Falconbridge had damned as "disorderly and turbulent." The directors of the company had not thought to look to the North American Colonies of Nova Scotia and New Brunswick for recruits, yet it was from that unexpected source that their new emigrants would come.[12]

Life in Nova Scotia was hard for both the white and the black refugees who were hurriedly settled there in 1783. Forced to create a new life in inhospitable weather, they were greatly frustrated by innumerable delays in the allocation of their promised land grants. In addition to the bitter cold and grinding poverty, tension between the black settlers and their white neighbors ran high, erupting in a race riot in Shelburne in the first year. As an impoverished and marginal group, the black refugees were cruelly exploited by affluent white settlers, while poor white refugees were furious that blacks undercut their capacity to make a living. Three years after their arrival, many of the black refugees were still waiting for their land allocation. Thomas Peters, the sergeant of the Black Pioneers from North Carolina, was settled at Digby, where land had been surveyed and allocated for the black refugees. Unfortunately the land in question turned out to be part of the clergy reserve, which was kept for the purpose of supporting the Anglican Church. In disgust, Peters moved to New Brunswick. Ralph Henry and his family were among some one hundred disgruntled black refugees who chose to follow him. The great majority of the black refugees stayed in Nova Scotia, creating townships at Birchtown near Shelburne, Digby near Annapolis Royal, and Preston near Halifax.

The one thing that these black communities had in abundance, which allowed them to persist in the face of unremitting hardship, was vibrant religious life. From the very first, the black refugees showed a preference for the emotionally expressive and spontaneous religion of the dissenters, rather than for the established Anglican Church. When the Baptist preacher David George arrived in Halifax from Charleston late in 1782, he found a warm welcome in the churches of New Light, who were despised by the Anglicans for their enthusiastic expression of faith through unrestrained shouting, fainting, and convulsions. This form of worship was responsive to George's highly charged preaching; however, he was discouraged that none of his own color was among the boisterous New Light congregation in Halifax. He decided to move to Shelburne, where black refugees from New York landed in the summer of 1783. At a camp in the woods near the settlement at Shelburne, he "began to sing," drawing an audience of enthralled listeners who came after work each evening "as though they had come for their supper." Every night, George recalled, they had "a little heaven together." Within a year he had a proper meetinghouse and a congregation of more than fifty.[13]

At the same time as he attracted converts, George attracted animosity from the white people in Shelburne, both as a religious dissenter and as the locus of a free black community. He and his congregation were a target for a riot in July 1784, when white soldiers and sailors "came with the tackle of their ship and turned [his] dwelling and every one of [the] houses quite over." George continued to preach in the face of repeated threats, until one night the mob beat him with sticks and drove him into "the swamp." He sought refuge at Birchtown, where the Methodist preacher now known as Daddy Moses had settled with his congregation, but George soon returned, unmolested, to his own meetinghouse in Shelburne.

A gifted and emotional preacher, George was tireless and fearless in his desire to "make a little heaven" in the wilderness. He traveled hundreds of miles to establish Black Baptist congregations at Saint John and Fredericton in New Brunswick, as well as Preston, near Halifax. On his return from a trip to Preston, his lower legs were so severely frostbitten that he was unable to walk for many months. The congregation at Shelburne made a wooden sledge to pull him to his meetinghouse every night so that he could continue to preach. From that time on George was always a little unsteady on his feet.[14]

George found converts at nearby Birchtown, although he chose not to continue preaching there, probably because of the influence of Daddy Moses, whose distinctive brand of Methodism had already claimed significant allegiance among the black refugees. A licensed Methodist preacher who visited Birchtown in 1784 was astonished to find fourteen Methodist classes meeting nightly, a wondrous circumstance due entirely to "a poor negro" who could "neither see, walk nor stand." Boston King had vivid evidence of the potency of Daddy Moses's preaching when his wife, Violet, fell to the ground in convulsions, crying for mercy, which continued for another six days "until the Lord spoke peace to her soul." Deeply impressed though King was with his wife's dramatic conversion, as well as similar conversions of many of his neighbors in subsequent weeks, he lingered in dark despair for many months before the Lord finally called to him in March 1784. For King, the liberation of the spirit was essential in the perilous journey from slavery to freedom; only when freed from both physical and spiritual bondage could the regenerated self emerge from the wilderness into the land of Canaan. He wrote of his experience of redemption, "Everything appeared to me in a different light. . . . I was now become a new creature." When the white American Methodist circuit rider Freeborn Garrettson visited Birch-town a year later, King found the inspiration to visit his "poor ungodly neighbours, and exhort them to fear the Lord, and seek him while he might be found." By 1791 he was preacher for the racially mixed Methodist congregation at Darmouth, next to Preston.[15]

On his occasional visits to Birchtown, Freeborn Garrettson tried, with little success, to contain the "enthusiasm" of the black Methodist congregation within accepted Wesleyan practice. Fearing contamination from the "pious frenzy" of the New Light sect, of which he profoundly disapproved, he despaired that no licensed preacher was available to guide to this volatile congregation along the proper path. Like the appalled Anglican missionaries who tried to minister to the black refugees, he failed to appreciate that their raucous spiritual expression owed little to the influence of New Light and reached back to a much older African past. The cultural practices that had nurtured the unregenerate self did not need to be abandoned in order for the followers of Daddy Moses to believe that they were reborn in God's grace.[16]

Garrettson was particularly concerned about contamination from the New Light doctrine that the sins of the body did not affect the union of the spirit with God, and that a sinner could find salvation as readily as one who abided by moral laws. The same dangerous antinomian tendency was found in the Methodist breakaway group who preached a doctrine of predestination founded by the Countess of Huntingdon. When John Marrant, a black sailor from Charleston who was ordained by the countess, arrived in Nova Scotia in December 1785, Garrettson was sure he was sent by the devil. Despite warnings that this black preacher "did not come from Mr. Wesley, and preached there was no repentance this side the grave," Marrant was permitted to preach in the meeting-house of Daddy Moses. The effect on his audience was electric. As Marrant described in his journal, "Many were not able to contain; but cried out to God to have mercy upon them . . . several sinners were carried out, pricked to the heart." Inevitably there was conflict with Daddy Moses as the two strove to gain spiritual ascendancy in Birchtown. For all his humiliation of the "the old blind man," Marrant was not able win over more than a minority of people, although these converts remained fiercely committed, even after Marrant left for America left three years later. The Countess of Huntingdon's Connexion continued to thrive under the leadership of Cato Perkins and William Ashe, whom Marrant probably knew from a previous life in Charleston.[17]

Rich spiritual experience was the only consolation for a life of appalling poverty in Nova Scotia. A white visitor to Birchtown was shocked by their huts, "miserable to guard against the inclemency of a Nova Scotia winter," and that they had to survive the long winter "depending on what they could lay up in the summer." In the opinion of this witness, "the wretchedness and poverty so strongly perceptible in the garb and continence of . . . these miserable outcasts" were as extreme as he had ever seen. Boston King later recalled that in the winter of 1789, when famine stalked the whole province of Nova Scotia, families at Birchtown were forced to sell everything they had to get a few pounds of flour. "When they had parted with all their clothes, even to their blankets several of them fell down dead in the streets from hunger," King wrote. Life was no better at Digby and Preston.[18]

Nearly all of the black refugees in Nova Scotia finally received their land by 1788. On average, the land allocation to the black refugees was forty acres, smaller than the lots allocated to whites, although "Colonel" Stephen Blueke, who was still a bulwark of the Anglican Church, received a grant of two hundred acres. In New Brunswick, the black settlers were also allocated land, but it was many miles away from their town lots in Saint John and Fredericton, "worthless in itself from its remote situation," as Thomas Peters bitterly complained. By 1790, Peters was fifty-three years old but undiminished in his determination to see his black constituency receive what was their due. In 1790, he left his family behind and made the voyage across the Atlantic to the unknown metropolis of London to put the grievances of the black refugees to the British government.[19]

Peters arrived in London in October 1790 and by November had tracked down his old commander in chief, Sir Henry Clinton, who provided him with a letter of introduction to the Home Office, urging the secretary of state to give credence to the "melancholy tale" Peters had to tell. Clinton also put Peters in touch with William Wilberforce, and through him Peters found the man he most wanted to meet, Granville Sharp. Peters had heard about the settlement in Sierra Leone, and it was the idea of the Province of Freedom more than anything that had propelled him across the Atlantic. Here was a potential home for the disaffected black refugees, he believed. By a stroke of luck Peters arrived in London at just the very time that Sharp was struggling to find ways to save his "poor little ill-thriven swarthy daughter."[20]

It was Sharp who helped Peters frame his petition to Pitt's government to request that the black refugees be resettled someplace where they could "by their industrious exertions become useful subjects to His Majesty." Nova Scotia was unacceptable, Peters argued, because of "a degrading and unjust prejudice against people of colour that even those who are acknowledged to be free . . . [were] refused the common rights and privileges of other inhabitants, not being permitted to vote at any elections nor serve on juries." It was impossible for blacks to get redress for wages denied or violent attack, Peters pointed out. Surely this was not what the government intended for its loyal black subjects?[21]

In response to these acutely embarrassing accusations of bad faith, the prime minister put pressure on the colonial governors of Nova Scotia and New Brunswick to ensure that outstanding land grants be allocated to the black refugees. Going further, he undertook to pay the necessary expenses to transport as many black settlers as wished to leave Nova Scotia. The freshly incorporated Sierra Leone Company, delighted with the prospect of new settlers for their colony, offered free grants of land to any who wanted to emigrate. New settlers were promised twenty acres for every man, ten for every woman, and five for every child, "subject to certain charges and obligations."[22]

John Clarkson, brother of Thomas Clarkson and friend of William Wilberforce, was on temporary leave as a lieutenant in the Royal Navy when he was engaged as the company agent to collect the emigrants in Nova Scotia and take them to Sierra Leone. He did a sterling job selling the company's offer in Nova Scotia, traveling from one black settlement to another, steadfastly refuting the negative interpretations offered by white critics. He was much impressed with the people he met, comparing them very favorably to the laboring poor of England. Clarkson first went to Preston, where Mingo Jordan had a large Methodist congregation, and was delighted when more than two hundred people indicated their willingness to emigrate. Boston King, the Methodist preacher at nearby Dartmouth, also chose to emigrate to Africa with his flock. At Birchtown, Clarkson addressed hundreds who crammed into Daddy Moses Wilkinson's Methodist meetinghouse. Patiently he explained to these eager listeners that the expression "subject to certain charges and obligations" did not signify that an annual rent would be levied on the land; rather it referred to "a kind of tax for charitable purposes such as for the maintenance of their poor, the care of the sick, and the education of their children." Clarkson's black audience accepted his explanation, and they especially warmed to his assurance that, unlike in Nova Scotia, where they were barred from voting or serving on juries, there would be no discrimination between white and black settlers in Sierra Leone. Clarkson's words were quickly transmitted to the rest of the community, and within three days the entire Methodist congregations of Daddy Moses and Luke Jordan had agreed to go. As well, Cato Perkins, William Ashe, and all who belonged to the Countess of Huntingdon's Connexion elected to follow Clarkson to Sierra Leone. The addition of David George's Baptist congregation from nearby Shelburne brought the total of emigrants from that area to 600 people. Digby contributed another large contingent of about 180 people, nearly all of them Methodists. The families of Thomas Peters and Ralph Henry were among 200 people, of both Methodist and Baptist persuasion, who walked overland from New Brunswick to be included in the exodus.[23]

The expectation was that only a few hundred black refugees would take up the offer to settle in Sierra Leone. Neither the British government nor the Sierra Leone Company was prepared for the scale of the migration. Half of the black refugees in Nova Scotia and New Brunswick were determined to leave, many of them abandoning their freehold land grants. A surviving list of emigrants from Birchtown and the Shelburne area reveals how much was left behind. Harry Washington, described as a farmer, born in Africa, and fifty years old (although he was probably fifty-three), was traveling with his wife, Jenny, and carrying an ax, saw, and pickax, plus three hoes, as well as two muskets and several items of furniture. He left behind two town lots, a house, and forty acres. It was the same story for Isaac Anderson, age forty, born in Angola, who was traveling with his wife, Sarah, and three children. Every head of household named on the list owned one or two town lots, at the very least, and most were abandoning forty acres of freehold land. David George, said to be forty-eight and traveling with a wife and six children, had the most substantial property of five town lots, two houses, and fifty acres. George managed to sell off at least part of his holdings before he left. Nathaniel Snowball was not so fortunate; Clarkson was obliged to pay off his debts before Snowball was permitted to leave with his extended family. Clarkson also cleared the debts of Thomas Peters and William Ashe.[24]

Fifteen ships were needed to carry nearly 1,200 people to Sierra Leone, at a cost of £15,500 to the British government. Alexander Falconbridge, who had actually been to Sierra Leone, was greatly disturbed at the "premature, hair-brained and ill-digested scheme" of injecting such a large number of settlers into a largely untamed and disease-ridden wilderness, "before they were certain of possessing an acre of land." The directors of the Sierra Leone Company paid no heed. So delighted were they with the response from Nova Scotia that they shelved plans to encourage white settlers to emigrate from England. Henceforth the only whites in Sierra Leone would be a handful of company employees.[25]

William Wilberforce, a company director, told Clarkson that he should call the new black settlers Africans, believing that this was "a more respectable way of speaking of them," but this was emphatically not how they conceived of themselves. In their eyes they were free British subjects and emphatically they were Christians. They had migrated as whole congregations and were led ashore by their preachers, singing the old Wesleyan hymn:

Wake! Every heart and every tongue
To praise the Savior's name.
The day of Jubilee is come!
Return ye, ransomed sinners, home.[26]

The new emigrants were dismayed to discover that even though several company ships had arrived before them not a jot of work had been done to clear the site. They had to hack a path through the tangle of thorny bush and sharp-edged elephant grass, then clear the original site razed by King Jimmy, where a settlement called Freetown would be built, even though it was reclaimed by jungle that proved "extremely difficult to penetrate." About six miles away to the east was Granville Town, where the original settlers lived. Alexander Falconbridge, who had returned to Sierra Leone as the company's commercial agent, had given Clarkson such a jaundiced view of the original settlers that Clarkson refused to be responsible for such an "immoral, idle, discontented, ungovernable, people" and threatened to flog any who attempted to come into Freetown. He made an exception for Elliot Griffiths, whom he appointed the company interpreter, hoping to make good use of Griffiths and his association with his powerful father-in-law, Naimbana.[27]

Once a site was cleared, the first task was to erect some form of shelter other than flimsy tents. Temporary huts were made from green saplings woven together and plastered with mud to support a thatch of grass, providing some protection from the heat but vulnerable to invasion from wildlife. One night soon after arrival, a gorilla carried off a girl, whose startled father had to wrestle with the animal to save her. Another settler only just managed to scare a big leopard away from his sleeping wife and daughter. The jungle concealed many varieties of poisonous snakes, and an unwary step might bring terrible death. One of the dogs died instantly from the bite of a beautifully marked snake about four feet long. Anna Maria Falconbridge claimed to have seen a snake that was nine feet in length.

As if these were not trials enough, Clarkson began to suspect that he had a serpent nursing at his breast. On March 22, 1792, Thomas Peters called on the governor to express his concerns about the parlous situation in Freetown. He was "extremely violent and indiscreet," Clarkson wrote in his journal, "as if he were desirous of alarming and disheartening the people." He decided that it must be Peters who was responsible for the "irritability of temper and peevish disposition" the settlers had begun to display. Although they had once been close, Clarkson was now ready to vilify his old friend as a man of "great penetration and cunning" who had been "working in the dark . . . to get himself at the head of the people." Self-evidently, Peters was already the "at the head of the people." It was he who was elected to go to England to petition the government on their behalf; he had garnered the support of the British government; he had marshaled Nova Scotia's black refugees to emigrate. Yet on arrival in Sierra Leone, Clarkson was appointed governor and Peters was denied any role in the administration of the new settlement. Clarkson's rancorous response was prompted by fear that Peters believed that he, not Clarkson, should have been the appointed governor.[28]

Turbulent discontent inspired by Peters's complaints brought Clarkson to the end of his tether, with "fainting fits and hysteric weeping frequently," yet he maintained a steely determination that he, and only he, would be in charge. In mid-April 1792, Clarkson engineered a confrontation with his imagined rival under a massive cotton tree and threatened that "one or other of us would be hanged on that tree" before the matter was settled. This was a naval officer's response to mutiny; as governor of Sierra Leone he had no judicial right to execute anyone. At a subliminal level at least, Clarkson knew that the challenge from Peters was justified, and perhaps this was why his reaction was so virulent. Petulant self-justification filled his journal and letters as he railed, "This wretch would have driven all the whites out of the place and ruined himself and his brethren." Everywhere Clarkson cared to look was evidence that Peters was not acting out of personal pique but giving expression to a shared disillusionment. The settlers had every reason to fret, he acknowledged, as they had been "deceived and ill-treated through life . . . and seeing no probability of getting their land, they began to think, they should be served the same way as in [Nova Scotia] which unsettles their minds and makes them suspect everything and everybody." Clarkson's response to this insight was not to share the decision-making; rather he organized to have Peters's activities watched and demanded stronger executive powers from the company.[29]

Just as the black settlers began to adjust to their new circumstances and create a viable community, the monsoon rain arrived. About three o'clock in the morning on April 2, Clarkson recorded, "A great deal of lightening, torrents of rain came down with heavy squalls of wind and several loud claps of thunder repeated by the deep roaring echoes of the mountains." The settlers' inadequate huts were badly damaged, and the next day a tornado ripped through the tattered dwellings. This first rainy season proved to be one of the wettest that the Koya Temne could remember. With inadequate shelter from the rain, and forced to sleep on the ground, nearly everyone came down with malarial fever. Anna Maria Falconbridge described a desperate situation, with more than seven hundred of the new settlers "under the affliction of burning fevers," and no more than two hundred "scarce able to crawl about." Handfuls of people died every day, to be buried with "as little ceremony as so many dogs and cats." The provisions brought from England by the company ships were completely spoiled, and the steaming monsoonal air carried the nauseating stench of rotting food. Boston King's wife, Violet King, was just one of 138 Nova Scotia settlers who died that season.[30]

In the midst of this terrible time, Clarkson was tested by demands from the settlers who had "imbibed strange notions from Thomas Peters as to their civil rights." They wanted a greater say in the management of their affairs, and they wanted to have their own elected representatives keep order and resolve disputes. In a conciliatory gesture, Clarkson agreed that they might elect black juries to hear disputes, but only if they submitted their choice to him for veto. By that time Peters was too ill to protest. He died on June 26 a sorely disillusioned man, leaving his wife, Sally, with seven fatherless children to support.

If Clarkson believed the settlers' "strange notions... as to their civil rights" would die with Peters, he was far wrong. Just before Peters's death, Clarkson received an unambiguous letter from an anxious settler chiding him that it was all very well to make promises; they needed to be kept. The king had promised them land when they left America, his correspondent reminded him, "but you know governor, the state you found us in Nova Scotia and New Brunswick." He went on to explain that they were in Sierra Leone with no land: We now not having got our lands... makes us very uneasy in mind fearing we shall be liable to the same cruel treatment as we have before experienced." The day Peters died, a petition from the Methodist congregation protested Clarkson's assumption of power over them. The eccentric spelling betrayed the authors as barely literate, and the tone of the letter was deeply deferential but far from submissive. The Methodist settlers told him they willingly agreed to be governed by the laws of England, but went on, "We do not consent to gave it into your honer hands with out haven aney of our own culler in it." They reminded Clarkson that he had promised them that "whoever came to Saraleon wold be free and should have a law and . . . all should be equel." So, the petition continued, "we have a right to chuse men that we think proper for to act for us in a reasnenble manner." In the matter of governance and the administration of justice, they were adamant: "To gave all out of our hands we cannot."[31]

By late July, the settlers were "driven to despair," according to the company secretary, because the survey for the farm lots they had been promised had not yet begun. They had only the rudimentary huts they had built on small town lots carved out of the jungle, and their only basis for subsistence was the credit at the company store paid for two days a week of work for the company. Their habit of trusting Clarkson was all that protected the company's handful of haughty, idle, and incompetent white employees from their collective wrath. Without Clarkson, the company secretary confided in his journal, "I should scarce think it safe to stay among them."[33]

CHAPTER 10

AT THE END OF THE WORLD
IN NEW SOUTH WALES

At the other end of the world, the convicts and marines in the remote penal colony of New South Wales faced lingering death from starvation, a prospect made all the more excruciating because they knew no more about what was happening in England than the goings-on on the moon. Lord Sydney had chosen New South Wales as a penal colony because of its extreme isolation; it was more than four thousand nautical miles away from the nearest European outpost at Batavia (present day Java) and nearly seven thousand miles from Cape Town. In April 1790, the desperate Governor Phillip decided that their sole ship, the *Supply,* which was only 170 tons, must sail to Batavia to get whatever supplies it could carry. It was a distant hope that the ship could return in time to ward off famine, but that slim possibility was more predictable than waiting on phantom ships from England. In the meantime, "labour and attention were turned on one object—the procuring of food." The basic commodity of flour had become "more tempting than the ore of Peru."[1]

The penalty for stealing food was increased from one thousand to two thousand lashes, as if such a penalty would make a difference. A convict in hospital, recuperating from his first five hundred lashes and waiting to receive the next installment of five hundred, somehow managed to get the irons off one of his legs to hobble to the nearest garden and gnaw on some turnips. It was against the law to buy another's rations, yet a trade in food persisted, sometimes with tragic consequences. A convict "with a wild and haggard countenance" collapsed in the street, and the autopsy revealed that he had not eaten for days; he had been selling his ration. Convicts found a ready market among those who "from their situation were not likely to be suspected," Governor Phillip later explained to the secretary of state, referring to officers who had the capacity to pay a bottle of rum for ten pounds of flour. Lieutenant William

Dawes was found to have been buying flour from a convict, though he protested that he was unaware the flour was part of the convict ration. The governor did not believe him, pointing out that Dawes had been previously reprimanded for buying dried peas from convicts. There was little Phillip could do about Dawes, who was a marine officer and therefore "not amenable to a general court martial in this country."[2]

While immune to legal proceedings in Sydney Cove, the officers acted as both judge and jury for any convicts who transgressed the governor's iron rules about food. Dawes was one of the officers who heard the case against "Black Jemmy" Williams, charged with stealing biscuits on April 11, 1790. Williams had been rolling some casks from the wharf to the commissary store when he noticed the cask of ship's biscuits was broken. He admitted that he took the biscuits that had fallen out, believing he had the customary right to the spillage. The court did not agree and sentenced him to suffer a second dose of five hundred lashes, laid on in "the usual manner." In the same court another black convict was sentenced to two thousand lashes for helping himself to some potatoes from an officer's garden. Marine captain Watkin Tench, who was also sitting in judgment with Dawes that day, ruefully recorded "the melancholy lengths" to which they were compelled to stretch the penal system.[3]

On April 19 the little *Supply* set sail for Batavia with all the colony's hopes on board "to the lowest abyss of misery," Judge Advocate Collins recorded. Unknown to him, Black Jemmy was also on board, having stowed away in order to escape another five hundred lashes on his cruelly scarred back. Black Jemmy was originally a seaman, and he was almost certainly helped by the crew to avoid detection until the ship was well on its way to Batavia. Although he was returned to Sydney nine months later, he escaped the very worst of the famine and the punitive brutality it spawned.[4]

On the evening of June 3, 1790, anxious eyes compulsively scanning the horizon were finally rewarded with the sight of a real sail. A large ship flying English colors was making its way into the harbor. The *Lady Juliana* had sailed from Plymouth ten months earlier and was carrying enough rations to fend off starvation, together with a cargo of 222 female convicts. Women were once objects of intense desire, but to the sunken-eyed, hungry officers who rowed out to meet the ship, the women on the *Lady Juliana* were no more than useless mouths to feed. Collins sourly observed that many were old and likely to require labor to assist them rather than to contribute to the new colony. Tench paid the women no heed; all he could think of was the mail. Letters torn open by trembling hands burst upon him "like meridian splendour on a blind man," releasing a flood of pent-up news. The colonists learned that there had been a revolution in France and that King George was now completely recovered from a strange malady they never knew he had. The unwelcome news was that another thousand male convicts were on their way.[5]

Scenes of ecstatic jubilation greeted the storeship *Justinian* when it sailed into the harbor a few days later, carrying enough supplies for a year. There were no such expressions of joy on June 29 when the ships carrying the promised male convicts arrived. Holding rags to their faces in a vain attempt to ward off the stench, marines in longboats received the cargo of naked, emaciated men, crawling with lice and encrusted with human excreta, "slung over the ship side in the same manner as they would sling a cask," the horrified chaplain reported. Scurvy-racked and unable to walk, they dragged themselves on hands and knees on to the shore, where they lay on the damp ground, stupefied from the intake of fresh air. Those whose hearts had failed them at the first exposure to air had been thrown overboard, their bruised bodies washed up on the rocks by the tide. Nearly three hundred had died on the voyage. The chaplain estimated that "the landed sick were near five hundred," many of whom died in the next few weeks. Those able to speak said that they had been kept chained belowdecks for the entire journey and systematically starved of rations. They had lain shackled to corpses for as long as they could bear the stench, just so they could get the dead prisoner's meager ration. Everything they had owned, even their clothes, had been stolen by the ship's captain, they told the chaplain.[6]

This fleet of convict transports was contracted to the slave-trading firm of Camden, Calvert, and King, which previously transported convicts to Africa. According to an army officer who accompanied the convicts, the dreadful mortality and hideous conditions were directly attributable to that contract. These English convicts had been shackled in the same "barbarous" way as a slave cargo, he wrote to the abolitionist

William Wilberforce, which made it "impossible for them to move but at the risk of both legs being broken." What made the Second Fleet utterly infamous was that unlike slave cargo, the convicts had no value, so no attention was given to keeping them fit and alive. "The slave trade is merciful compared with what I have seen in this fleet," the officer concluded. What did have value in a settlement that had been without supplies for more than three years were the convict rations and clothing. As soon as their debilitated human cargo was unloaded, the masters of the ships set up a store on the wharf to sell the held-back clothes and rations, which "were eagerly bought up."[7]

These ships brought no immediate release for John Martin, now two years beyond the expiry of his sentence. The papers relating to the sentences of First Fleet convicts were not on board the Second Fleet either. Some good fortune came his way, however. Martin found himself a wife, Ann Toy, whom he formally married two years later. His friend John Randall, whose first wife had died, married Mary Butler almost immediately after the *Lady Juliana* had discharged its cargo.

Randall was kept on as one of three official game shooters for the settlement, even though game meat was no longer a desperate need, along with two white gamekeepers. The position allowed him to maintain an independent existence within the ironbound penal system at Sydney Cove, ranging widely through the bush, often out for days at a time, tracking and shooting kangaroo. He and his fellow gamekeepers also acted as guides for Tench and Dawes when they went exploring the country north and west of Sydney, sometimes for weeks at a time. While working in the bush, Randall maintained good relationships with the Aborigines, in contrast to the white game shooter John McIntyre, who had earned their powerful enmity. Tench noted with interest that Aborigines he met on his expeditions regarded McIntyre "with every mark of horror and resentment." It was no surprise to him when McIntyre was fatally speared.[8]

On December 9, 1790, the three gamekeepers were hunting in familiar territory at Botany Bay, south of Sydney. On previous hunting trips they had constructed a hut of boughs, after the Aboriginal fashion, and it was in this hut that they sheltered overnight, waiting for the elusive kangaroo to emerge at dawn. About midnight they found themselves surrounded by Aboriginal men with spears. McIntyre was deliberately speared in the side, but Randall and the other white man were not threatened. There was no doubt that the attack was premeditated and specific. The weapon used was specially designed to cause the maximum damage, with ingenious stone barbs attached with gum resin to the spearhead, which broke off within McIntyre's body when the spear was drawn out, thereby guaranteeing a slow and excruciatingly painful death. Friendly Aborigines at Sydney Cove supplied the identity of the assailant, a warrior they called Pemulwuy.

While Tench could see that McIntyre had given serious offense to the Aborigines and probably deserved his ritual punishment, the governor insisted that this killing was entirely unprovoked. He determined that there must be a massive reprisal, and Tench was ordered to lead an expedition to Botany Bay to bring in Pemulwuy for execution, as well as the heads of ten Aboriginal men. Dawes, who had been taking pains to study the Aborigines and learn their language, was appalled to be included in this order and initially refused to be part of the action, although he was eventually persuaded to do his duty by the chaplain. Randall and the other gamekeeper with McIntyre at the time of the attack were chosen as guides for the grisly expedition.

More than fifty men left the settlement at dawn on December 14, 1790, carrying muskets, hatchets for decapitation, and bags for the heads. When they reached Botany Bay, they were unable to find a single Aborigine. The overheated, insect-bitten party trudged back to Sydney, only to be ordered out again. This time, Tench was determined to have an element of surprise. He instructed the guides to find the quickest route to Botany Bay "without heeding difficulty or impediment." Randall and his fellow guide led them to a swampy area, which they advised was "bad to cross, but might be got over." Desperate for the advantage, Tench urged his men on, only to see them become mired in quicksand up to their chests, where they would have smothered had not the ropes intended for the Aboriginal victims been used to pull them free. Badly shaken and encrusted with mud, they continued a rapid march to the designated Aboriginal village, where there was not a soul to be seen. The Aborigines had been gone for days.[9]

Rather than a lesson for the indigenous Australians about European superiority, the punitive expedition was a complete farce—"the most teadious march as ever men went," as one exhausted marine recorded in his diary. The expedition proved a humiliation for Tench, and it cost Dawes his place in the colony. Owing to his insubordination on this occasion and his criminal behavior in purchasing rations from starving convicts, Dawes was denied promotion and recalled to England a year later. If anyone gained an advantage from these farcical events, it was John Randall. Having failed to lead the head-hunting marines to Pemulwuy, he incurred no personal enmity from the Aborigines and continued to hunt game unmolested. At the same time, he had demonstrated his trustworthiness and loyalty to the governor, which stood him in good stead. He was permitted to live an almost entirely independent life, armed and at liberty to move outside the settlement, more or less as he chose. When at home, he enjoyed the pleasures of a proper family. Among the very first children born in Sydney Cove was his daughter Frances; a second daughter, Lydia, was born in July 1791.[10]

Two other convicts able to enjoy a considerable measure of freedom were Daniel Gordon and Caesar, both of whom were a thousand miles away on Norfolk Island. In order to avoid mass starvation, the commanding officer on Norfolk Island allocated lots of land to be cleared and cultivated by small groups of convicts so that they could become self-sufficient. Daniel Gordon was not well disposed to farming; he found that he could make a living from his old profession as tailor to the officers. Caesar, on the other hand, was supporting himself on his lot in November 1791. He was also supporting his common-law wife, the Irish convict Ann Poore, who was one of the convict women from the *Lady Juliana* sent to Norfolk Island to improve the gender ratio. Their daughter, named Mary-Ann, was born in March 1792. For all his apparent industry, Caesar was returned to Sydney a year after his daughter's birth, with neither wife nor child. A new commander had arrived on Norfolk Island, who decided to get rid of "any such characters who might be dangerous or troublesome." Caesar had been in no trouble during his time on the island, so it must have been the anticipation of strife that saw this hardworking convict torn away from his family. On this small island where the men outnumbered the women two to one, conflict was brewing with the soldiers and retired marines recently sent to the island, who determined that they should have the benefit of convict labor, and the benefit of convict women as well. Once again, Caesar was reduced to hauling carts in the streets of Sydney Cove like a beast of burden, on pitifully short rations.[11]

At Sydney Cove the convicts tried all manner of means to get away. From the first day, when "stragglers" tried to follow the Aboriginal track to Botany Bay in hopes of joining the ships of a French scientific expedition at anchor there, people sought to escape. A group of twenty men and one pregnant woman attempted to walk to China, believing it to be a place a hundred miles or so to the north where there were "a copper-coloured people, who would receive them and treat them kindly." Plenty of absconders died in their attempt; most were driven back to the settlement by a combination of starvation and terror. Black Jemmy very nearly got away. He made it more than four thousand miles north to Batavia before he was discovered as a stowaway on the *Supply* and was sent back as crew on the return passage. When he arrived back at Sydney Cove, the captain was so full of praise for this young man that the governor was inclined to forgive the outstanding punishment, until convinced that to do so would only encourage more stowaways. The punishment was cut in half. Black Jemmy's back was again shredded with 250 strokes of the cat. Less than a year later, he stowed away on the *Atlantic* bound for Calcutta. This time he got as far as the River Ganges before being discovered by the naval agent on board, who refused to accept Black Jemmy's claim to be a free man whose sentence had expired. Once more he was shipped all the way back to New South Wales to have his claim verified.[12]

The record of sentences of the convicts on the First Fleet eventually arrived in the colony in May 1791, some four years after the fleet had sailed. Those whose time had long since expired, like John Martin, were given the options to take up land as free settlers or sign on for an additional eighteen months of labor in return for clothing and rations. Most vehemently declared that they would quit the place. They were free to leave, they were told, if they could find a ship willing to take them. Here was the rub: few ships came to remote Sydney Cove, where the sight of a sail remained an occasion for great excitement. Those ships that did come had little need of fresh crew. Faced with a choice, John Martin did not at first elect to take land and continued to work for rations. If he was among the majority of emancipated convicts itching to get away, the wherewithal eluded him. Early in August 1792, the governor announced that only a select few of the ex-convicts would be permitted to leave, and then only if they carried a signed certificate to that effect. A new clause was to be inserted into shipping contracts to penalize the master of any ship that took away anyone who did not hold such a certificate. That same month, Martin confirmed his future in the colony by marrying Ann Toy, who still had her sentence to serve.[13]

The *Atlantic* arrived back from India in June 1792 with a load of despised dhal instead of the expected ration of flour, as well as the stowaway Black Jemmy, who was still insisting that he was a free man. The judge advocate checked the record to find that, yes, Black Jemmy made an accurate count, having been sentenced to seven years in May 1785. No further punishment was necessary, Collins decided, and Black Jemmy was "at liberty to get away in any ship that would receive him on board." A young man with recent experience as a seaman and excellent recommendations from the ship's captain, he was better placed than most to secure a berth. He was probably one of two ex-convicts who left on the *Atlantic* when it took the retiring Governor Phillip to England in December of that year. One way or another, Black Jemmy finally made his escape from New South Wales, albeit to a perilously uncertain future. Any black seaman who worked in the Atlantic or the Caribbean ran the risk of being snatched by man hunters and sold into slavery. That ever-present risk may have influenced the choice of the ex-seaman John Martin to continue in the place of his incarceration. After all was said and done, there was no chattel slavery in New South Wales, however brutal and coercive its penal system. The nearest slave market was more than six thousand nautical miles away at the Cape.[14]

Martin's option of working in return for rations from the store became less and less viable as the expected ships from England again failed to arrive. That the colony was so dependent on stores from England rather than harvesting the abundant natural resources was a source of astonishment to the magistrate at the new penal settlement of Parramatta, west of Sydney. "The quantities of fish in the harbour is amazing," he wrote, "I should imagine the fishery under proper regulations might be of great advantage." He watched helplessly as recently arrived convicts, already weak from their traumatic journey, died at a terrifying rate for want of adequate food. "If the convicts had but an opportunity to fish," he despaired, "but there is no trusting of them with a boat." Just as distressing was the daily business of his court, where he found himself "obliged to punish those whom hunger drove to steal a few cobs of corn or a turnip." Half-starved convicts were still required to do backbreaking work, "yoked to draw timber twenty-five in a gang," as one Irish convict later recounted. "The sticks were six feet long, six men abreast. We held the stick behind us and dragged it with our hands." This when they were being fed a few ounces of salt meat a day.[15]

It was of particular concern to the magistrate that the fundamental staple of flour was absent from their ration. The substitute, cobs of Indian corn, was "little use in point of nourishment," he wrote; "they have no mills to grind it and many are so weak that they cannot pound it." Since a fishery was not in operation, the only way to survive the increasingly severe rations was to grow a garden. The magistrate noted with approval that ex-convict settlers who had taken land grants on the northern boundary of Parramatta had had plenty of vegetables and corn, as well as several pigs, to provide for their families. If periodic starvation could be avoided, he concluded, one must have the capacity to become self-sufficient. John Martin reached the same conclusion. In November 1792 he took up a fifty-acre grant of land about three miles northeast of Parramatta.[16]

John Randall finished his sentence in April 1792. With a wife who still had time to serve, as well as his small daughters, Francis and Lydia, Randall chose to stay and take his chances as a farmer in the colony. It was surely no coincidence that on the same day Martin received his fifty-acre grant, Randall was given a grant of sixty acres adjacent to him, a place commonly known as the Northern Boundary Farms. To call this place "farms" was a complete misnomer; the land in question was a tract of wilderness of which grants were given to emancipated convicts on the condition that after eighteen months the grantees would have cleared the virgin bush and raised enough crops for their subsistence, so they could be "off the store" within that time. Those taking up the grants were given two pigs as initial livestock. To assist in clearing the land, they were supplied with a hatchet, two spades, and a shovel.[17]

At the Northern Boundary Farms the eucalyptus trees reached a hundred feet into the unclouded sky, while the undergrowth was a tangle of bushes armed with hidden prickles. Areas of open vegetation, which looked like grassy sward on which stock could graze, proved to be clumps of razor-sharp spear grass that hid snakes with venom potent enough to kill a pig in minutes. Even when the huge trees could be felled, it was found that the extensive root system was bound into the soil in an uncompromising mass. Torrential rain that swept in from the ocean drained away almost as soon as it settled, leaving the ground parched and hard-baked. There was little prospect that a man with no experience of rural labor could wrest a viable farm out of this howling wilderness, in the opinion of Watkin Tench, who paid a visit to the area just about the time that Randall and Martin took up their grants. In a year or so, he predicted, any inexperienced ex-convict would "have the honour of returning to drag a timber or brick cart for his maintenance."[18]

By the end of 1792 the only the black convicts still yoked to the carts or hauling timber were John Moseley, Black Jack Williams, and Caesar. How Moseley survived at Sydney Cove is something of a mystery. He never came to the attention of the indefatigable chroniclers of the early settlement, David Collins and Watkin Tench. Throughout his time in New South Wales he escaped scrutiny, despite his conspicuous color and background. Freed from servitude after twelve years, he did not marry or father children in the colony; perhaps he still considered himself married to the mother of his child in England. Black Jack, as John Williams was known, was due for emancipation in August 1791, yet he was kept in servitude. His sentence must have been extended when a pardon had saved him from the hangman in 1788. Such was the capricious nature of the governor's mercy that his senior partner in the crime, the wily Daniel Gordon, who had twice cheated the gallows and been sent to Norfolk Island as a miscreant, was nonetheless a free man. The "ignorant black youth" the governor had wanted to save was faced with another thirteen years of forced labor before he was free. Caesar had been given a secondary sentence of life, as well as twice being sentenced to death and twice pardoned, so he had no hope of emancipation. After being forcibly returned to Sydney Cove without his family, this "incorrigibly stubborn black," as Collins described him, made himself the most notorious convict in the colony when he "once more fled from honest labour" into the bush, leading a gang of armed convict absconders who plundered farms on the outskirts of the settlement, until his flamboyant career was terminated by bounty hunters in 1797.[19]

For Martin and Randall, felling massive trees to wrest farms from the wilderness and building huts from the rudimentary material they could find was terribly hard work. In the stressful first year, it was not so much their lack of prior farming experience that was against them, as the weather. During the first few months that they worked on their land grants, the daytime temperature hovered between 102 and 114 degrees in the shade. The ground was littered with the lifeless bodies of birds that dropped from the sky. The two men and their wives struggled to clear enough land for a hut, to plant a garden, and to sow a crop of Indian corn, in the face of fierce winds that blew from the west like the blast from an oven.[20]

On December 7, 1792, a wildfire swept through the tinder-dry bush, threatening huts and destroying gardens. Fanned by scorching westerly winds, the fire spread across the Sydney basin, speeding through the tops of the eucalyptus trees with a deafening roar as it greedily consumed the highly combustible, oily leaves. A neighbor tersely recorded in his journal that at midday it was 107 in the shade and "the whole country was in a perfect blaze." The roaring inferno was beaten back from around Parramatta, except for one of the established farms, where a spark from the burning treetops flew into the thatch of the hut, instantly incinerating all the outbuildings and thirty bushels of wheat.[21]

Having escaped the fire, Randall and Martin desperately needed to sow crops by the end of summer, because the colony was again feeling the pinch of approaching famine. They managed to establish their farms in time to benefit from the rains that broke out in April 1793. That effort was at no small cost. On February 13, 1793, in a week when the temperature gauge registered between 112 and 116 degrees, John Randall and his wife, Mary, buried their infant daughter, Lydia.[22]

In the long run it was Martin who proved to be the adequate farmer, with twelve of his fifty acres in grain within the first few years. Within five years he was the only one of the original grantees remaining at Northern Boundary Farms, "a sober industrious man, yet very poor." Randall continued to hunt game for the governor and this, rather than farming, was what kept his family well provided for. He sold his land in order to join the New South Wales Corps and resume his earlier career as a soldier. However hard, Randall's life in New South Wales had one priceless compensation. For a man born in slavery to see his three surviving children with the privileges of any freeborn English person, guaranteed by custom and law, was a significant achievement, and perhaps he thought it worth the bitter tribulations that had brought him to this strange place at the very end of the world.[23]

CHAPTER II

PROMISES UNFULFILLED
IN SIERRA LEONE

Lieutenant William Dawes returned to England from New South Wales in the spring of 1792, hankering to extend his rapport with native people into missionary work. He carried a letter of introduction from the chaplain of New South Wales to William Wilberforce, the parliamentary leader of the abolitionist movement and director of the Sierra Leone Company. Wilberforce was quick to recognize the worth of a half-pay officer who was "an avowed friend of religion and good order." Dawes was taken into the Evangelical fold of the Clapham Sect, and in August 1792 he was appointed to be one of two councilors who, with Governor Clarkson, were to be the governing council of Sierra Leone. He spent much of the voyage to Sierra Leone in prayer, anticipating the challenge of bringing Christianity to the pagan Africans.[1]

When Dawes disembarked at Freetown in September 1792, he was inevitably disappointed in the society he found. The black settlers had no need of proselytizing, neither from him nor from the company chaplain he had brought with him. They had their own preachers, to whom they were deeply attached. The Methodists, who were well over half of the Freetown settlers as well as the original settlers from Granville Town, supported five preachers, in addition to the revered Daddy Moses. The Countess of Huntington's Connexion, led by Cato Perkins and William Ashe, was the next largest congregation, while David George's Baptist flock accounted for the rest. "I never met with, heard, or read of, any set of people observing the same appearance of godliness," Anna Maria Falconbridge observed, adding that whatever time she woke in the night, she could hear "preachings from some quarter or another." On Sunday, all the settlers dutifully attended the formal Anglican service, led by Clarkson, before retiring to their meetinghouses to spend the rest of the day in a more enthusiastic celebration of their faith.[2]

Far from being impressed with the intense religiosity of Freetown, Dawes and the chaplain both were shocked by the raw fervor of the black preachers and their total ignorance of doctrinal matters. To Dawes's stern eye, the enthusiasm of the black dissenters, with their wild shouting and ecstatic visions, smacked of impiety. By contrast, Clarkson saw no reason "to cry down these different sects, and the black preachers for their ignorance, extravagant notions, and apparently ridiculous way of expressing their thoughts." The exuberant religion the black settlers brought with them disturbed him far less as the "strange notions . . . as to their civil rights" that were still causing him no end of grief.[3]

By the time Dawes arrived in summer of 1792, the black settlers were still adjusting to their new circumstances. The moment the torrential rains had passed, an army of fierce ants swarmed out of their nests, marching through the settlement and destroying everything in their path. The only thing that would deflect the ants from their mission was the use of boiling water or firebrands. It was in trying to deflect the invasion that one settler's new house was burned to the ground. Ants were not the only terrifying invaders to be confronted; leopards and snakes continued to be a threat. Houses were made weatherproof and safe from wild beasts, so that, little by little, the terrors of Africa lost their fearsome aspect. The seasoned survivors at Granville Town were able to pass on their hard-won knowledge of local conditions when Clarkson relented his opposition and incorporated them into the company's fold. Falling back on the survival skills of plantation slavery, the women created vegetable gardens and raised poultry to supplement the store food and the men built boats to fish or hunted antelope and wild boar in the forests. While the settlers adjusted to the strange and sometimes terrible environment of Africa, they had less inclination to adjust to the changed conditions that governed their new home.

The metropolitan fantasies entertained by the directors of the Sierra Leone Company, who envisaged vast profits from plantation crops and trading centers, bore no relationship to the harsh reality of creating a free community on the slave coast of Africa. None of the directors had ever been to West Africa, and they could not begin to imagine what it was like living in mud huts during a torrential monsoon. Nor did they understand that the rugged terrain meant that only a limited amount of land was available for farming. Once the Nova Scotia settlers began to hack into the jungle, Clarkson realized that there would not be enough arable land to provide the large grants the settlers had been promised. He had to persuade them to accept only one-fifth of land they had been led to expect. Without reference to the directors' instructions, Clarkson softened the blow by agreeing that the settlers could hold elections for their own peacekeepers, reviving Sharp's original conception of a tithingman for every ten families and a hundredor for every hundred, though the settlers were still denied representation on the governing council.

With good grace the settlers accepted their reduced land allocation, but they reacted with fury when Clarkson told them that the directors would not allow them to have any land on the riverfront. Access to the water was an absolute necessity in Sierra Leone. There were no carts or horses; communication and transport were all by means of water. Isaac Anderson, with Luke Jordan and a dozen or so of Jordan's congregation, were already working on land along the river. Clarkson's request that they move reignited a bitter grievance that had soured their lives before. As Anderson violently expostulated, this same trick had been played on them in Nova Scotia, wherein white men had occupied the entire waterfront, built wharves along it, and then charged money for access. The entire Methodist congregation had not crossed the ocean to suffer the same discrimination all over again. In deference to the settlers' fears of further injustice at the hands of self-interested white people, Clarkson hastily rescinded the company instructions.[4]

In this highly charged environment, Clarkson chose not to act on the orders from the company directors to institute a quit rent of two shillings an acre on the land the settlers had been promised. The quit rent was a cornerstone of the directors' investment strategy, and company profit predictions were based on the returns from this rent. Clarkson felt personally betrayed by this policy, communicated to him only after he got to Sierra Leone, and was extremely apprehensive of what it could mean to his fragile settlement. The company investment strategy meant little to him; he just wanted to see the black refugees established as viable freehold farmers, with himself as their protective patriarch and guide. Following his own instincts, Clarkson rationalized that the directors would surely abide by his decisions and that their policies "must give way to the general spirit of my promises." It was a high-risk strategy for a servant of the company who was about to go on extended leave.[5]

As for the "cool, correct, sensible" William Dawes, who was to be acting governor in Clarkson's absence, there was little about him that encouraged Clarkson's confidence. A marine officer with four years' experience at a penal settlement was hardly equipped for managing a colony of free black refugees established on the principles of equality, Clarkson felt. He was anxious that Dawes understand that "these people have been deceived through life and have scarcely ever had a promise made that was performed." Could Dawes be capable of acting with appropriate sensitivity, given that his experience had been of the "arbitrary proceedings" of a penal station?[6]

Despite his anxiety about Dawes, Clarkson went on leave in order to be married in December 1792. He took David George with him for a term of study with Baptist clergy in England. George carried a petition to the company directors, expressing, "Our ardent desier is that the same John Clarkson return back to bee our goverener." The settlers had taken stock of Dawes and did not like what they saw. "He may be a very good man," they told Clarkson as he was leaving, "but he does not show it." That keen-eyed observer Anna Maria Falconbridge, whose husband was in the process of drinking himself to death, felt that Dawes would never win the confidence of the settlers. The "awful severity in his looks and actions" may have been appropriate for a penal colony, she thought, but it would never do in Freetown. As soon as Dawes took charge, she astutely predicted, "anarchy and discord [would] again return in full force" among them.[7]

Dawes showed severity in more than his looks. Stern piety ruled his actions. One of his early directives was to make it mandatory for everyone to attend church services every morning and night. In establishing the twice-daily observances, Dawes was staunchly supported by the second councilor for the company, Zachary Macaulay, a young man of twenty-four who arrived in Freetown in early January 1793. Macaulay took seriously the admonition of the chairman "that the point to be laboured is to make the colony a religious colony." The twice-daily church services were meant to undermine the influence of the self-taught black preachers, who appeared to Dawes and Macaulay to be ignorant and dangerous. Of particular concern to Macaulay was "the reigning folly of Methodists of this place in accounting dreams, visions and the most ridiculous bodily sensations as incontestable proof of their acceptance with God and their being filled with the Holy Ghost." This was *not* the Christianity that Dawes and Macaulay envisaged taking root in heathen Africa. At his twice-daily sermons the chaplain was careful to demonstrate that people could not commune directly with God since "the Holy Spirit acted always in strict conformity to the word of God as delivered in Scriptures," which they were unable read. Sermons of this nature became so unpalatable to the Methodists that they refused to attend. Within a year the dispirited chaplain had given up and returned to England.[8]

Besides his habit of dropping to his knees in prayer at any time of the day or night, Dawes was pious in his attachment to his employer's instructions. A month after he became acting governor, he summoned the settlers to inform them that they must relinquish the lots currently occupied. He had drawn a town plan that allocated them new lots, away from the waterfront, which would be reserved for the company, as the directors required. The settlers responded to this pronouncement with angry dismay, according to Anna Maria Falconbridge, informing Dawes that they were "free British subjects, and expect to be treated as such" and would never "tamely submit to being trampled on." They reiterated Clarkson's promise to them that waterfront land would be available equally to all, white or black. Clarkson's word no longer carried any weight in Freetown, so Anna Maria reported with great indignation. Dawes responded with the suggestion that it was Clarkson's nature to make "prodigal and extraordinary promises without thinking of them afterwards." Adding further insult was the suggestion that Clarkson had no power to fulfill such promises as he "more than probable *was drunk* when he made them." Shocked beyond comprehension, the settlers refused to believe that Dawes spoke for the views of the company, but they were faced with no real alternative to his plan. Most acquiesced to the scheme and reluctantly moved to new lots. Isaac Anderson, Luke Jordan, and Nathaniel Snowball refused and continued living on the town lots they had established along the river, vigorously resisting any pressure to move. Macaulay came to regard this particular area as "Discontented Row."[9]

All of Dawes's actions, both religious and civil, were enthusiastically endorsed by his second councilor. Macaulay's previous experience of six years as an overseer on a slave plantation in the West Indies made him an odd choice for a colony run by abolitionists, yet the directors set much store by this young man. He had repented of youthful wildness and excessive drinking to become an Evangelical convert and member of the Clapham Sect. The company chairman, Henry Thornton, described him to Clarkson in glowing terms as a zealous Christian who felt he was "doing a duty to God by going out." Once in Sierra Leone, Macaulay immediately initiated a campaign to convince the directors of the acting governor's sterling performance. According to his version of events, the settlers were happier with the resolute Dawes when he made them do their duty than they were when being harangued by Clarkson in his attempts to persuade them. That made short work of Clarkson and his problematic promises. Not even Clarkson's good friend Wilberforce could (or would) save him from being dismissed from the company's service in May 1793.[10]

Macaulay's glowing reports about Dawes contrasted sharply with Anna Maria Falconbridge's scathing account. She was witness to his first attempt to make the settlers do their duty. Finding that the settlers would not bend to his will, Dawes threatened to leave Sierra Leone, a strategy he had seen employed to great effect by Clarkson. The settlers responded with one voice, so Anna Maria reported, saying, "Go! go! go! we do not want you here." A policy of insult and disobedience continued in the hope that they could drive Dawes away. With the help of Elliot Griffiths, the local Africans were harnessed to the cause. Soon after he assumed the governorship, Dawes was alarmed by louder than usual drumming from the nearby Koya Temne village. He broke out the muskets and armed the settlers to repel an attack that did not come. Days later, a similar commotion sent the settlers running to Dawes, begging to be armed. This time he refused, having deduced that this was a ruse by the settlers to get guns that they could use against the company servants. Macaulay reported that one of the Methodist preachers pointedly compared Dawes to Pharaoh, reminding his flock that his oppressive rule must be endured until "God in his own good time would deliver

Israel." Others were not so patient. After news arrived of the execution of Louis XVI, hints were dropped to Dawes that such a fate could easily be his.[11]

Isaac Anderson and Cato Perkins were senior members of the Nova Scotia community. Perkins, who was in his midfifties, was the senior member of the Huntingdon Connexion, while Anderson, age forty, was an elder in the Methodist church. Together they had met a lot of challenges since escaping from enslavement in South Carolina, yet perhaps their biggest to date was to travel to London in order to make a direct appeal to the company directors. The message they carried, so they indicated in a letter to Clarkson, was "Things will not go well in the colony unless people you brought with you from Nova Scotia have justice done them."[12]

In their written petition to the directors, Anderson and Perkins expressed humble gratitude for all the company had done for them while at the same time reminding the directors that it was the promise to better their conditions that had induced them to leave Nova Scotia. Such promises—"far better than we ever had before from white people"—had not been realized under Clarkson's governorship, yet they had borne the hardship and waited patiently "without groaning." Now they feared the promises would never be fulfilled. "We have not the education which white men have," they wrote, "yet we have feeling the same as other human beings and would wish to do everything we can for to make our children free and happy after us." They perceived the problem clearly: "Mr. Dawes seems to wish to rule us just as bad as if we were all slaves which we cannot bear... [and] we are afraid concerning the happiness of our children for as we have not justice shewn us we do not expect our children will after us." Under the regime he established, the settlers had land and no option but to work for the company, which set both the price of their labor, which they thought too low, and the price for the goods they bought, which was artificially high. It was a form of labor exchange little better than bondage, they claimed. At the heart of their concern was a palpable terror of losing the capacity for a sustainable, independent life, and as consequence their children could be reenslaved. No hint of blame was attached to Clarkson for having lured them across the Atlantic Ocean with promises he had no right to make.[13]

These two earnest black men had not a hope in heaven of convincing the directors that injustice was a feature of their great scheme for Africa, or that the company's white employees were inadequate to the task. The company chairman, Henry Thornton, dismissed their concerns in a few lines to Clarkson, suggesting that the complaints related to "vague promises" that he had made. For his part, Clarkson expressed surprise that the settlers "should fancy themselves oppressed and think they should complain without cause." Still, he admonished Thornton, the directors were obliged "to pay some little attention to their requests." Once he had grasped the validity of the complaint, Clarkson insisted that the directors must take the matter seriously.[14]

A second letter by Anderson and Perkins, written into formal English by Anna Maria Falconbridge's second husband, was presented to the directors in November 1793. This missive was much more direct. "We always supposed we were sent from Nova Scotia to Sierra Leone by His Majesty (God bless him)," they wrote, arguing that the king, not the company, should appoint the governor. If that were not to be, they had an alternative: "We have a right to a voice in naming the man who will govern us . . . we *will not* be governed by your present agents in Africa." With the intention to jolt the abolitionist sensibilities in the directors, they concluded, "The manner you have treated us has been just the same as if we were *slaves,* come to tell our masters of the cruelties and severe behavior of an *overseer.*" It did no good. They got no answer from the company other than the offer of a return berth aboard a company ship sometime in February or March 1794. In the meantime, Anderson found work as a servant, while Perkins was taken into the training school of the Countess of Huntingdon. The two men returned to Freetown deeply disillusioned; "sent back like fools," they bitterly reported to Clarkson.[15]

Clarkson was dismayed at the treatment of these two emissaries, observing sadly that Dawes and Macaulay exercised "a kind of religious influence" with the directors. He felt that the Clapham Sect was imbued with a sense of religious superiority and moral righteousness that meant "all those who may be said to be possessed of an independent heart and honest spirit, who would not *cringe* to any man alive" would be ignored. He was proved right when the directors released their annual report, which bristled with indignation that the settlers should make demands of them. Slaves who ran away from their masters rather than being "emancipated on a prudent principle of discrimination," proved to be "a less favourable specimen of the character," the directors explained. As self-emancipated people they did not understand obligations of "respect and obedience" and were unable to exercise "due regulation and command of their tempers." Henceforth, the settlers must to learn to curb their "inadequate or enthusiastic notions of Christianity" and subordinate their "false and absurd notions . . . concerning their rights as freemen" to the long-term objectives of the company. Above all, they should show more gratitude.[16]

A grievance that Anderson and Perkins did not raise with the directors was the very cordial relationship between the company's white servants and the slave traders. Dawes and Macaulay knew that they could not afford to alienate the powerful slave-trading interests that surrounded them, given that the primary purpose of the company was to establish trade in the region. Anna Maria Falconbridge was especially censorious about their attitude, going so far as to accuse Dawes of having traded in slaves. When Macaulay was acting governor in Dawes's absence, Isaac Anderson and Luke Jordan complained bitterly to Clarkson that he allowed the slave traders to come to the settlement and "abuse" the settlers. They were dismayed in August 1793 when Macaulay insisted that a crowd of settlers must deliver up five slaves who had escaped from a slave ship. When the settlers protested that it was Clarkson's policy that a person was free from the moment he or she entered Freetown, Macaulay gave the haughty reply that Clarkson did not know what he was talking about. British subjects had a right to buy and hold slaves, he said, and the people of Freetown had "no more power to detain a slave than . . . a bale of goods." Horrified, the settlers refused to surrender the runaways and sent them into the hinterland, supplied with arms to defend themselves.[17]

On that same day, Frank Patrick, from Norfolk, Virginia, was arrested for stealing wine, shoes, and tools from the company store, in addition to being suspected of stealing money found buried nearby. Patrick had been dismissed from company employ six months earlier when he had refused to obey orders and "chose to be impudent" by calling Dawes "a white rascal." Since company employment was the only source of credit at the store, Patrick and his family were on hard times. A jury of black settlers found him guilty, but it was Macaulay who determined the sentence of several hundred lashes, to be followed by eleven months' hard labor on the company trading ship, *York*. Days later, as the insensible Patrick was being carried aboard the *York* after his second dose of flogging, he was rescued by James Jackson, his old friend from Virginia. Jackson carried Patrick to his house, threatening to shoot anyone who tried to take him away. The standoff was short-lived. Jackson was arrested and Patrick was taken to serve his time on the *York*.[18]

Jackson appeared in court in November on charges arising from his attempt to protect Patrick. He argued that because the settlers had no land to sustain them, the company was obliged to give them employment so they could obtain the goods at the store, and that Patrick should have had a right to appeal his severe sentence. Macaulay privately derided Jackson's speech as insolent, but he imposed only a small fine, thinking the matter would blow over. He was wrong. A month later, the *York,* with its entire cargo of trade goods, was on fire as the result of the "carelessness" of someone on board. Few settlers were willing to help save the vessel, while some were heard "rejoicing in the calamity as a just judgement of heaven on their oppressors." Neither was this the end of the matter. The issues flagged by Patrick and Jackson continued to reverberate painfully through the colony for the next seven years.[19]

On June 13, 1794, the slave ship *Thomas* was tied up at the Freetown wharf. Although slave ships provided work for the settlers in loading and unloading goods, the workers despised the ships' captains and saw no reason to be courteous. On this occasion two men working as company porters encouraged a crowd of settlers to attack the captain when he taunted them with the specter of enslavement, "saying in what manner he would use them if he had them in the West Indies." One of the porters tried to bash him with a hammer. The injured captain complained to the acting governor. When the porters unapologetically confirmed their actions, they were instantly dismissed. Within days Freetown was in uproar. Macaulay was so alarmed, he summoned all the white employees to his house and told David George to bring the few Baptist settlers who supported the company. Some kind of riot took place on June 20, 1784. According to the official report, a mob of settlers plundered the company offices and threatened the governor's house.[20]

None of this would have happened, Luke Jordan and Isaac Anderson lamented in a letter to Clarkson, if Macaulay had respect for the elected spokesmen and took their advice; instead, he wrote, "the gentlemen here thinks proper to use us in a very improper manner." Matters deteriorated further when company employees arrested three people, triggering another day of turbulence and demands for the prisoners' release. The third day of unrest was Sunday. Macaulay distributed a statement to be read in church, in which he leveled the awesome charge of "the overthrow of God's altars in this place and the overthrow of those fair prospects for civilising Africa." Macaulay fully understood the impact of such pronouncements issued on the Sabbath. He reinforced his charge by asserting, "[Africa] will cry loudly for vengeance on you, if not in this at least in another world." His threats in relation to this world were no less terrifying. Without the company the settlers would be "exposed to the treachery of the slave-traders," he pronounced, "doomed to groan chained in the hold of a slave ship, or drag out a miserable life under the smart of a West Indian whip." If they did not like the way the company ran Sierra Leone, he told them, they should go back to Nova Scotia. A slave-trading brig had been purchased for just such a purpose, and any disaffected person was offered a free return passage.[21]

No one could face the prospect of expatriation to Nova Scotia. Protest sputtered out. Eight men, including James Jackson and Ralph Henry, were identified as ringleaders and marked out for exemplary punishment. All of these dissidents were from "that firm body of malcontents," the Methodist congregation of Daddy Moses. Macaulay was astute enough to see that the Methodists' self-validating religious experience, as well as their refusal to defer to ordained clergy, fed resistance to company rule. "Their government is pure democracy," he noted with distaste, "without subordination to anyone." He did not grasp that it was faith itself that made the Methodist meetinghouse such a seedbed of sedition. When Daddy Moses preached about the delivery out of oppression and over the mighty waters into the land of Canaan, his congregation had a very firm idea of what that meant in their own lives. Youthful arrogance and his previous experience as overseer on a slave plantation prevented Macaulay from comprehending that these as agents of sedition were acting out of powerful beliefs about the rights that came with liberty. Having emancipated themselves from slavery during the American Revolution with the rhetoric about the inalienable rights of free men ringing about their ears, they had struggled for nearly two decades to make this rhetoric a tangible reality.[22]

Lacking the judicial powers to deal with sedition, Macaulay organized for the eight men to be taken to England to be tried under English law, sending a number of witnesses against them but making no provision for any witnesses for their defense. Whether these eight men could be tried in an English court was a moot point. They never were taken to court, or even kept in prison. Whatever decision the directors made with regard to them remains a mystery; the record of their deliberations was destroyed in a French attack on a company ship in October 1794.

By December 1794, Granville Sharp was imploring Henry Thornton to arrange some kind of subsistence for the families left behind in Sierra Leone and to pardon the accused men so they could go home. His advice was never heeded. After another two years had gone by, it was John Clarkson who was pleading with Thornton on behalf of the accused men, who he considered were "treated in a very unjust way." One of the men, so Clarkson had been told, was "almost hungered to death." Given up by the benevolent society that had supported him and facing eviction by his landlady, he appeared to be "in the very jaws of destruction." Little came of Clarkson's intervention. The directors' abhorrence of his Jacobin sympathies completely prejudiced them against his views. It was assistance from the settlers themselves that eventually saw this man and two others returned to Sierra Leone. Clarkson's informant gave him specific news that James Jackson "went on board some ship, where he has never been heard of from and it is supposed he has met with some untimely end." No one explained what happened to Ralph Henry.[23]

Little could be done to rescue the black settlers in England, because soon after they left, Freetown was destroyed in an unexpected French attack. A ship rigged in the English fashion and flying British colors sailed into the river, drawing a large number of unsuspecting settlers to the wharf. Macaulay was casually observing the ship through a spyglass from his house on a hill above the town when he suddenly realized it was a French gunboat primed to attack. Ordering the British flag to be lowered, he quickly hung a white tablecloth over his balcony at the very mo-

ment the French guns opened fire. Despite his hasty surrender, the devastating bombardment continued for about an hour and a half, according to David George's reckoning, killing one settler and wounding
several others. Macaulay, who was fluent in French, went aboard the ship
to negotiate while the sailors ransacked the town. Acting quite independently of the ship's captain, these ragged *sans-culottes* swarmed ashore
and set about taking everything they could lay hands on. They destroyed
all the company property, including the ships, and were assisted in this
orgy of destruction by the indigenous Koya Temne. Macaulay observed
with cold fury that "the natives too employed themselves day and night
in carrying off whatever escaped the vigilance of the French."[24]

Many settlers were disgusted that the governor had refused to allow
them any resistance. Unlike the white employees of the company, they
had experienced war and were prepared to fight another one. However,
Macaulay had the white tablecloth fluttering from his balcony before
they could even get to the ammunition. Soon enough the settlers realized they had no need to fight; they mollified the French sailors by
indicating that they were Americans and allies of the French. As a consequence, their huts were spared. What property the sailors did not
want—planks, nails, other materials from the wrecked company building—they were permitted to take. "They restored us some things," a settler later recalled, "and some we got out of the water and on the beach,
some we saved from the fire . . . we divided our spoil with the distressed
European civilians, that they might have subsistence as well as ourselves." The dozen or so company employees were given shelter in the
settlers' homes, much to Macaulay's grateful surprise.[25]

Once the French had gone, Macaulay decided the settlers' plucky
salvaging looked very much like theft. Accusing the settlers of "aiding
the pillage," he demanded that everyone sign a declaration to say he or
she would return any salvaged material. Those who refused to sign were
denied any schooling for their children, medical treatment, and company employment. Even in the face of such stern sanctions, only about
120 settlers signed the declaration, and they were mostly Baptists. Universally the Methodists refused. It was a matter of powerful principle
that they be treated with respect and given recognition for their common
humanity. They might have reacted differently, Moses Wilkinson and

his fellow preachers explained to Clarkson, if Macaulay "had the least consideration to come and ask." They resented being called thieves for saving what little they could, when Macaulay had not even allowed them to defend themselves against a bombardment and the wholesale plunder of their "little affects."[26]

"We are the people of the Methodist connection that are calld people of a ranglesome nature," they wrote to Macaulay, vainly hoping to convice him that while they would not be ruled by dictatorial edict, they were "willing to be under the complement of any proposhall that is just." Macaulay ignored them, determined to have nothing less than complete capitulation. When one of the elected representatives suggested that kindness might promote a better atmosphere, Macaulay bluntly replied that if kindness meant giving up company property on the basis of "fanciful notions about [their] own deserving," then he was happy to be considered cruel. Unable to negotiate with the acting governor, the Methodist settlers dispatched another petition of grievance to the company directors in London. While they waited for a reply, their sense of bitterness and betrayal multiplied. Daddy Moses, Luke Jordan, and Isaac Anderson wrote to Clarkson, "We wance did call it Free Town, but since your absence we have a reason to call it a town of slavery."[27]

CHAPTER 12

IN BONDAGE TO THIS
TYRANNOUS CREW

Freetown was substantially rebuilt in 1796, making it the largest town on the west coast of Africa. About four hundred timber and shingle houses were neatly laid out along nine streets, each with a poultry yard and a garden plot, as well as orange, pineapple, and apple trees. An assortment of goats, sheep, and cattle cropped the grass-covered streets. In a double-storied house near the wharves, the widow Mary Perth ran a boarding-house and shop. Baptist preacher David George held a license to operate a tavern from his home. The waterfront was a site of frenetic activity, where at any given time there might be one or two visiting slave ships and the trading vessels of the Sierra Leone Company, as well as the canoes of hundreds of Africans who brought produce to trade each day. Above the bustling town, standing aloof on Thornton Hill, was the governor's palisaded house, proudly flying the Union Jack. Further distant, on the sides of the heavily forested mountains, bright green patches indicated the settlers' farms. For all the reassuring signs of comfort and security of Freetown, the colony of Sierra Leone was in turmoil.

The families who belonged to the Methodist congregation—well over half the black settlers—were without access to medical attention, school for their children, and company employment, all because they refused to sign the declaration about salvaging company property after the French attack in 1794. In desperation, they sent anguished appeals to John Clarkson in England, begging him come back and rescue them from the authoritarian regime of Zachary Macaulay, who formally replaced William Dawes as governor in March 1796. Like "Mosis and Joshua was bring the children of Esaral to the promised land," Clarkson had undertaken a divinely inspired project when he brought them from Nova Scotia, but they had not yet reached the Promised Land, they persistently reminded him. "Honoured Sir, leave us not in the wilderness to the oppressing masters," they begged. "Be amongst us...as Mosis and Joshua did—be with us to the end." What was under threat was their fundamental stake in Sierra Leone: the land they had been promised, for which they were now obliged to pay a huge quit rent.[1]

Clarkson's gentle replies did not reveal that he had known about the company decision to charge quit rent for the land ever since they arrived. As William Dawes had never attempted to collect the rent, Clarkson clung to the hope that the company would continue to honor his promise of no tax on the land. However, Dawes's reluctance as a rent collector was not for lack of commitment to the principle; rather, he feared the consequences of trying to impose the rent. Zachary Macaulay was made of sterner stuff. Once he was in complete control, Macaulay decided the time had come for the settlers to pay. Macaulay redrafted all the titles for the allotments, to which he added a quit rent fixed at one shilling per acre. This "trifling sum" was to be paid from the beginning of 1797. Additionally, 7.5 percent interest was to be paid on the settlers' debts to the company, including the outstanding amount for quit rent for the past three years.[2]

Neither Macaulay nor the directors in London understood how bitterly the quit rent had been opposed in the American colonies; neither did they know that the colonial government of Nova Scotia had been forced to abandon the concept because settlers, black and white, refused to pay a quit rent of two shillings for every hundred acres. Blithely, the Sierra Leone Company intended to impose a tax a hundred times higher than in Nova Scotia. When Macaulay cut the amount in half, requiring only one shilling an acre, he naively believed that he was being generous and fully expected the settlers to be grateful to him. To his chagrin, most of the settlers did not even bother to claim their new titles. Nathaniel Snowball, a runaway from Virginia who was a prominent member of the Methodist congregation, bitterly rejected the new claims, telling Macaulay that "he looked on them just as he would on a claim that would bind him a slave forever." Macaulay thought his statement absurd, failing to grasp that Snowball was expressing the view of the entire community. Characteristically, Macaulay's resolution of the impasse was to insist that those who had not claimed their new grants held no title to the land they occupied. He announced his intention to evict them.

Snowball would be first to go, along with the rest of those turbulent Methodists who still lived on lots fronting the river on "Discontented Row."[3]

In July 1796, Nathaniel Snowball and Luke Jordan found themselves arraigned in court for unjustly occupying company land. It was a landmark case, to which all the settlers paid close attention. A succession of witnesses swore that Clarkson told Jordan and Snowball they could have the land, whereas Macaulay tendered written evidence that no such promise was made. The black jurors could not agree among themselves about this contradictory evidence, so the governor hastily declared a mistrial and called together a new jury to hear the case again. Expecting "a speedy verdict" from his special jury, Macaulay was infuriated that they debated the matter till after midnight, eventually deciding in favor of Jordan and Snowball.[4]

The two men were by now so distrustful of Macaulay that they determined to leave Freetown for good. Even before the trial, Snowball had negotiated with the Koya Temne for another grant of land about four miles west of Freetown, at Pirates Bay. The intention was to take his departure "as the Ezerlites did," he explained in a letter to Clarkson. By the end of 1796, Snowball and Jordan had collected a large group of Methodist settlers to move to Pirates Bay, where they would be "no longer in bondage to this tyrannous crew." Jordan's fellow Methodist preacher Boston King, who had just returned from two years of studying to be a missionary at the Wesleyan Kingswood school in England, believed that at least half of the settlers intended to join the exodus. They would have done so had King not gone from family to family to read them a letter from Clarkson, pleading for them to stay together as a coherent community and not go "wandering about amongst the natives." On the strength of Clarkson's pleas, several important Methodists, including Isaac Anderson and Daddy Moses himself, chose to stay put. Yet for all Clarkson's significant influence, Snowball and Jordan were able to take thirty Methodist families to Pirates Bay the following year, where they set up their own independent colony, electing Snowball as their governor.[5]

It wasn't just the quit rent that drove so many families to Pirates Bay. Also under threat were the black churches, which sustained the intense spiritual life of the settlers. From the moment that Macaulay became governor, he embarked on a calculated assault on these churches. It was his view that the settlers were supremely arrogant in substituting their "visionary and delusionary experience" for the received wisdom of the catechism. He complained to his fiancée that these unlettered ex-slaves suffered "a proud conceit of their own spiritual gifts," which led them to scorn religious instruction, "fancying themselves wiser then their teachers." He was hard-pressed to decide which of the black sects was the worse: "our mad Methodists" led by Daddy Moses and Luke Jordan, or the Countess of Huntingdon's Connexion, led by the "reprobate" Cato Perkins. The rowdy Methodists appalled him with the creed of "which shall bawl the loudest," while the "rank antinomianism" of the Countess of Huntingdon's Connexion filled him with disgust. The Baptists were the least objectionable, he thought, though their morality was extremely lax. As a reformed drunk himself, Macaulay found it unacceptable that the Baptist preacher held a license to sell spirits, even though it was his means of supporting a large family of ten children. He eventually forced David George to relinquish the license, insisting that God's law required men to tread "the rugged path of abstinence."[6]

When Macaulay returned to Sierra Leone from leave in England in March 1796, he was determined to bring the settlers in line with the observances of the established church. With him came the new chaplain, John Clarke, a Scottish Presbyterian who shared Macaulay's horror at the raucous, undisciplined religious observance of the settlers. After visiting the various meetinghouses, Clarke was dismayed at "the unwillingness of the preachers to receive information" and their ignorance of the true principles of Christianity. Macaulay observed with approval how the new chaplain "level[ed] the whole weight of his ability to counter the ruinous actions by which the people [were] misled." Clarke's zeal was indefatigable. In addition to giving sermons to the various congregations aimed at instructing them on their shortcomings as Christians, he instituted a weekly lecture to combat their "gross ignorance of the first principles of religion."[7]

At first, the black preachers were delighted to have a vigorous and educated minister to preach in their meetinghouses. Within two months, the welcome of Daddy Moses and Cato Perkins had been angrily withdrawn and only David George continued to allow Clarke to

occasionally preach in the Baptist meetinghouse. Few settlers bothered
to attend either his sermons or his lectures. As Clarke was brusquely informed by one settler, what was required of a preacher was not "fine ha-
rangues," but words "that must agree with what I feel." When Clarke
made personal visits to invite settlers to come to Christ, he was curtly informed: "We don't want you . . . we are in Christ already and have been
for these last 22 years." Clarke's only true adherent among the black community was Mary Perth, whose busy life included being housekeeper
and teacher for the several dozen African children who lived at Governor Macaulay's house. The exacting toll of her workload had told on
Mary, as Clarke estimated the indefatigable widow to be about seventy
when she was only fifty-five. Clarke was delighted with the steadfast devotion of this "militant saint," whom he extolled as more "like one who
has come down from heaven to earth, than like one who is only preparing for glory." The rest were dangerously deluded, he believed, stubbornly deaf to his earnest proselytizing.[8]

In late May 1796, even David George was tested to the breaking
point when confrontation between Clarke and fourteen black preachers
almost ended in blows. On May 30, the mild-mannered Baptist preacher
burst in on Macaulay in a blind rage, accusing Clarke of having said that
the black preachers were blasphemers, and demanding to know whether
the governor was planning to shut down their meetinghouses. He was
mollified by assurances that nothing was further from Macaulay's intentions, and the strife subsided. George must have thought the governor
had played him for a fool when, a few weeks later, he read the proclamation of a new law that regulated marriage, removing the authority to
marry from the black preachers and giving sole authority to the governor
or an ordained minister in the Anglican Church. Nothing would mol-
lify George on this occasion. He protested "most outrageously," in
Macaulay's view, that this law represented "a violation of religious rights
and liberty of conscience" and would be resisted, "even to blood." By the
time George had alerted the Methodists and Huntingdonians to what
the proclamation said, the town was in pandemonium. A protest meeting led by Daddy Moses condemned the governor with such fervor that
George was quite frightened. Regretting his earlier angry outburst, he
felt obliged to withdraw.[9]

The Methodists were ready for a fight. They were fortunate that the literate Elliot Griffiths was a convert of Daddy Moses. He wrote a letter, dictated by one of the Methodist elders and signed by 128 settlers, protesting that the new law was an encroachment on their religious rights. The letter began by saying that as Methodists they were sorry to confirm the governor's poor opinion of their loyalty, but first and foremost they must be loyal to "the Governor of the universe." They expected the temporal governor to respect their honesty in expressing their belief that the proclamation was "very disgusting" to them as "dissenters. As they explained, "We are dissenting and . . . as such we consider ourselves a perfect church, having no need of the assistance of any worldly power to appoint or perform religious ceremonies for us." That bold assertion alone was enough to enrage Macaulay, without the final barbed comment, "We cannot persuade ourselves that politics and religion have any connection, and therefore think it not right for a governor of the one to be middling with the other."[10]

In court a few days later, Macaulay took the opportunity to lecture those assembled on the meaning of the law. If the settlers were not so ignorant, he said, they would know that marriage was "the business of the makers of law not preachers of the gospel." As for the Methodists, he described their letter as seditious from beginning to end not only was it disrespectful and insulting, but the "spirit was that of rebellion itself." With terror his listeners recalled that the last time the governor talked about sedition, eight men had been torn away from their families and sent to England. Macaulay was well aware of the terrifying effect his words had on his audience, later confiding in his journal that such harsh condemnation was necessary to prevent the Methodist meetinghouse from turning into "a kind of Jacobin club." Barely had he returned to his house on Thornton Hill when some of the Methodists were at his door "almost dead with fear" to beg his pardon and explain that they had not understood the petition they had signed. It was an "easy termination" of that little fracas, so Macaulay liked to think.[11]

Macaulay regarded the Baptists as the most tractable of the settlers and encouraged their loyalty by awarding them the lion's share of company patronage, with the result that they were deeply distrusted by the rest of settlers. Luke Jordan and Nathaniel Snowball complained to Clarkson that George and his followers seem[ed] to think they could "do no greater service to the company and the colony than to invent and carry all the lies in their power to the governor against those who differ[ed] with them in things which pertain to religion." Much as Macaulay appreciated the Baptists' loyalty, he was far from satisfied with their religion and regularly took pains to instruct George in the error of his ways. A few months after the confrontation over the marriage law, George was flattered to receive an invitation to accompany Macaulay on a long walk to the governor's mountain farm, about three miles away. As they walked, Macaulay, with Bible in hand, proceeded to show George how his religious practice broke three commandments: his people were unchaste; he neglected the children's religious instruction; he encouraged his flock in licentiousness by not denouncing alcohol. George had been preaching for a quarter of a century, yet the arguments he mustered in defense of his creed were no match for hours of scriptural quotation from Macaulay. Finally, the old man was so overwhelmed that he burst into tears of humiliation. Macaulay was exultant at the efficacy of his religious instruction, writing to his fiancée: "Rivers of water ran down David's eyes because men had not kept God's law."[12]

Others were not so readily cowed by this young man's arrogance. The governor may have believed he had achieved a satisfactory end to the religious rights dispute; the Methodists and Huntingdonians were far from satisfied that religious diversity would continue in the colony. The Sunday schools that Macaulay had instituted for their children were a particular source of concern. Although they desperately wanted education for their children, they believed that religious instruction was the responsibility of their own preachers. Stubbornly the Methodists resisted the governor's efforts to force their children into Clarke's catechism classes. Their resistance came at no small cost. The original settlers from Granville Town refused to send their children the six miles to Sunday school in Freetown, so the governor closed down the schools the company ran for them until they did as they were told. Even in the face of these harsh sanctions, they would not comply.[13]

No matter how many times he lectured them, those of the Methodist and Huntingdon persuasions remained obdurate in resistance to his schemes. As far as Macaulay could see, all his endeavours yielded nothing but "opposition, reproach and ill-will." In the main, the settlers didn't trust him, they didn't believe that the words he read to them were the same as the words written on any paper he wanted them to sign, and they were generally insolent toward him. He began to regret even the limited amount of settler representation the colony permitted. In an exasperated moment, he decided Sierra Leone was an object lesson in the folly "of those who extol *vox populi*, as *vox Dei*." Those ideologues would change their tune if they had to suffer "the wayward humour, the perverse disputing, the absurd reasoning, the unaccountable prejudices, the everlasting jealousies, the presumptuous self-conceit, the group ignorance and the insatiable demands" of the settlers of Sierra Leone.[14]

In December 1796, Macaulay found more reason to pour scorn on the concept of popular representation when the election for hundredors and tithingmen was swept by "factious" fellows who opposed him on the quit rent. In Macaulay's view the men elected were ignorant and perverse, "destitute of the capacity of joining together two ideas or comprehending the simplest proposal." He resolved to ignore the elected representatives and thereby "reduce them to insignificance." When they called on him to discuss their anxiety about a new constitution he was proposing, he told them "they were disturbing themselves foolishly and to go home and mind their own business." Not one of them was "capable of reading or writing a sentence distinctly," he scornfully recorded in his journal, observing that when they were sworn into office they insisted on having one of the black settlers read the declaration, for fear they might be signing something injurious to them.[15]

Whether they could read or not, the settlers understood that the matter in question was one of huge significance. For more than twenty years, the defining issue for them had been to live as free people and not to submit to the indignities and deprivations that had marked their lives as slaves. Owning land—not renting it or working it for somebody else —was critical in their self-definition, as was regulating their own community. It was equally important that men should be responsible for the maintenance of their families and that the women and children should not labor as they had in slavery. For a time after their arrival, the male heads of households had been prepared to endure the indignity of working for credit to redeem goods at the company store—a condition of labor they saw as akin to bondage—only because they were waiting for the land allocation that they hoped would provide the foundation of an independent life.

The ownership of land was an essential element in the settlers' definition of freedom, yet they did not invest agriculture with any special mystique. Most were artisans, sailors, tradesmen, or fishermen who found ways other than farming to make their living. Masons and carpenters helped rebuild the slave factory at Bance Island after the French attack. Quite a few settlers engaged in small trading ventures; others worked on visiting ships at the wharves. Even if their work was sometimes tainted with the odium of the slave trade, they were at liberty to choose their employment and set the terms of their labor. Macaulay did not understand why so few chose to grow the trade crops that the company needed. It was his opinion that they were simply too lazy to climb the hills to reach the farming lots that they had been allocated.

By 1796, some thirty settlers had created farms out of the mountain lots, and these were producing quite well, despite continuing problems with livestock being stolen by the Koya Temne or taken by mountain leopards. These farmers had already achieved a measure of self-reliance growing trade crops such as coffee, pepper, and ginger, as well as the African staple crop of rice with interspersed plantings of cassava and yams. Harry Washington, who had experience of agriculture on farms at Mount Vernon, was one of the more successful farmers. So too was Isaac Anderson, who had been a slave artisan in Charleston. Anderson was full of pride about the achievement of his farm when he sent John Clarkson a barrel of rice from the crop he had produced. In a letter written for him by Boston King, Anderson quoted Deuteronomy: "Thou shall not mushel the ox that treadet out the corn." As one of the most passionate critics of the company, Anderson was not about to be muzzled by the governor's scorn.[16]

On January 5, 1797, the settlers met to discuss how to get rid of the quit rent, which was many times what they had successfully resisted paying in Nova Scotia. They were determined never to submit to a condition that reduced them to perpetual tenancy. "Who could say that now they were not slaves?" Macaulay recorded one of the settlers as saying. The governor was not about to tolerate any dissent on the issue, warning that "the smallest degree of clamour and tumult" would see them deprived of every service provided by the company. It would be "an unequal war" to send petitions to England, he warned them. His reputation in England was high, whereas they were already branded as turbulent, discontented, and ungrateful. Instead of working themselves into a lather of distrust, he said, the settlers needed to understand that the white men in Sierra Leone were "their natural advisors," whose energy was entirely harnessed to promoting the settlers' happiness.[17]

The demand for the first payment of the quit rent was proclaimed in June 1797, at which time the Baptist settlers reluctantly agreed to pay rather than face the governor's wrath. The great majority held out against it. On August 5 the elected representatives wrote to the governor to remind him that they had abandoned land in Nova Scotia in the expectation that they would receive land on the same conditions in Sierra Leone, and that they were never told that the land belonged to the company, to which they must pay quit rent. "Sir if we had been told that, we never could come here," they wrote; "we are astonished why the company could not tell us after three years we was to pay a shilling per acre ... if the lands is not ours without paying a shilling per acre, the lands will never be ours." Rather than pay, they said, the settlers would apply to the Koya Temne for more land that they could hold without such conditions.[18]

About two weeks later, the governor called a public meeting of heads of households for which he had prepared a long address. Even though Macaulay knew that very few of the settlers could read, he had printed one hundred copies so the community would be able to measure the full weight of his disdain. His address lasted for more than an hour and was delivered with all the assurance of an orator. He denied that the black settlers had left freehold land in Nova Scotia and insisted that they had always known about the quit rent. The problem with ignorant people, he concluded, was that they were susceptible to "every prating, malicious, designing talebearer" who wished to misrepresent the good intentions of the company. "You have often been made to see the folly of acting thus," he told his stunned audience, "yet you still return like the sow to flounder in the same dirty puddle." With admirable restraint, Isaac Anderson rose to respectfully beg the governor for a right of reply, but Macaulay turned on his heel, leaving them to peruse their copies of what he had just said.[19]

At a subsequent meeting with the governor, Anderson was no longer restrained. Macaulay recorded that Anderson was in a blind fury as he remonstrated that the settlers were "an abused, oppressed and injured people, not one promise made them having been fulfilled." The governor responded by browbeating Anderson until he fell silent. Very soon after this humiliation, all the Methodists turned in their grants, saying that to accept the grant was to accept the status of a slave. Anderson went with Elliot Griffiths to negotiate with the supreme chief of the Koya Temne, reasoning that he had originally ceded the land to the settlers, so it was he and not the Sierra Leone Company with whom they should deal.[20]

Macaulay suspected that Anderson and his fellow Methodists "cherished hopes of... throw'g off the jurisdiction of the company servants, and constituting one of their own number a kind of dictator, who assisted by a council, should rule them after the manner of the Natives." With the company servants vastly outnumbered by the settlers, Macaulay began to fear insurrection. He put in place a private signal to rally the few whites and the thirty or so obedient Baptists to his fortified house in case of trouble. He was sure that he would have to hang two or three troublemakers, despite having no legal capacity to enact a capital punishment, and was prepared "to risk holding up my hand at the Old Bailey" in order to protect the company's interest.[21]

At this stage, however, the settlers had not abandoned their cherished belief in themselves as dutiful subjects of the king, living in a British colony. Anderson felt they should appeal directly to the king, and he took the opportunity to make such an appeal when a British frigate called at Freetown. Together with the two other elected tithingmen, Anderson presented a petition on January 16, 1798, addressed to the captain as the king's representative on the West African coast. The petition explained how the black settlers had been given land by the British government as a consequence of their "good behavior in the last war." The king had heard their complaints about living in a cold country and made the offer to remove them to Sierra Leone where they would be more comfortable. Things had not turned out in accordance with the terms of His Majesty's offer, and they were now "shamefully called upon to pay a quit rent of a shilling an acre for the land" they held. Did they remain the king's subjects? If so, they sought to apply to the Crown to be "righted in all the wrongs" done to them. Without hesitation, the captain turned the petition over to Macaulay, who decided to ignore it, although he did advise his employers that it was prudent not to collect the quit rent, at least in the short term.[22]

An industrious calm settled on Sierra Leone once the demand for the quit rent was withdrawn. Boston King reported to Clarkson early in 1798 that the farm allotments had produced "such a noble crop" that he had "no doubt that the gratter part of the people may become independence." There was palpable joy that the abrasive governor was due to leave the colony. Just as Macaulay was counting the weeks to his departure, an edict arrived from the directors that the quit rent must be paid. The directors' concession to settler concerns was that the revenue would be used for development within Sierra Leone. A more perceptive man than Macaulay would have recognized that the settlers were entirely consistent in their opposition to the quit rent and that their reasons had nothing to do with how the revenue was spent. He could hardly have failed to notice that their mutinous spirit had melted away as soon as the quit rent was abandoned, indicating that the quit rent alone was the cause of rebelliousness.[23]

Macaulay was single-minded in his devotion to the company and took account of none of these things. He duly informed the settlers that new titles had been drawn up incorporating the quit rent conditions, for which they must apply by December 15, 1798. About a dozen families accepted the grants and the rest refused, even though the refusal meant that their children were barred from the free company school. A new grant register excluded the names of all those who refused their grants and listed their allotments under the designation of "unallocated land." Among those whose land was reallocated in this fashion were some of the colony's most successful farmers, such as Isaac Anderson, Harry Washington, and Nathaniel Wansey. Macaulay's action drove nearly every settler into the rebellious coalition, including previous supporters of the company. Watching these events with mounting anxiety was the man who was to replace Macaulay as governor, a twenty-three-year-old stripling named Thomas Ludlam. "From that period," Ludlam wrote in his later report, "the colony had no peace."[24]

Early in 1799, another issue of contention was added to the explosive situation in Freetown. Ever since Macaulay's harsh sentencing of Frank Patrick in 1793, resentment had been accumulating about the interpretation of the law by the white judges and a perceived white bias in the administration of the law. "We do not think our selves dun jestises in the colenny not by no meains," the black representatives wrote to the governor, insisting that they be permitted to appoint one judge and two justices of the peace from among the settlers. Macaulay pointed out that none of them was sufficiently versed in English law to be a judge. Conceding that they were "unlaint people," the settlers argued that they could become versed in the law with the help of the white men who currently sat as judges. Macaulay was unmoved, although he did allow them to put their case to the directors in London, confident of the directors' negative response. For all his iron will, Macaulay grew more and more uneasy during the weeks leading to his departure, admitting in private letters that he slept with loaded muskets in his bedroom.[25]

Macaulay left Sierra Leone for good in April 1799. He took with him twenty-five of his young African charges to be educated at a special school in Clapham. These African children were Macaulay's sole source of satisfaction from his tour of duty in Sierra Leone. He believed that they, not the turbulent settlers, represented the future of the Sierra Leone Company's civilizing project in Africa. The company chairman, Henry Thornton, was delighted by the vision of Macaulay's "triumphal entry into this island with a train of twenty or thirty little black boys and girls at his heels, the trophies which he brings with him from Africa." Mary Perth accompanied Macaulay in order to assist with the children, the trip to England giving her the opportunity to get expert medical help for her ailing daughter, Susan.[26]

As soon as Macaulay departed from Freetown, the settlers took matters into their own hands. Without waiting to hear back from the company directors, they selected the Methodist preacher Mingo Jordan as judge and Isaac Anderson as one of two justices of the peace. The elected hundredors and tithingmen then formed into a bicameral parliament of sorts, passing resolutions about the day-to-day management of Freetown and Granville Town, quite independent of the company. In September this de facto government resolved that the proprietors of the colony were all those people who had come to Sierra Leone with Clarkson, together with the original settlers from Granville Town, since it was to these people that the Koya Temne had given the land. In making their bid of independence, the settlers were not to know that Macaulay had been appointed the permanent secretary of the Sierra Leone Company and in that capacity had applied to the British Parliament for a royal charter to give the company formal jurisdiction over Sierra Leone.

What the company was asking for was incontestable control, including full judicial power to repress dissent. As the company directors explained in a subsequent report, "The unwarranted pretensions of the disaffected settlers, their narrow misguided views; their excessive jealousy of Europeans; the crude notions they had formed of their own rights; and the impetuosity of their tempers" would inevitably lead to "most ruinous effect" unless the company had the legal capacity to "repress the turbulence and assumption of the colonists." So it did not matter what the elected hundredors and tithingmen in Freetown decided. Once the royal charter was granted, there would be no more elections in Sierra Leone.[27]

At the same time as asking for a royal charter, the directors were negotiating to take into Sierra Leone some five hundred Maroon warriors from Jamaica. These were the descendants of runaway slaves who had intermarried with the Caribs long before Jamaica became a British colony, and who lived in self-regulated communities in the mountains. They had not been defeated in the Maroon War of 1795 but had surrendered in response to a treaty offer from the British commander, which was subsequently repudiated by the colonial government, leading to their deportation to Nova Scotia. Utterly miserable in frigid Nova Scotia, the Maroon chiefs had petitioned the British government to move them to a more appropriate place. Desperate to find a solution, the British government seized the offer from the Sierra Leone Company. To sweeten the deal, Parliament allowed a substantial sum of money to the company to fortify Government House in Freetown and to garrison a detachment of soldiers in the colony.

Ludlam knew about these developments when he formally assumed the governorship of Sierra Leone in November 1799. He also knew that the directors refused to allow the black settlers to select a judge. He decided that it would be wise to withhold this information until he had received the additional authority of the royal charter, as well as the military backup, from England. His instinct was to first tackle the greatest source of perceived injustice by removing any restrictions on children attending the schools. His masterstroke was to abandon the quit rent. The son of a mathematician, Ludlam had done the sums to show that the quit rent required the settlers to pay the full value of the land every twenty years. He felt they were right to regard it as unacceptable. No money had ever been collected by the end of 1799, and he argued the case that it never could be collected.[28]

The new governor's conciliatory gestures may have worked had not he felt duty-bound to inform the settlers on December 5, 1799, that a black judge would not be permitted. Two days later, the governor received an unapologetic message that the settlers "had resolved to persist in their appointment of judges . . . to make and execute laws themselves." To prove that they [could not] "get justice from the White people," a list of grievances was submitted. None of the items listed was substantial, but the cumulative effect was to create a picture of persistent discrimination and humiliation at the hands of the company's white servants. Having made the case, the settlers moved to elect a judge and a justice of the peace, as if this were normal procedure.[29]

On May 20, 1800, Ludlam called a meeting to explain why he was obliged to reject these judicial appointments. The twenty-seven people who attended listened patiently to the governor explain that for a judge to apply for the appropriate penalties, he must be versed in English law and able to read. In any case, he added ominously, under the royal charter being drawn up in England, all such decisions would be the king's prerogative. If the settlers did not accept the decision they would be tried for treason. Here was the first intimation that the company was about to get far greater power over the settlers' lives than it currently managed to exercise. The governor failed to mention that a detachment of soldiers was to be stationed in Freetown to protect the company and uphold the charter. Neither did he reveal that more than five hundred new settlers, of a notoriously aggressive nature, were to arrive in the colony within months.[30]

Ludlam hoped that his hint about the royal charter would induce "perplexity and doubt" among the dissident settlers. Quite the opposite was the case. The settlers decided that they must move immediately if they were to secure their democratic independence. On September 3, nearly all the heads of black households in Freetown attended a gathering at Cato Perkins's Huntingdon meetinghouse to formulate a new code of laws to regulate trading practices, animal husbandry and farming procedure, and domestic and social behavior. The governor's authority was deemed to extend no further than the company's business. The "paper of laws" required every black settler to be bound by the law or leave Freetown. It was displayed in the town on September 10, 1800, when it was seen by a white company employee who called it treason and demanded it be taken down.[31]

Two weeks later Ludlam was so troubled by stories of "meetings of a most seditious and dangerous nature" that he called to his house all the company employees, about thirty loyal settlers, and all the African seamen from the company ships "for the purpose of forming a strong guard and assisting the civil power in the execution of its warrants." On September 25, the new code of laws was once again displayed, drawing curious crowds the following day. A witness later reported that "people being on farms, hearing of this news, gathered themselves together to hear and understand" at one of the settlers' houses. The frightened young governor overreacted. He sent a group of loyal black settlers he had armed and deputized as marshals to arrest several men on charges of treason. The marshals burst into the house just as the meeting was breaking up.[32]

In the melee that followed, three men were arrested, while the supposed ringleaders, Isaac Anderson, Nathaniel Wansey, and Frank Patrick, escaped out of the town with about forty men. They set up camp by the bridge on the road to Granville Town, where they were joined by Harry Washington, whose farm was nearby. The next day rewards were posted for Isaac Anderson and Nathaniel Wansey for "treasonable and rebellious practices." Frank Patrick was charged with "aiding and assisting" them. In Ludlam's subsequent account of events, he claimed that he tried through an intermediary to negotiate with Anderson, but the rebel leader's insolent verbal response was that "the prisoners must first be released and then they might be induced to treat." The prisoners themselves sent an anguished plea to Anderson: "For mercy's sake come in . . . let us fulfil our promises and hear the governor's answer." Anderson's reply to this appeal came on Sunday, September 28, in a note that read, "We de sire to now wether you will let our mens out if not turn out the women and chill dren." Anderson was not literate; the unsigned note was written by someone else, and while the tone was combative, the intention of this clumsy missive was not unambiguous, as Ludlam chose to believe. It did not necessarily mean that Anderson intended to attack Government House "and would give no quarter," as Ludlam later claimed.[33]

The Sierra Leone Company subsequently tried to portray Anderson and those with him as dangerous hotheads who wished to annihilate the company employees and loyal settlers. Significantly, the men with Anderson were all middle-aged—Anderson himself was about fifty, Nathaniel Wansey was forty, Frank Patrick was forty-five, and Harry Washington was sixty—and they were largely without arms. They had some guns but no ammunition, which was almost all stored at Government House. Apparently, on September 28 or 29 they stole a gun and some powder from the governor's farm, as well as powder and shot from the farm of another company servant. This was hardly evidence of preparation for an armed coup; they were as likely to have wanted the arms for hunting game for food.

With Anderson's old friend Cato Perkins as his go-between, Ludlam made a final attempt at negotiation, proposing to ask the captain of the next British ship to arbitrate the issues, making it clear that those charged with treason would still be subject to trial and punishment. When he had received no reply by September 30, he felt it was time for decisive military action. He was especially concerned that the disgruntled ruler of nearby Koya Temne was itching for a fight and had sent an ominous message that unless this dispute was soon resolved, he would send his warriors into Freetown to sort it out. At that very moment, as if life were imitating fiction, a large British transport ship, the *Asia*, arrived in Freetown Harbor carrying more than five hundred Maroons and forty-seven soldiers of the Twenty-fourth Regiment. Ludlam could not have prayed for a more timely "intervention of providence."[34]

On October 1, the Maroon chiefs called on the governor to discuss the allocation of land they were promised. They were surprised to find all the company employees huddled together under armed guard. Ludlam pointed out that "the rebellion then raging in the heart of the colony" would put the promised land grants in jeopardy. According to his account, the Maroon chiefs made "a unanimous and hearty offer" to put an end to the rebellion. What they actually said, according to the white agent who accompanied them, was that they "like[d] King George and white man well." "If them settlers don't like King George nor his government," they continued, "only let the Maroons see them." Significantly, the Maroons refused to sign the land grant agreement when it was presented to them. Having once been betrayed by the breach of a treaty they had been persuaded to sign, they had determined never to sign any agreement again. Ludlam was in no position to argue. He thought it was "prudent not to insist," as to do so might "sour their minds and indispose them to render those services which we so much wanted."[35]

The offer of the Maroons' chiefs was no vainglorious response. They were extraordinary warriors and had never been defeated in battle. When they took to the field they gave no quarter. After months at sea they were desperate for some physical activity, so they were pleased to be invited to "stretch their legs a little," as Henry Thornton, the company chairman, later joked. They were never told that this so-called rebellion was a dispute over settlers' rights between the company and people resettled from Nova Scotia, as they were. When the Maroons were subsequently confronted with the quit rent, they opposed it with just as much vigor.[36]

However keen to "stretch their legs," Maroon chiefs were not baying for a fight. They persuaded Ludlam to try one more time to negotiate with Anderson to forestall bloodshed. Yet another message was sent to Anderson's camp with Cato Perkins. The Maroons' white agent recorded this message as saying that "unless they came in by 10 that evening or sent some proper persons to treat for them, further dallying would be at an end." In Ludlam's self-justifying retrospective account, he claimed the letter promised he would abide by his offer of arbitration if Anderson and his men were to surrender, and that their punishment would "not extend to loss of life."[37]

When Anderson received the letter, he needed some time to consult with his men, some of whom were absent from the camp. No one who was present could read or write. His verbal reply did not reach the governor's house till after ten o'clock that night. According to one eyewitness account, Anderson's message was that "in the time given they could not see one of their principal persons, but the *terms* pleased them well and they would be in in the morning." Ludlam's retrospective account insisted that Anderson gave a deliberately evasive answer. There was no opportunity to negotiate in the morning; Ludlam ordered the plan of attack to be put into effect that very night. A violent thunderstorm threw into disarray the plan to surround the camp and cut off any retreat, but one division of Maroons did manage to surprise the unsuspecting camp at dawn. Two of Anderson's men were killed, while the rest escaped into the mountains.[38]

Next day, a notice was posted to say that if the rebels surrendered on the outskirts of the town by four o'clock that afternoon, mercy would be extended to them; if they did not, the Maroons would be sent to hunt them down. The effect this would have on people who could not read and who needed more time to comprehend the content of the notice was never taken into account. Most did give themselves up over the next few days, including Harry Washington and Frank Patrick, but their surrender was not at the time and place specified in the notice, so in Ludlam's view "they could claim no benefit from it." Isaac Anderson and Nathaniel Wansey found refuge among the Koya Temne.[39]

Within a week, Ludlam had thirty-one men in his custody, but he still had not received the charter of justice that would allow him to try them on criminal charges. Keen to avoid the expense of holding the prisoners, his expedient solution was to establish a military tribunal made up of an officer from the *Asia* and two from the Twenty-fourth Regiment. The court-martial was in session from October 10 and each of the prisoners was tried for "open and unprovoked rebellion." Six men were banished for life to the British garrison at the slave fort of Goree, a sure sentence of death. Harry Washington and twenty-three others were banished across the Sierra Leone River to the Bullom Shore. Frank Patrick's trial was held over until he could be tried for a capital crime. All of those charged with rebellion lost their land in Sierra Leone, which was distributed to the Maroons, along with the houses, stock, and crops. Soon after the military tribunal had finished its work and the *Asia* had sailed away, Isaac Anderson was handed to the governor.[40]

The long-awaited charter arrived in the colony on November 6. It was carried ashore with great ceremony, accompanied by a cannon salute. No one recorded the response of the traumatized black settlers to this event. Ludlam himself was as traumatized as anyone. He announced that he was resigning his post at the end of 1800. His replacement was none other than William Dawes, who returned to Sierra Leone for his second tour of duty, this time with much-strengthened powers over the lives of the settlers. One of Ludlam's very last duties as governor was to act as judge in the trial of Isaac Anderson and Frank Patrick on December 22, 1800. The new charter did not allow for the charge of treason, so the men were indicted for capital felonies: Anderson for sending a threatening letter and Patrick for taking away a gun. Both were found guilty and hanged immediately. There was no process for appeal.[41]

The personal tragedy and appalling loss in human resources that resulted from these dubious and draconian decisions—forty of the colony's most respected settlers dead or banished—was of no consequence to the directors of the company. They believed that Sierra Leone was much better off without them and "the crude notions they had formed of their own rights." Runaway slaves from America had made "the worst possible subjects," William Wilberforce complained in disgust, "as thorough Jacobins as if they had been trained and educated in Paris." They had, of course, been trained and educated in the American Revolution. Their radical notions about their rights as free men and women, which so bewildered and angered their abolitionist sponsors, were not adopted from the French revolutionaries but were forged in their tortuous negotiations to secure their freedom and to make it a tangible reality in their lives. George Washington believed that he must stake everything to defend the right to freedom and self-determination; it should have been no surprise that a man he once held as property believed the same.[42]

EPILOGUE

On February 15, 1796, the criminal court of New South Wales was interrupted by the news that the outlaw known as Black Caesar had been killed by bounty hunters for a reward of five gallons of rum. Judge Advocate David Collins considered this moment one of the more significant in his long tour of duty in the penal colony. In an uncharacteristically splenetic outburst, Collins penned a brief obituary to the dead man, who had caused him more grief than any other convict in the colony. "Thus ended a man who certainly, during his life, could never have been estimated at more than one remove above the brute," he wrote. For sixteen years, the judge advocate had impassively presided over incidents of murder and child rape, yet nothing of this kind could be attributed to Caesar, whose crime had been to steal food. Collins was unperturbed by venality in convicts; he *expected* it. What so disturbed him about this refractory convict was the persistent refusal to be reduced to the condition of a slave. The battle of wills he had waged with "this incorrigibly stubborn black" had finally been resolved by the offer of a lavish reward for his capture, dead or alive. For next six months until Collins quit the colony in August 1796, he was pleased to report no further incidents of armed runaways in the bush, and he left for England confident that the dangerous precedent of convict resistance had been snuffed out once and for all.[1]

Collins returned New South Wales in 1805, only to find himself issuing futile proclamations and rewards to curtail runaway convicts' forming alliances with Aborigines and disaffected settlers to create a parallel community beyond the boundaries of the settlement. A special name was coined for this threat to judicial authority: bushrangers. Over the next five decades, bushrangers were reviled and relentlessly hunted by colonial authorities at the same time as they captured the popular imagination as potent symbols of freedom in a carceral society. The bushranger, of whom Caesar was the prototype, became the most significant figure of resistance in Australian history, lionized in folk memory and immortalized in song as the man "who'd scorn to live in slavery bound down by iron chains."[2]

That Caesar and his fellow black convicts were sent to New South Wales to labor without a wage and subjected to arbitrary punishment that could scar them for life was less of a testament to shabby treatment by their British allies than the tortuous process of negotiating freedom among the poor at the end of the eighteenth century. A whole range of coerced labor, such as impressment and indenture, was used to harness the energy of the British underclass—for whom freedom meant little more than the capacity to chose between one form of servitude and another—while the savage criminal code created a new category of un-free labor for distant imperial projects. Those men and women sent as convicts to New South Wales were a cross section of the urban poor, of whom the eleven black convicts were a representative percent. Little distinguished the seamen who transported them and the marines who guarded them; they were invariably impressed into service and faced with equally brutal treatment.

Dominated by chains and the lash, penal servitude was coercive and violent, but it was not the equal of chattel slavery. Except for the rebellious Caesar, the small cohort of black convicts achieved emancipation from servitude within five to twelve years. Among the very first generation of Australian-born children were half a dozen with African fathers, guaranteed the privilege and status of the freeborn by custom and law. They included Caesar's daughter, Mary Ann, who was given a land grant in the new colony of Van Diemen's Land. Free land grants given to the freeborn and emancipated convicts alike could, with luck and judicious management, lift them into the ranks of "the middling sort." John Moseley, who ran away from Edward Hack Moseley in Virginia at the age of fifteen, was a case in point. Like John Randall, Moseley chose to sell his land rather than farm it, and while Randall became an enviable member of the racketeering New South Wales Corps, Moseley progressively worked his way to modest prosperity as a dealer in Sydney Town, employing three women servants. In his comfortable old age, it was with consummate irony that Moseley could describe himself in a previous life as "a tobacco planter from America."[3]

Four years after the state-sanctioned death of Caesar, the hanging of Isaac Anderson and Frank Patrick on the other side of the world in Sierra Leone was not recorded; neither was any obituary penned. No one knows what impact their executions had on the traumatized black settlers, but it did little to retard their push to be a self-determining community with the full entitlements of liberty. The Sierra Leone Company was never able to collect the contentious quit rent, and the powerful nexus between the settlers' "enthusiastic" religion and the "false and absurd notions . . . concerning their rights," which had so disturbed the company directors in 1794, remained as strong as ever. Within a few years, the men banished to the Bullom Shore unobtrusively returned with their families to take up land in Sierra Leone once more.[4]

When the disillusioned Sierra Leone Company relinquished the colony to the Crown in 1808, the new British governor was dismayed to find that the settlers from Nova Scotia still maintained their distinctive churches and a feisty attachment to their rights as free men and women. Thomas Perronet Thompson was an abolitionist and William Wilberforce's nominee for the job. Like his patron, Thompson was appalled by the pretensions of "runaway slaves . . . full of every species of ignorant enthusiasm and republican frenzy." These "negro *sans cullotes*," as he called them, entertained ridiculous notions of equal status with whites, and they enraged him by defying his authority, constantly reminding him, "This is Free-Town," subverting the very name of the place to "purposes of insubordination and rebellion." He changed the name to Georgetown but it made no difference; neither he nor subsequent governors could bring them to heel. These self-emancipated slaves embodied "everything . . . vile in the American," in Thompson's disgusted view. He continued, "The most absurd enthusiasm is their religion and wild notions of liberty are their politics."[5]

That the abolitionist sponsors of the Sierra Leone project refused to accept aspirations for self-determination from people who had freed themselves from slavery was a bitter paradox, as was the British government's sending runaway slaves in chains to penal servitude at the other end of the world. The most profound paradox was that in fleeing the Founding Fathers, whose rhetoric of liberty denied their aspirations, these runaways carried to the far corners of the globe the animating principles of the revolution that had so emphatically excluded them.

ACKNOWLEDGMENTS

Foremost I acknowledge the work of historians to whom I am most indebted: Ellen Gibson Wilson, Sylvia Frey, Stephen Braidwood, Gary Nash, and Ian Duffield. Many individuals have contributed valuable insights to this project, and I especially thank Ira Berlin, Christopher Brown, Deirdre Coleman, Ron Hoffman, Graeme Hodges, Woody Holton, Rhys Isaac, Jim Kohen, Iain McCalman, Mike McDonnell, Andrew O'Shaughnessy, Georgina Pinkas, Marcus Rediker, Beverly Runge, Cinder Stanton, Judith van Buskirk, Jim Walvin, Ruth Whitehead, Henry Weincek, and Al Young. Thanks also to Jack Robertson and staff at the Thomas Jefferson Library, Jim Horn and the staff of the Rockeller Library, Robert Ritchie and the staff of the Huntington Library, and Phil Chase and the team at the George Washington Papers. I am grateful for the unstinting assistance of the archivists at the National Archives of the United Kingdom, the manuscripts section of the Library of Congress, the London Metropolitan Research Office, the Clements Library at the University of Michigan, the archives of the University of Illinois at Chicago, the New-York Historical Society, the Public Archives of Nova Scotia, and the Mitchell Library of New South Wales.

The complicated and laborious research for this book was made possible by a five-year Australian Research Council Professorial Fellowship, two Australian Research Council Discovery Grants, a Senior Scholar's Award from the Fulbright Foundation, the Coca-Cola International Fellowship from the International Centre for Jefferson Studies, and a Visiting Fellowship at the Rockefeller Library, Colonial Williamsburg.

A special thanks to gracious hosts, Grace and Tain Tompkins; my agent, Bella Pomer; my editor, Gayatri Patnaik; my various research assistants, Emma Christopher, Fiona Pollack, Eleanor Morrisby, and Luke Clarke; and John Stokes, who drew the maps. There are no words sufficient to thank my husband and sometime research assistant, Michael

Lynch, without whom I would be lost. My remarkable mother and pioneer feminist, Betty Vivian Pybus, died while this book was in progress. Now I understand that I should not have allowed my research to take me away from her, as it so often did. Every book teaches a new lesson.

APPENDIX

Biographies of Significant Black Refugees

ANDERSON, ISAAC

Born in Angola and enslaved in South Carolina, Anderson ran away to the British in Charleston in 1775. In 1776 he left with the royal governor, Lord William Campbell, for New York, where he married Sarah, who had been enslaved to Harry Smith of Charleston. Both were evacuated to Nova Scotia in 1783. In Nova Scotia, Anderson and his wife lived in Birchtown, where he worked as a carpenter. Anderson first came to prominence as a critic of the Sierra Leone Company in 1792, when he protested the prohibition on waterfront land. In 1793 he went to London to present the settlers' grievances to the company directors, and during his many months in London he worked as a servant. In 1796 he was elected a hundredor and was one of the settlers who carried a petition of protest to the captain of the *Daedalus* in 1797. He was re-elected as a hundredor in 1798 and 1799 and was appointed justice of the peace by the settlers in 1799. By July 1800 he had emerged as the head of the anticompany settlers in Sierra Leone, and a warrant for his arrest on charges of treason was issued on September 16, 1800. After he fled from Freetown on September 17, 1800, a reward was offered for his capture. He sought refuge among the indigenous Koya Temne people but was handed over in November 1800. Anderson was tried in December 1800 on the capital charge of sending a threatening letter and subsequently hanged.

ANDERSON, PETER

A runaway slave from Virginia, Anderson joined Lord Dunmore's Ethiopian Regiment in 1775 and was captured at the Battle of Great Bridge. Late in 1776, while awaiting execution in the jail in Williamsburg, he escaped and hid in the woods until he was taken aboard a British warship in 1777. He was possibly at the taking of Savannah and was at the siege of Charleston. In November 1782, he was evacuated to England, and his enslaved wife and three children were left behind in Virginia.

BURKE, SAMUEL

Originally from Charleston, Burke had been taken to county Clare, Ireland, in 1774 and had gone from there to the Bahamas as a servant to the governor Brigadier

Montfort Browne in 1776. Burke served as a recruiter for Brigadier Browne's Loyalist regiment in New York and married a free black widow, Hannah. Burke and his
wife were at the reconquest of Charleston in 1780. After being wounded at Hanging
Rock, he was evacuated to England with his wife. In London he worked selling paper flowers.

CAESAR

Caesar's origins are unknown, but he was probably bought to England in the final
British evacuation in 1783. He was living in the parish of St. Paul, Deptford, when he
was sentenced to transportation for seven years at Maidstone, Kent, in March 1786,
and was transported to New South Wales in May 1787. At Sydney Cove, Caesar was
tried for theft at the Criminal Court in April 1789 and sentenced to penal servitude
for life. The following month he absconded with stolen arms but was recaptured
three weeks later. He absconded again in December of that year but was driven back
to the settlement by Aborigines. Reprieved from hanging by the governor, he was
sent to Norfolk Island in March 1790. His daughter, Mary Ann Poore, was born on
Norfolk Island two years later. Caesar returned to Sydney in March 1793 and absconded in July 1794. By December 1795 he was the leader of a gang of convict
absconders and was killed by bounty hunters in February 1796.

GEORGE, DAVID

Born in Essex County, Virginia, of African parents, George was enslaved to a man
named Chapel. As a boy he ran away into the South Carolina backcountry, where he
was enslaved first by the Creek Indians and then the Natchez, until he was given to
the Indian agent George Galphin at Silver Bluff, where he married Phyllis and had
several children. He was converted by the black Baptist preacher George Liele, and
together he and Liele established the first black Baptist church in America. After defecting to the British in 1779, George ran a butcher's stall in Savannah and supplied
provisions to the British outposts along the Savannah River. George took his family
to Charleston in 1782 and from there was evacuated to Halifax, Nova Scotia. George
established Baptist churches at Shelburne, Preston, near Halifax, and at St. Johns,
New Brunswick. He took nearly all of his Baptist congregation to Sierra Leone.
When he left for Sierra Leone in 1791, with Phyllis and six children, he was forty-
eight years old. In Sierra Leone he and Phyllis had four more children. At the end
of 1793, George went to England to study with the Baptists, and when he returned

in 1795 most of the settlers in Sierra Leone regarded him with suspicion. He was the leader of the pro-government settlers in Sierra Leone and also worked as a missionary to the indigenous Koya Temne. He died in 1810.

GORDON, DANIEL/JANEL/JACK

Jack Gordon appears to have been abandoned or freed by Benjamin Gordon during the siege of Charleston in 1779. He came to New York and was listed as embarked to go to Nova Scotia in April 1783, but apparently he went to Portsmouth, England, instead. In April 1785, Janel Gordon was sentenced to transportation beyond the seas for seven years at Winchester, England, for theft.

At Sydney Cove, Gordon was sentenced to death in February 1788 for the theft of wine (with John Williams) and was pardoned on the gallows. In August 1789, Gordon was tried for the theft of food and clothing from his fellow convicts, and this time his trial was aborted. He was subsequently sent to Norfolk Island, where he was listed as a free man in 1790. He was still on Norfolk Island, working as a tailor, in 1805, and he returned to Sydney in 1806. In October 1818 he died.

GRIFFITHS, ABRAHAM ELLIOT

When he was a servant in London in the 1780s, Griffiths became a protégé of Granville Sharp, who paid to have him taught to read and write. As one of the corporals of the Black Poor in London in 1786, he was prominent in the original expedition to Sierra Leone in 1787 and wrote letters to London newspapers on behalf of the settlers. After his white wife, Rebecca, died in Sierra Leone, he became the interpreter for the supreme Koya Temne ruler, Naimbana, and married his daughter, Clara. In 1792 he also became interpreter for the Sierra Leone Company and converted to Methodism. Distrusted by the Sierra Leone Company, Griffiths was suspected of inciting the settlers against the company and also of forging currency. He escaped punishment following the 1800 attempt to establish settler independence, but was imprisoned in 1802 for debt to the company and died in jail.

HANDLEY, SCIPIO

A self-employed fishmonger, Handley was sentenced to death for carrying messages for the royal governor of South Carolina, Sir William Campbell, late in 1775. He escaped from jail in 1776 and sailed to New York with the exiled Lord Campbell. In New York he joined the Royal Navy and went to Barbados, returning when Savannah was captured in 1780. Badly wounded by a musket ball in his leg at the siege of Savannah, Handley was left unfit for further active duty and was evacuated to England in 1782.

HARRIS, WALTER

As an enslaved house servant of Mrs. Mary Byrd of Westover plantation in Virginia, Harris was married with several children and known simply as Wat. In 1780 he was taken as a guide by General Benedict Arnold and later transferred to Lord Cornwallis, with whom he went to Yorktown. He was smuggled out of Yorktown on the *Bonetta*. After about a year in New York he went to England. He was part of the original expedition to Sierra Leone, and it is not known whether he survived beyond 1788.

HENRY, RALPH

Henry ran away to join Lord Dunmore's Ethiopian Regiment in 1776, probably when his owner, Patrick Henry, was the first governor of Virginia. He went with Lord Dunmore to New York, where he married his wife, Miney, a runaway from Philadelphia, and he worked for the Royal Artillery Department. He and his wife and child were evacuated to Nova Scotia late in 1783 and settled at Preston, until they left for Sierra Leone in 1792. Henry was identified as a leader of a riot against the officials of the Sierra Leone Company in 1793 and was sent to England to be tried for insurrection. The case never came to trial, and Henry appears to have died in England.

JACKSON, JAMES

Enslaved to Richard Sweepston of Mecklenburgh, Virginia, Jackson ran away in 1779 with his wife, Peggy, and their two children, who were enslaved to William Eggerson in Norfolk. They were taken to New York by the British and evacuated to Nova Scotia in 1783. In 1791, Jackson and his family went to Sierra Leone and in 1793 he was identified as a leader of a riot against the officials of the Sierra Leone Company and was sent to England to be tried for insurrection. The case never came to trial and Jackson struggled for years to survive in England. In 1796 he signed on as a seaman and was believed to have died at sea.

JOHNSON, THOMAS

A free man from Charleston, South Carolina, Johnson claimed to have been a confidential servant of John Izard, who, he said, gave him a house and ten acres on the Izard estate at Cedar Grove. He was recruited as a guide in the British Legion commanded by Banastre Tarleton in 1780 and later was working for Tarleton at

Yorktown. He and his wife, Margaret, and children were smuggled out of Yorktown to New York on the Bonetta. They were evacuated with the British Legion to Nova Scotia, where the family settled at Guysborough. In 1784 Johnson and his wife went to England and were living at the workhouse in the parish of St. Marylebone, where their third child, Elizabeth, was baptized. In 1787 they were listed among the families receiving weekly payments from the Committee for the Relief of the Black Poor. Although they agreed to migrate to Sierra Leone, the family did not join the expedition.

JORDAN, LUKE

Enslaved to George Jordan of Nasemond County, Virginia, Jordan and his wife, Rachel, from the plantation of Solomon Slaughter, ran away with their four children in 1779. They were taken to New York by a British warship and were evacuated to Nova Scotia in 1783. Jordan and his family lived at Birchtown, where he was a Methodist preacher and worked as a sailor. In 1792 he took his wife and ten children to Sierra Leone, where he was a leader of the black settlers and a consistent critic of the Sierra Leone Company, finally leaving Freetown to establish a separate settlement at Pirates Bay in 1796.

KING, BOSTON

Enslaved to Richard Waring in South Carolina, King was apprenticed to a brutal builder, from whom he ran away after the siege of Charleston in 1780. He worked for the British, attached to a provincial regiment as a guide and servant first at Camden and then at Nelson's Ferry. He arrived in New York at the end of 1781, where a year later he married Violet, who had been enslaved to Colonel Young of Wilmington, North Carolina. He learned to read a bit during a brief enslavement in New Jersey. He and Violet were evacuated to Nova Scotia and lived at Birchtown, where they became converts of Daddy Moses. King was called to become a preacher himself and had a congregation at Darmouth. He and Violet went to Sierra Leone in 1792, but Violet died soon after arrival. King then married Phillis. In 1794 he went to England to study with the Methodists in order to become a missionary and become fully literate. He returned to Sierra Leone in 1796 and subsequently ran a school for the Bullom people. He died in 1802.

MARTIN, JOHN

A seaman from the American colonies who came to England during the American War, Martin was tried at the Old Bailey in July 1782 for stealing clothing and sentenced to transportation for seven years. He was transported to New South Wales in May 1787. At the time of landing at Sydney Cove, Martin had technically only one year to serve. He married Ann Toy in August 1788. In November 1792 he was free and received a grant of fifty acres, and by 1806 he was a successful farmer, also employed as a constable. He had no children with his first wife, who died in 1806. He married Mary Randall, the daughter of his fellow black First Fleeter, John Randall, in July 1812, and they had eleven children. When he died in December 1837, his age was given as eighty-eight.

MOSELEY, JOHN

As youth enslaved to Edward Hack Moseley, Princess Ann County, Virginia, Jack ran away with two other youths in August 1775. He worked briefly for an Irish ship's captain, John Cunningham, in Portsmouth, before joining Lord Dunmore's Ethiopian Regiment in 1776. In New York he worked for the Wagon Master General's Department and in October 1783 he got a berth aboard HMS *Loyalist,* bound for England. He was indicted under the name John Shore at the Old Bailey on April 21, 1784, for impersonating a fellow seaman on the *Loyalist* in order to receive his wages. As John Moseley he was sentenced to death, and in March 1785 he was reprieved to transportation for life to Africa. A daughter was born in 1785, mother unknown. He was transported to New South Wales in May 1787. In April 1800 Moseley received a conditional pardon and in 1801 he received a land grant. In 1828 he was recorded as a dealer in Essex Lane, Sydney, employing three women as servants. His death was in 1835.

PATRICK, FRANK

Enslaved to Richard Brown in Norfolk, Virginia, Patrick ran away to the British in 1779 and was taken to New York on a British ship. Patrick was evacuated to Nova Scotia and lived at Birchtown before he went to Sierra Leone in 1791. He was dismissed as a laborer for the Sierra Leone Company in 1793 for being disrespectful and was subsequently found guilty of stealing from the company store. Zachary Macaulay sentenced him to a severe flogging and hard labor aboard the company ship *York.* He joined the anticompany alliance to establish settler independence in 1800 and fled from Freetown with Isaac Anderson in September of that year. A reward of fifty dollars was offered for his capture. He surrendered in October. On December 22 that year, Patrick was found guilty of taking away a gun and subsequently hanged.

PERKINS, CATO

Enslaved to John Perkins of Charlestown, South Carolina, Perkins ran to the British during the siege of Charleston and probably went with General Clinton to New York, where he worked as a carpenter. He was evacuated to Nova Scotia and lived in Birchtown, where he was converted by John Marrant, of the Countess of Huntingdon's Connexion, a Methodist splinter group. Perkins went to Sierra Leone in 1792, where he led a strike of carpenters against the Sierra Leone Company for better conditions later that year. In 1793 Perkins went to London to present a petition of protest to the company directors. During his months in England he studied with the Huntingdon Connexion. During the 1800 attempt to establish settler independence, he acted as an intermediary between the governor and Isaac Anderson.

PERTH, MARY

Enslaved to John Willoughby of Princess Anne County, Virginia, Mary and her daughter Patience were among eighty-seven people who ran to Lord Dunmore in 1776. In New York she married Caesar Perth, who had been enslaved to Hardy Waller of Norfolk, Virginia, and worked for the wagon master general. The couple went to Nova Scotia on *L'Abondance* in 1783 with Mary's daughter Patience and two orphans from the Willoughby plantation. The family settled at Birchtown, and in 1792, Mary, Caesar, and their daughter Susan went to Sierra Leone. When Caesar died in 1793, Mary opened a boardinghouse and shop. In 1794, she went to work for the governor Zachary Macaulay as housekeeper and teacher, responsible for the many African children living at Macaulay's house. When Macaulay returned to England in 1799, taking twenty-five African children with him, Mary and her ailing daughter Susan went also. Although Susan died in England, Mary returned in 1801 and reopened her boardinghouse and shop. She remarried in 1806 and died in 1813.

PETERS, THOMAS

Born in Nigeria, Peters was sold in Louisiana in 1760 and after three unsuccessful attempts to escape he was sold to William Campbell of Wilmington, North Carolina, in 1770. Peters ran from Campbell in March 1776 with his wife, Sally, and their daughter, Clairy. He served as a sergeant in the Black Pioneers throughout the war. His family was evacuated to Nova Scotia in 1783 and settled near Digby, but when he did not receive the promised land grant, Peters moved to St. John, New Brunswick. In 1791, Peters went to England to petition the government, and on his return he organized for nearly 1,200 people to relocate to Sierra Leone in 1792. In Sierra Leone,

Peters came into conflict with the governor John Clarkson over the failure of the Sierra Leone Company to provide land promised to the black settlers. He died of malaria in 1792, about fifty-four years old, leaving a widow and seven children.

PROVEY, JOHN

Although Provey claimed to have been born free and a servant to a lawyer in North Carolina, he was more likely a runaway. He joined the British fleet off Cape Fear in 1775 and became a servant to Clinton's secretary, William Smith. He went with Clinton to Rhode Island, where he became a servant to Lord Percy (later Duke of Northumberland), who took him to England. He married Ann in England and had a daughter, and the family was part of the original expedition to Sierra Leone, but all died before the ships left England.

RANDALL, JOHN

Probably a slave of Captain John Randall of Stonington, Connecticut, Randall could have been recruited as a musician for a British regiment. He was most likely evacuated with his regiment to England in 1783, and he was sentenced at Manchester Quarter Sessions in April 1785 to transportation for seven years to New South Wales for stealing a watch chain. At Sydney Cove, Randall married Esther Howard in February 1788, but she died in October 1789 having borne him a daughter, Frances. By then Randall was employed as a game killer for the community and sharing a hut with fellow black convict John Moseley. He was married again to Mary Butler in September 1790, and they had four children. Mary died on July 29, 1802. In November 1792, Randall was free and had received a grant of sixty acres north of Sydney. In November 1800, he sold his farm and joined the New South Wales Corps at Sydney and was discharged in April 1810. In 1814 he was a landholder outside Sydney, and also a constable, with a third family of four children. He died in 1822.

SNOWBALL, NATHANIEL

Enslaved to Mrs. Shrewstin of Norfolk, Virginia, Snowball ran away to join Lord Dunmore in 1776, taking with him his wife, Violet, and son, Nathaniel, who were enslaved to Richard Murray of Princess Anne County, and his brother Timothy, who was enslaved to Cornelius Colbert of Norfolk. The family was taken to New York and evacuated to Nova Scotia. They lived at Birchtown, where they were members of Daddy Moses's congregation. They left for Sierra Leone in 1792, where

Nathaniel was an outspoken critic of the Sierra Leone Company. Together with Luke Jordan, he led an exodus to a new settlement at Pirates Bay, where he was elected governor in 1797.

THOMPSON, JOHN
Possibly born free on Long Island, Thompson was a servant to Col. Edward Fanning and carried messages for him in 1775. He was caught and imprisoned in 1776 but escaped to rejoin the British. Until 1781 he was in Fanning's Loyalist regiment, and then he joined the Royal Navy. He was discharged from HMS *Warwick* at Portsmouth in 1784, and he applied to the Loyalist Claims Commission for compensation for his supposed property loss. His daughter was baptized at the London parish of St. George in the East in 1783. He and his white wife, Ann, went to Sierra Leone. He died there in 1790 when he was an ambushed during a dispute with the indigenous Koya Temne.

TWINE, JOHN
Although he claimed to be free, Twine was probably enslaved to a tavern keeper in Petersburg, Virginia. Having been impressed into the Continental army, Twine deserted to the British at Trenton in 1777. He went to Charleston with the army in 1780 and then went north with Lord Cornwallis. He was wounded in the thigh at Camden. In 1782 he and his wife, Hannah, were evacuated from Charleston to England and were aboard the ships that left on the original expedition to Sierra Leone, but they did not arrive.

WANSEY, NATHANIEL
Enslaved to James Stewart of Newcastle, Pennsylvania, Wansey ran to the British when they occupied Philadelphia in 1778 and went with the British army to New York, where he married Chloe, who had come to New York with General Matthews in 1779. They were evacuated to Nova Scotia in 1783 and went to Sierra Leone in 1792. Wansey was a leading critic of the Sierra Leone Company, and as chairman of the tithingmen he was a leader of the 1800 attempt to establish settler independence. After the attack by Maroons in October 1800, he found refuge among the Koya Temne people and led an attack on Freetown in November 1801 and again in April 1802. Repulsed, he fled farther north to the Mandinka people but was handed over to the company. It is not known what became of him, though he was almost certainly executed.

WASHINGTON, HARRY

Born in Africa, probably in the region around the Gambia River, Harry was purchased by George Washington in 1763 and put to work to drain the Great Dismal Swamp. In 1766, Harry was taken from the Dismal Swamp to Washington's Mount Vernon estate. He ran away in July 1771 but was returned within a matter of weeks. He was working as a hostler at Mount Vernon in August 1776 when he again ran away to join Lord Dunmore. Taken to New York by Lord Dunmore at the end of 1776, he became a corporal in a corps of Black Pioneers attached to the Royal Artillery Department, and he went to Charleston in 1780, returning to New York sometime in 1782. He was evacuated to Nova Scotia on *L'Abondance* in July 1783 and settled at Birchtown, where he married Sarah. A convert to the Methodist congregation of Daddy Moses, he relocated to Sierra Leone, with his wife and three children, leaving behind a town lot and forty acres of freehold land. In Sierra Leone he had a farm to the east of Freetown until 1800, when he joined Isaac Anderson's attempt to establish settler independence from the Sierra Leone Company. He was sentenced by a military tribunal in October 1800 to be exiled to the Bullom Shore, where he was elected leader of the exiled community, but he might have returned to Sierra Leone following a later amnesty. His death was not recorded.

WEAVER, RICHARD

An enslaved man from Philadelphia, Weaver ran to the British army in 1777. He went to England with his wife and several children in 1779 and was in England by 1782. He accepted the bounty from the Committee for the Black Poor and he, his wife, and daughter were part of the original expedition to Sierra Leone in 1787. At the founding settlement of Granville Town, Weaver was elected the first governor. He survived at least until 1789 but may not have been alive when the people from Nova Scotia arrived in 1792.

WHITECUFF/WYCUFFE, BENJAMIN

A free man from New York who worked as a spy for the British, Whitecuff was twice captured and nearly executed by the Americans. He escaped from America and came to England via the West Indies and joined the Royal Navy. He served at the siege of Gibraltar and was discharged in 1783. He was baptized in Deptford in 1783 and married Sarah soon after. They were part of the original expedition to Sierra Leone in 1787, but Whitecuff died before the ships left England and Sarah died soon after reaching Sierra Leone.

WILKINSON, "DADDY MOSES"

Enslaved to Mills Wilkinson of Nasemound County, Virginia, Daddy Moses led a group of runaways to Dunmore in 1776. He was crippled and blind in 1779, which suggests that he had survived the smallpox epidemic of 1776. He became a charismatic preacher among the runaways in New York, and he was evacuated to Nova Scotia with his large congregation in 1783. He reestablished his church at the settlement at Birchtown, where he owned two town lots and forty acres. He was a significant influence in persuading most of the Methodists to leave Nova Scotia and go to Sierra Leone in 1792. In Sierra Leone he was the most influential religious leader, and his congregation was consistently identified with resistance to the Sierra Leone Company, though he took no part in political action.

WILLIAMS, JAMES "BLACK JEMMY"

At the age of sixteen James Williams was sentenced at the Old Bailey in May 1785 to seven years' transportation for the theft of clothing and shoes. He said he had been on an errand to deliver letters from the captain of a West Indian ship. He was transported to New South Wales in May 1787. At Sydney Cove, where he was known as "Black Jemmy," he was twice sentenced to five hundred lashes. In April 1790 he stowed away on the *Supply* bound for Batavia but was returned to Sydney. In October 1791, he stowed away on the *Atlantic* bound for Calcutta and was not discovered until the vessel had reached India. When he returned to New South Wales in June 1792, no further punishment was inflicted on him, as his sentence had expired. He was allowed to leave on the first available ship.

WILLIAMS, JOHN "BLACK JACK"

When he was fifteen and a resident in St. Nicholas's parish, Deptford, in London, John Williams was sentenced to death, later reprieved to transportation for seven years. He was transported to New South Wales in May 1787. At Sydney Cove, where he was known as "Black Jack," he was tried in February 1788 (with Daniel Gordon) for the theft of wine from the stores and again was sentenced to death, with the sentence commuted. His extended sentence finally expired in 1804, and he subsequently became a sealer in Bass Strait, living with several Aboriginal women, whom he kept as his slaves. He was drowned in 1830.

ABBREVIATIONS USED IN THE NOTES

ADM	Records of British Admiralty
ANSW	Archives of New South Wales
AO	Records of the British Auditor
ASSI	Records of the Justices of Assizes in United Kingdom
BL	British Library, London
CJ	Journal of the House of Commons
CL	Clements Library, University of Michigan
CO	Records of British Colonial Office
CRBP	Committee for Relief of the Black Poor
FO	Records of British Foreign Office
HL	Huntington Library
HO	Records of British Home Office
GLRO	Greater London Research Office
LOC	Library of Congress
ML	Mitchell Library, State Library of New South Wales
NA	National Archives, United Kingdom
NYHS	New-York Historical Society
OBSP	Old Bailey Session Papers
PANS	The Public Archives of Nova Scotia
PRO	Domestic Papers of the National Archives, United Kingdom
RG	Nova Scotia Commissioner for Public Records Collection
T	Records of British Treasury
UIC	University of Illinois at Chicago
ViMtV	Mount Vernon Ladies Association Archives
VSL	Virginia State Library
WO	Records of British War Office

PROLOGUE

1. For accounts of the supposed rebellion in Sierra Leone, see the appendix to the Sierra Leone Company Minutes for 1800, CO 270/5, and the Sierra Leone Commissioners of Enquiry 1827, vol. 2, CO 267/2, NA.

2. The Book of Negroes can be found in the Carleton Papers PRO 30/55/100, NA. It can also be found online as a searchable database at http://www.gov.ns.ca/nsarm/virtual/africanns/book.asp.

3. The question of the numbers of runaways in the revolution is controversial. My research indicates that only about one-fifth of the 80,000 to 100,000 claimed by Aptheker, and later by Frey, actually ran to the British. For further discussion of this thorny issue, see Pybus, "Jefferson's Faulty Math."

4. The quote is from Isaac, *Landon Carter's Uneasy Kingdom*, 17. It must be said that historians such as Gary Nash, Ira Berlin, Graeme Hodges, and James and Lois Horton have been determined to put slaves at the center of their own story when writing about the Revolution.

5. For free black refugees in Jamaica, see John Pulis, "Bridging Troubled Waters: Moses Baker, George Liele and the African American Diaspora to Jamaica," in Pulis, *Moving On*. For the Bahamas, see Michael Craton, "Loyalist Mainly to Themselves: The 'Black Loyalist' Disapora to the Bahamas," in Shepherd, *Working Slavery, Pricing Freedom*, 44–64. For St. Lucia, see Tyson, "The Carolina Black Corps," 648–64. For the Mosquito Shore and British Honduras: Linebaugh and Rediker, *The Many-Headed Hydra*, 269. For black refugees in Germany: Jones, "The Black Hessians," 287–302, and Selig, "The Revolution's Black Soldiers," 15–22.

A NOTE ON SOURCES

1. The petition of William Blue, October 1823, MS Ab 31/52, ML. Works cited: Duffield, "Constructing and Reconstructing 'Black' Caesar"; Quarles, *Negro in the American Revolution;* Norton, "Fate of Some Black Loyalists"; Braidwood, *Black Poor and White Philanthropists;* Nash, "Thomas Peters: Millwright and Deliverer."

CHAPTER I

1. Harry Washington declared himself born in Africa when he signed up to go to Sierra Leone: "List of the Blacks at Birchtown who gave their names for Sierra Leone in November 1791," CO 217/63, NA. For Harry's likely African origin, see

Sweig, "The Importation of African Slaves," 516–23. For the purchase of Harry and his subsequent deployment at Mount Vernon, see Washington, *Papers of George Washington: Colonial Series*, vol. 7, 300, 314–15, 442–43, 516. Nan and Harry were on list of taxable property that Washington submitted in 1766, but children under sixteen were not listed. Washington was the manager of the Dismal Swamp scheme until 1768, when it passed over to his brother John. For an account of the company Washington formed to drain the Dismal Swamp, see Royster, *Fabulous History of the Dismal Swamp Company.*

2. Washington had been elected delegate for Fairfax County on February 20, 1775. Washington to John A. Washington, March 25, 1775, Washington, *Papers of George Washington: Colonial Series*, vol. 10, 368.

3. The surviving records of the second convention can be found in Scribner, *Revolutionary Virginia*, vol.2, 347–86, although Patrick Henry's speech was never written or recorded verbatim. Washington to Fairfax, August 24, 1774, in Washington, *Papers of George Washington: Colonial Series*, vol. 10, 155.

4. Escape of Harry is noted in Washington, *Diaries of George Washington*, vol. 3, 45.

5. For Tidewater plantation life, see Kulikoff, *Tobacco and Slaves*, and Isaac, *Transformation of Virginia*. Quote from John Adams's diary, September 24, 1775, in Butterfield, ed., *Diary and Autobiography of John Adams*, 183.

6. Madison to Bradford, November 26, 1775, Madison, *Papers of James Madison*, vol. 1, 130.

7. Dunmore to Dartmouth, May 1, 1775, CO 5/1353, NA, and Deposition of Dr. William Pastuer 1775 in *Virginia Magazine of History and Biography* 13 (1905): 29. For Loyalist reassurances, Byrd to Wormeley, October 4, 1779, Ralph Wormeley Papers, University of Virginia. The quote from a patroller is found in Holton, *Forced Founders*, 147.

8. Dunmore to Dartmouth, June 25, 1775, CO 5 /1353, NA.

9. For the attack on Hampton, see Scribner, *Revolutionary Virginia*, vol. 4, 69–70, 416. Jefferson to John Randolph, November 29, 1775, in Jefferson, *Papers of Thomas Jefferson*, vol. 1, 269.

10. For Moseley, Virginia Runaways project: http://teacherlink.org/content/social/ instructional/runawayintro/home.html. For John Cunningham, see Scribner, *Revolutionary Virginia*, vol. 5, 360. In the Book of Negroes John Moseley said that before he joined the British in 1776 he "lived with John Cunningham, Portsmouth, Virginia as a freeman."

11. Madison to Bradford, June 19, 1775, in Madison, *Papers of James Madison*, vol. 1,

153; for Dunmore's Proclamation, see Scribner, *Revolutionary Virginia,* vol. 4, 334.

12. Jefferson's convoluted argument was eventually struck from the final document by the Congress; see Jefferson, *Papers of Thomas Jefferson,* vol. 1, 426. Washington to Reed, December 15, 1775, in Washington, *Papers of George Washington: Revolutionary War Series,* vol. 2, 553.

13. *Virginia Gazette* (Purdie), November 24, 1774. Edmund Pendleton, December 14, 1775, Fourth Virginia Convention, in Scribner, *Revolutionary Virginia,* vol. 5, 139. Pendleton to Lee, November 27, 1775, in Pendleton, *Letters and Papers of Edmund Pendleton,* vol.1, 133.

14. For Creole slave life, see Kulikoff, *Tobacco and Slaves;* Stanton, *Slavery at Monticello;* and Schwarz, *Slavery at the Home of George Washington.*

15. *Virginia Gazette* (Dixon and Hunter), November 27, 1775. For capture and punishment of runaways, see Scribner, *Revolutionary Virginia,* vol. 6, 305, 485, and vol. 7, part 1, 284.

16. Dunmore to Howe, November 30, 1775, in William Bell Clark, ed., *Naval Documents of the American Revolution,* vol. 2 (Washington, 1967), 1210–11. Ruffin notice, January 6, 1776, see Scribner, *Revolutionary Virginia,* vol. 4, 426.

17. Dunmore to Dartmouth, February 20, 1776, Memorial of Neil Jamieson AO 13/58/197. Quote from Thomas Ludwell to Richard Henry Lee, December 23, 1775, Lee Family Papers, University of Virginia. For Great Bridge, see Clark, Morgan, and Crawford, *Naval Documents of the American Revolution,* vol. 3, 24–27, 187–89.

18. Woodford to Howe, December 5, 7, and 17, 1775, in "The Woodford, Howe and Lee letters," *Richmond College Historical Papers,* vol. 1, (1915), 110–33. For captive runaways, see Scribner, *Revolutionary Virginia,* vol. 5, 58–59, 103, and vol. 6, 69. For Peter Anderson's escape (he is called James Anderson in the Virginia documents), see Loyalist Claims Commission, AO 12/99/354, AO 13/27/226,230, NA. For death of slaves in jail see petitions for compensation to the Virginia Assembly House of Delegates, 1776–77, VSL.

19. Lund Washington to Washington, December 1775; Lund Washington to Washington, December 3, 1775, Washington, *Papers of George Washington: Revolutionary War Series,* vol. 2, 571, 481–82.

20. For detail on John Willoughby Sr., see *Virginia Magazine of History and Biography,* vol. 1 (1894), 499–50, and *Virginia Gazette* (Purdie), May 10, 1776. For Moseley's and Willoughby's arrest and forced removal, see Scribner, *Revolutionary*

Virginia, vol. 5, 141, 142, 207, 369–71. For Cunningham, see Scribner, Revolutionary Virginia, vol. 5, 361, 408, and Virginia Gazette (Purdie), January 19, 1776.

21. The Willoughby petition can be found in Journal of the House of Delegates of the
Commonwealth of Virginia, 55.

22. Notice of auction of Dunmore's slaves: Virginia Gazette (Purdie), June 12, 1776.
For sale of captured slaves to the West Indies, see Scribner, Revolutionary Virginia, vol. 6, 425.

23. An analysis of fugitive slaves in Virginia prior to 1775 can be found in Windley,
Profile of Runaway Slaves, 162–64. Barry Sawyer ran off from his master in
Princess Anne County, as did Shinea Sawyer and her four-year-old daughter,
Chloe Sawyer, both of whom were enslaved to a man in the town of Norfolk.
In that party also were two other children, Nelly and Tom Sawyer, age seven
and three respectively, who were the property of a yet another man in Norfolk
County. For a glimpse of the number of women with Dunmore, see "List of
women embarked at Mill Point, May 21 1776" published in Virginia Gazette
(Purdie), August 31, 1776.

24. The account of Mary's proselytizing comes from "A Letter from the Rev. Mr.
Clark," 464. Wesleyan Methodists laid heavy emphasis on the reclaimed sinner
as a slave redeemed, as expressed by St. Paul in the Epistle to the Galatians 5:1:
"Stand fast therefore in the liberty wherewith Christ has made us free and be not
entangled again with the yoke of bondage."

25. A fellow runaway from Mills Wilkinson named Cuff was captured by the Patriots in January 1776; see Scribner, Revolutionary Virginia, vol. 5, 423. He was subsequently sent to the West Indies for sale; see petition of Mills Wilkinson to
Virginia legislature for compensation, May 21, 1777, VSL. Moses Wilkinson's details are in the Book of Negroes. Black Methodist preachers were not
unknown in Tidewater Virginia at the time. Harry Hosier, a black man, traveled
and preached with itinerant preachers in Virginia during and after the revolution.

26. Quotes from Henry in Meade, Patrick Henry, 107–8. Information on Ralph
Henry is found in the Book of Negroes.

27. Lund Washington to Washington, January 1776, in Washington, Papers of George
Washington: Revolutionary War Series, vol. 3, 129.

28. Runaway notice, Virginia Gazette (Purdie), April 5, 1776. Isaac, Landon Carter's
Uneasy Kingdom, 3–15. There is no record of any of Landon Carter's runaways
with the British. It would have been difficult for them to have gotten to Gwynn

Island, as they landed on the south side of Rappahannock on June 26 in King and Queen County, still a long way from Gwynn Island and they were without a boat.

29. *Virginia Gazette* (Purdie), March 8, 1776. Narrative of Andrew Snape Hamond in Clark, Morgan, and Crawford, *Naval Documents of the American Revolution,* vol. 5, 321–22, and Dunmore to Germain, March 30, 1776, CO 5/1373. For evidence of the 300 graves, see Fenn, *Pox Americana,* 58.

30. For background on the smallpox epidemic, see Fenn, *Pox Americana,* and Ranlet, "British, Slaves, and Smallpox in Revolutionary Virginia," 218.

31. *Virginia Gazette* (Purdie), May 31, 1776; Dunmore quotes in Clark, Morgan, and Crawford, *Naval Documents of the American Revolution,* vol. 5, 669; and Dunmore to Germain, June 26, 1776, CO 5/1373. Narrative of Andrew Snape Hamond in Clark, Morgan, and Crawford, *Naval Documents of the American Revolution,* vol. 5, 839–41, 1079.

32. *Virginia Gazette* (Dixon and Hunter), July 20, and *Virginia Gazette* (Purdie), July 19, 1776.

33. Clark, Morgan, and Crawford, *Naval Documents of the American Revolution,* vol. 5, 1250–51. Several indentured convicts ran away in April 1775. One, Joseph Wilson, was captured with the British off Hampton in October 1775. It is not clear who ran off in July 1776, as there are no existing records that speak of slaves or indentured servants at that time. For indentured convict servants see Dalzell and Dalzell, *George Washington's Mt. Vernon,* 152–55. Description of the runaway Harry as "a man about forty years old, valuable," from Lund Washington's list, no date, from Willard Collection, LOC. Lund's list has been incorrectly dated April 1781, but was most likely drawn up in late 1782 or early 1783 as the basis for a claim against the British. Harry Washington's statement in the Book of Negroes implies that Lund's retrospective claim that Harry left Mount Vernon in April 1781 is incorrect.

34. Dunmore to Germain, July 31 and September 4, 1776, CO 5/1353; Clark, Morgan, and Crawford, *Naval Documents of the American Revolution,* vol. 5, 1312–14. Andrew Snape Hamond's narrative suggests that there were about 200 effective black troops on Gwynn Island, whereas the Diary of Miguel Antonia Edwardo, a visitor to the fleet in late June, estimated 300: Clark, Morgan, and Crawford, *Naval Documents of the American Revolution,* 1344–45. For Ralph Henry, see the Book of Negroes and Rivington's *Royal Gazette,* February 6, 1779. More than 100 people recruited by Dunmore were evacuated from New York as free persons in 1783.

CHAPTER 2

1. For the Thomas Jerimiah case, see Olwell, *Masters, Slaves and Subject,* 232–34. Campbell to Dartmouth, August 13, 1775, in Clark, Morgan, and Crawford, *Naval Documents of the American Revolution,* vol. 11, 94. Campbell to Dartmouth August 18, 1775, in Davies, *Documents of the American Revolution,* vol. 20, 93–98.

2. Memorial of Scipio Handley, Loyalist Claims Commission, AO 13/119/431, AO 12/47/117, and AO 12/109/160, NA.

3. The area known as the Indian Lands was a large territory west of Charleston, which had been ceded by the Cherokee. The Book of Negroes indicates that Mary was not the only runaway from the Indian Lands in 1775, so she may have been part of a group. The Anderson quote is from the Book of Negroes. I am grateful to Ruth Holmes Whitehead of the Museum of Nova Scotia for the information about Robert Lindsay. Free blacks in Charleston did own slaves; in the decade after the Revolution there were nearly fifty such people, who between them had ownership of 277 people: Kroger, *Free Black Slave Masters.*

4. Laurens to Capt Thornborough, in Clark, Morgan, and Crawford, *Naval Documents of the American Revolution,* vol. 5, 164; Laurens to Richardson, December 19, 1775, in Laurens, *Papers of Henry Laurens,* vol. 10, 576; Laurens to Bull, January 20, 1776, Laurens, *Papers of Henry Laurens,* vol. 11, 49.

5. For Peters, see the Book of Negroes and Nash, "Thomas Peters: Millwright and Deliverer." Memorial of John Provey, AO 12/101/155, NA.

6. Clinton to Martin, May 10, 1776, inclosing "Oath to be administered to Negroes serving in Capt Martin's Company," and "List of names of Negroes belonging to Capt Martin's Company," undated, Clinton Papers, CL. Clinton, *American Rebellion,* 25–26.

7. See Loyalist Claims Commission, AO 12/19/343, AO 12/99/356, AO 12/30/290, AO 12/9/355, NA.

8. Frank Griffin, WO 71/155, NA.

9. Memorial of Samuel Burke, AO 12/99/358–59, NA.

10. Memorial of Benjamin Whitecuff, AO 13/56/628, NA.

11. Quote from William Beekman papers in van Buskirk, *Generous Enemies,* 135. Peter Jay to John and James Jay, September 1, 1779, in the papers of John Jay, Columbia University. The Book of Negroes shows John Jay's slave Frank was evacuated with the Wagon Master General under the name Massey, while the boy enslaved to Frederick, called Peter Robinson, was evacuated carrying a certificate of freedom signed by General Birch.

12. June 7, 1779, Daniel Jones, "Orders Relative to Refugee Negroes," in van Buskirk, *Generous Enemies,* 135. Rivington's *Royal Gazette,* November 4, 1780.

13. In New Jersey there were four times as many fugitives in the seven-year period of the war as in the previous seventy years: Hodges, *Root and Branch.*

14. 1790 Census for New Haven and New London; Boas, *Stonington During the American Revolution; Lists and Returns of Connecticut Men;* White, *Connecticut's Black Soldiers.* For John Randall in New South Wales, see Gillen, *Founders of Australia.* Joseph Holt wrote of Randall, "the black played on the flute and tambour" when he was accepted into the NSW Corps: Holt, *A Rum Story,* 66–67. Two Connecticut deserters were Alexander Mourice, AO 12/100/7, and Gad Saunders, PRO 30/55/100, NA.

15. Memorial of John Twine, AO 12/54/142, NA. Recruitment of deserters, Orderly Book of Sir William Howe, January 27–May 1778, CL.

16. *Pennsylvania Ledger,* October 15 and 22, 1777. Richard Weaver, AO13/79/703, Benjamin Whitecuff, AO13/56/268; Nathaniel Wansey, Book of Negroes.

17. For an account of the destructive raids into Portsmouth and Norfolk, see Collier, *Detail of Some Particular Services.* The fleet returned immediately to New York with all its refugees: "Return of Persons that came off from Virginia with General Mathew in the Fleet August 24, 1779," CO 5/52/63, NA. Pendleton to Woodford, June 21, 1779, in Pendleton, *Letters and Papers of Edmund Pendleton,* vol. 1, 290–91.

18. This account of the demography of the 1779 runaways comes from my analysis of Virginia runaways from the Book of Negroes.

19. Samuel Burke memorial, Loyalist Claims Commission, AO 12/99/358–59, NA.

20. Quote from Jones, *History of New York,* vol. 2, 76. For housing and employment in New York, see Wilson, *Loyal Blacks,* 64 and Wray Papers, vol. 7, CL.

21. For Colonel Tye, see Hodges, *Slavery and Freedom,* 96–104. Contemporary accounts of his raids from *Pennsylvania Gazette* and *Weekly Advertiser,* June 21, 1780, are reproduced in Kaplan and Kaplan, *Black Presence,* 82.

22. For an account of Ward's Blacks, see Braisted, "Black Pioneers and Others," in Pulis, *Moving On,* 23–27.

23. For the importance of the Exodus story in African American religious experience, see the first chapter of Raboteau, *Fire in the Bones.* As an interactive and self-validating faith, enthusiastic Methodism was disparaged by the Anglican Church because it undermined established hierarchy. Quote on Moses from John Clarkson Journal, 1792, NYHS.

24. Stephen Blueke, who had assumed Colonel Tye's place as "colonel" of the Black Brigade, was a significant member of the Trinity congregation, along with his wife, Margaret. For Trinity see Hodges, *Root and Branch,* 34, who notes that the Lutherans also performed some baptisms and marriages for runaways.

CHAPTER 3

1. Memorial of Peter Anderson, AO 12/99/354, AO 13/27/226, 230, NA.
2. Campbell, *Journal of an Expedition Against the Rebels of Georgia,* 20–29. Paybook of Campbell's 71st Regiment, GD 174/2/2172, Scottish Records Office.
3. Regimental Order Book, Siege of Savannah, July 30, 1779, Library of Congress and *Georgia Royal Gazette,* November 18, 1779. Quote in Prevost to Clinton, November 2, 1779, PRO 30/55/14; Memorial of Scipio Handley, and AO 13/119/431, NA.
4. "An Account of the Life of Mr. David George from Sierra Leone in Africa, given by himself in Conversation with Brother Rippon and Brother Pierce of Birmingham," in Rippon, *Baptist Annual Register 1790–1793,* 473–77.
5. Galphin to Laurens, December 22, 1777, in Laurens, *Papers of Henry Laurens,* vol. 12, 175, and Campbell, *Journal of an Expedition Against the Rebels of Georgia,* 53–56. Galphin was not much use to the British, who charged him with treason in 1780, and he died before he came to trial.
6. Pass issued to George signed by Edward Cooper, December 11, 1779, RG 1/170/332, PANS.
7. Proclamation, June 30, 1779, PRO 30/55/17 also printed in Rivington's *Royal Gazette,* July 3, 1779, and February 12, 1780. Quote from John André, "Suggestions for gaining dominion over the American Colonies," undated [1780], Clinton Papers, CL.
8. For Harry Washington, see "List of Negroes employed in the Royal Artillery Department, October 1781," Wray Papers, CL; "Abstract of the Number of Men etc Victualled at Gibbs Landing," April 6–9, 1780, Frederick Mackenzie Papers, CL. Memorial of Samuel Burke, Memorial of John Twine, AO 12/19/339–43; AO 13/63/402; AO 12/99/357, AO 13/26/369; AO 12/54/32, NA.
9. André to Cathcart, March 4, 1780, Clinton papers, CL. Wright to Germain, July 31, 1779, CO 5/665/305, N.A. Henry Laurens's claim that "thousands of Negroes" were with the British was a sweeping overestimation: Laurens to Read, February 9, 1779, Smith, *Letters of Delegates to Congress,* vol.12, 39. Memorial of Thomas

Johnson, AO 13/70b/301–2, NA. For the beheaded guide Harry, see Memorial of McKinnon, AO 13/4/321, NA.

10. For Gordon, see Book of Negroes; King, "Memoirs of the Life of Boston King," 107.

11. Ibid.

12. Tarleton, *History of the Campaigns of 1780 and 1781*, 89–90.

13. Clinton expressed concerns about Arnold's unpopularity in Clinton to Dundas, January 23, 1781, Clinton Papers, CL. The distaste for Arnold—"a man so detestable"—was expressed by the Hessian officer in Ewald, *Diary of the American War*, 296. For Walter Harris: Memorial of Walter Harris PRO AO 12/99/334, NA; Mary Willing Byrd to Jefferson, in Jefferson, *Papers of Thomas Jefferson*, vol. 4, 690–92, and Morgan, *Slave Counterpoint*, 284–85.

14. Quote from Isaac Jefferson in "Memoir of a Monticello Slave," reprinted in Bear, *Jefferson at Monticello*, 7–10. Considered with the evidence of Jefferson's memorandum books, it seems that Isaac and his mother, Ursula, as well Mary Hemings with her three small children and the cook Sukey went with the British. Isaac remembered his father, George, and Sukey's husband, Jupiter, going with them also, but the evidence implies that they were not in Richmond at the time and that they returned with Mrs. Jefferson on January 21. They were taken to Portsmouth, not Yorktown, as he claimed.

15. Madison to Madison, January 18, 1781, and Jones to Madison, January 17, 1781, in Madison, *Papers of James Madison*, vol. 2, 293, 289.

16. For the negotiation with Arnold, see Jefferson, *Papers of Thomas Jefferson*, vol. 4, 330–31. The Hessian officer, Johann Ewald, reported that after the army reached Portsmouth about 300 runways were deployed to build defensive earthworks at Great Bridge (Ewald, *Diary of the American War*, 278). When General Phillips arrived from New York to take command from General Arnold, he could report that he had employed some 250 runaways who had recently come in and that these people should be mustered into a corps and given some small payment, as well as their food, since "these negroes have undoubtedly been of the greatest use" (Phillips to Clinton, April 3, 1780, PRO 30/11/96, NA. Pendleton to Madison, May 7, 1781, in Pendleton, *The Letters and Papers of Edmund Pendleton*, vol. 1, 354). Isaac Jefferson in Bear, *Jefferson at Monticello*.

17. Carter to the Commanding Officers at Portsmouth, October 30, 1781, Robert Carter Papers, vol. 3, Special Collections Library, Duke University. Log of HMS *Savage* commanded by Captain Thomas Graves, ADM 51/862, NA. Washing-

ton's runaways were the overseer, Frederick; Sambo, a carpenter; Gunner, a brick maker; Stephen, a cooper; and Watty, a weaver. Lucy, Deborah, Esther, Peter, Lewis, Peter (2), Thomas, and Frank were house servants, and James, Tom, and Daniel worked as laborers at one of the farms. They are named in an undated list probably drawn up for a claim against the British in 1782 or 1783. I do not believe they included Harry, as claimed on the list. See the undated list of Lund Washington, Willard Collection, LOC.

18. The correspondence between Washington and his manager on the sale of his slaves began in March 1778 and was dominated by Lund's frustrations at his cousin's scruples and his saying he would not sell them without their consent even though the general fervently wished "to get quit of the Negroes": Lund Washington to Washington, April 8 and 11, 1778, September 2, 1778, ViMtV. The cash entry for the sale of Abram, Orford, Tom, Jack, Ede, Fatimore, Phillis, Bet, and Jenny is recorded on January 18, 1779, in Lund Washington's Account Book, ViMtV, and on the same date in Ledger B, George Washington Papers, LOC. By February 1779, Washington had hardened his resolve to sell slaves who were neither couples nor parents of children and was waiting for the appropriate time: Washington to Lund Washington, February 24 and 26, 1779, George Washington Papers, LOC.

19. Washington to Lund Washington, April 30, 1781, in Fitzpatrick, *Writings of Washington*, 14–15. Lafayette to Washington, April 23, 1781, and Washington to Lafayette, May 4, 1781, in Idzerda, *Lafayette in the Age of Revolution*, 60, 85. Lund Washington to Washington, December 3, 1775, Washington, *Papers of George Washington: Revolutionary War Series*, vol. 2, 480.

20. For New Kent runaways see the Book of Negroes and Jones, "Black Hessians," 292. For Washington's 1771 inventory of New Kent slaves, see Washington, *George Washington Papers: Colonial Series*, vol. 8, 591. The evidence of slave defections is complicated by the fact that detailed records of tithable property have been destroyed. For Dismal Swamp Company, see Charles Royster, *Fabulous History of the Dismal Swamp Company*, 271–72. The executed slave is mentioned in a letter to Charles Lee, in Fitzpatrick, *Writings of George Washington*, vol. 29, 460–61.

21. See Jameson to Madison, March 10, 1781 and Pendleton to Madison, May 7, 1781, in Madison, *Papers of James Madison*, vol. 3, 16, 111.

22. Quote from Ewald, *Diary of the American War*, 305. For provisioning of army, see Bowler, *Logistics and the Failure of the British Army in America*, 72–73. Lafayette to Washington, July 20, 1781, in Idzerda, *Lafayette in the Age of Revolution*, 258.

23. Jefferson to Gordon, July 16, 1788, in Jefferson, *Papers of Thomas Jefferson,* vol. 13, 362–64. Jefferson's losses in Betts, *Thomas Jefferson's Farm Book,* 503–5. Jefferson's Statements of his Losses to the British at his Cumberland Plantations in 1781, January 27, 1783, in Jefferson, *Papers of Thomas Jefferson,* vol. 6, 224–25.

24. Isaac Jefferson in Bear, *Jefferson at Monticello,* 11.

25. Quote by Josiah Atkins, June 24, 1781, in Fenn, *Pox Americana,* 129.

26. Leslie to Cornwallis, July 31, 1781, PRO 30/11/6; Cornwallis to O'Hara, August 7, 1781, PRO 30/11/89; O'Hara to Cornwallis, August 9, 1781, PRO 30/11/70; Cornwallis to O'Hara, August 10, 1781, PRO 30/11/89; O'Hara to Cornwallis, August 17, 1781, PRO 30/11/70; NA. For "a vast concourse" of runaways transferred to Yorktown, see Parker to Lafayette, August 1, 1781, in Idzerda, *Lafayette in the Age of Revolution,* 334.

27. Tilden, "The Doehla Journal," 245.

28. St. George Tucker, "Journal," October 17, 1781, College of William and Mary.

29. Ewald, *Diary of the American War,* 335–36. Cornwallis to Clinton, October 15, 1781, in Cornwallis, *Correspondence,* vol. 1, 125.

30. Isaac Jefferson in Bear, *Jefferson at Monticello,* 10.

31. Quote on Washington's response from Courtland Letter, October 17, 1781, in Schoff Revolutionary War Collection, CL. Tucker, "Journal," October 17–19, 1781.

32. Cornwallis Orderly Book, June 28 to October 19, Boston Public Library. Ebenezer Denny quoted in Fenn, *Pox Americana,* 130. Ewald, *Diary of the American War,* 342.

33. General Orders, October 9, 1781, in Fitzpatrick, *Writings of George Washington,* vol. 23, 262. Months after Yorktown, Washington wrote to the French admiral Marquis de Grasse on behalf of a friend trying to recover slaves who, "in endeavouring to make their escape from York," had been taken on board a French warship and "unavoidably carried off with the Fleet to the West Indies." Washington to de Grasse, February 6, 1782, in Fitzpatrick, *Writings of George Washington,* vol. 23, 489. Pendleton accused the French of "plundering" slaves: Pendleton to Madison, September 2, 1782, in Madison, *Papers of James Madison,* vol. 5, 97. In July 1782 Governor Harrison told Washington that he was "wearied out from frequent applications" to the French about runaway slaves, "without being able to procure them." Harrison to Rochambeaux, June 26, 1782, and Harrison to Washington, July 11, 1782, in McIlwaine, *Official Letters of the Governors of Virginia,* vol. 3, 257, 266. French officer quoted in Ranlet, "British, Slaves, and Smallpox in Revolutionary Virginia."

34. Articles of Capitulation PRO 30/11/58, NA. Washington to Ross, October 24, 1781, in Fitzpatrick, *Writings of George Washington,* vol. 23, 262. For inoculation, see Craik to Washington, May 13, 1777, in Washington, *Papers of George Washington: Revolutionary War Series,* vol. 19, 409.

35. For the detail on the sales, see Stanton, *Free Some Day.* The term *salvage* was commonly used to refer to the recapture and repatriation of runaways, as in Lund Washington in Fitzpatrick, *Writings of George Washington,* vol. 22, 14.

36. For runaways in Philadelphia: Pennsylvania Gradual Abolition Act 1780; Harrison to Virginia Delegates in Congress, July 6, 1782; Madison to Pendleton, August 6 and September 24, 1782, *Letters of Delegates to Congress,* vol. 19, 199–20. For Washington's slaves: Washington, *Diaries of George Washington,* vol. 4, 277–83, and Washington, *Papers of George Washington: Confederation Series,* vol. 6, 304–5.

37. Nelson to Cornwallis, October 26, 1781, PRO 30/11/90, NA. For Washington's suspicions: Fitzpatrick, *Writings of George Washington,* vol. 23, 252, 364, 315, 336.

38. During the subsequent transfer of officers on parole, more runaways were taken to New York. According to eyewitness accounts of their arrival there, all of the ships were incredibly crowded, "packed together with two servants for each officer": Uhlendorf, *Revolution in America,* 480. Ewald reported that the ship that carried the German officers also carried "143 officers' servants and camp followers among whom twenty-four had their wives and children." To these were added another fifty people of both sexes whose faces were hidden. These, he correctly surmised, were American deserters and black runaways who were being smuggled out to avoid retribution: Ewald, *Diary of the American War,* 343.

CHAPTER 4

1. King, "Memoirs of the Life of Boston King," 110.

2. On receiving orders to this effect in August, Carleton sent his resignation, insisting he was unwilling to continue as a "caretaker of refugees." Lord Shelburne accepted his resignation but never sent a replacement. Carleton was left to manage an unpalatable situation as best he could: Carleton to Shelburne, August 14, 1782, Carleton to Leslie, July 15, PRO 30/55/59, PRO 30/55/43, NA.

3. George Liele eventually went to Jamaica as an indentured servant to Moses Kirkland, where he went on to become famous as a Baptist preacher: Rippon, *Baptist Annual Register,* vol. 1, 332.

4. At least thirty accompanied Hessian and provincial regiments to East Florida. Lists of Loyalist refugees from Savannah to East Florida compiled for the governor, Patrick Toyn, gave the names of several dozen free black people in addition to

some 5,000 enslaved people evacuated to that colony. Toyn to Townshend, return of Refugees from Georgia, CO 5/560/469, NA. Memorial of Scipio Handley, AO 12/47/117, AO 12/109/160, AO13/119/431, NA.

5. Leslie to Carleton, June 27, 1782, and Carleton, "Answer to General Leslie's Queries," PRO 30/55/43 and PRO 30/55/45, NA. There was an abortive agreement with Mathews to allow American commissioners to inspect embarkations and remove American-owned property, but little happened as a result. See Mathew to Leslie, August 17, CO 5/1095/44, NA. Leslie to Wright and Johnson, October 9, PRO 30/55/91. See also Leslie to Carleton, October 10, FO95/10, NA.

6. Leslie to Carleton, November 18, 1782, CO 5/8/384; South Carolina Delegates Petition, PRO 30/55/65, NA. More than a few departing runaways chose to go to Jamaica, even though it was a notorious slave colony. The departing royal governor took to Jamaica ten people he had personally emancipated for the service they had rendered the Crown, including another black Baptist preacher, George Vineland. Several other couples arrived in Jamaica from Charleston carrying certificates of freedom signed by General Clinton. Nineteen men and nine women went to Jamaica as a company of Black Pioneers, and another thirteen accompanied the Seventy-first Regiment. Even though the total number of blacks evacuated to Jamaica was never documented, the free black population in Jamaica increased markedly in the wake of the American Revolution, rising by two-thirds between 1775 and 1787. Wilbur Henry Siebert, "Loyalist Exodus to the West Indies: Legacy of Revolution" in Toth, *American Revolution in the West Indies,* 213.

7. For troop returns to England see WO 1/12/33, NA. Memorials of Samuel Burke, John Twine, Peter Anderson, AO 12/54/142; AO 12/19/339–43; AO 13/63/402; AO 12/99/357; AO 12/54/142, NA. No doubt the hasty evacuation of Charleston was distressing; however, the highly partisan contemporary historian beggars belief with his account of British soldiers chopping off the fingers of abandoned runaways as they clung to the sides of departing boats: Ramsay, *History of the Revolution in South Carolina,* vol. 2, 32. For slaves who bought their freedom, see McCowan, *British Occupation of Charleston,* 106.

8. Cruden quote, CO 5/109/30, NA. For St. Lucia, see Tyson, "The Carolina Black Corps." For Jamaica, see Pulis, "Bridging Troubled Waters," in Pulis, *Moving On,* 187; and Siebert, *Legacy of the American Revolution,* 212. The scattered record of embarkations and arrivals over the period between 1782 and 1785 yields a total number of 6,940 African Americans who were evacuated to East Florida, St. Lucia, Jamaica, Nova Scotia, New York, and England, although that count does not

include those who left on the multitude of small vessels that were not part of the official evacuation fleet, or members of the Royal Navy. A more reliable figure would be close to 8,000. Some were undoubtedly sequestered slaves taken as replacements for confiscated Loyalist property. My speculation that more than 15 percent were free echoes the view of those who have made a detailed study of the evacuation of Charleston and who have suggested that 80 percent of the blacks who left were enslaved: Barnwell, "Evacuation of Charleston by the British in 1782," 8–26; Olwell, *Masters Slaves, and Subjects,* 270.

9. Oswald's private letter to the secretary of state on his deliberations in Paris, November 16, 1782, Richard Oswald Papers, CL. For the original draft treaty with amendments, see Oswald to Melbourne, November 30, 1782, CO 5/110, 377, NA. Laurens was exchanged for Lord Cornwallis after the fall of Yorktown. As he was mourning the death of his son, he had delayed going to Paris till the last day: Wharton, *Revolutionary Diplomatic Correspondence of the United States,* vol. 6, 90–91. The addition to Article Seven was entirely Laurens's initiative, as he boasted in a letter to his old friend John Lewis Gervais, describing himself as "your friend who suggested and insisted upon that Article." Laurens to Gervais, March 4, 1784, in Laurens, *Papers of Henry Laurens,* vol. 16, 403. John Adams and Benjamin Franklin were implacably opposed to slavery. John Jay owned slaves (one of his enslaved servants had run away from him in Paris), yet he was committed to emancipation and had tried unsuccessfully to have slavery abolished in New York.

10. Laurens to Gervais, December 14, 1782, in Laurens, *Papers of Henry Laurens,* vol. 16, 73–74. For the business dealings between Oswald and Laurens after the treaty, see Laurens, *Papers of Henry Laurens,* vol. 16, 264–68, and Rawley, *London, Metropolis of the Slave Trade,* Chapter 5. Oswald died before Laurens's land could be transferred to him.

11. King, "Memoir of the Life of Boston King," 110.

12. Court-martial of Jacob Duryee, July 11, 1783, WO 71/155, NA.

13. Byrd to Jamieson, April 1783, quoted in Olwell, *Masters, Slaves, and Subjects,* 285. There were at least two of Mary Willing Byrd's runaways listed in the Book of Negroes evacuated to Nova Scotia.

14. Baurmeister, April 19, 1783, in Uhlendorf, *Revolution in America,* 556. Thomas Willis, an employee of the police, was paid a piece of gold to kidnap a runaway called Caesar, whom he bound and beat with a stick through the streets of Manhattan and onto a ship. Luckily, Willis was caught in the act. He was given

a court-martial and Caesar was set at liberty once more. Wilson, *Loyal Blacks*, 65.

15. Court-martial of Jacob Duryee, WO 71/155, NA. Court-martial of Samuel Doremus, Daniel Maffis, Reuben Walter, William Grant, Bristol Banter, Harry Scobie, Serg. Thomas Cadmus, Serg. William Vanriper, and Caesar Trotten, August 12, 1782, WO 71 96/126–37. "Return of the men of regiments and prisoners on the Provost to be given to Lord Montague to serve in his corps in the West Indies, September 27, 1782, Carleton Papers, PRO 33/55/50, NA. Hodges, *Root and Branch*, 155–56, gives an account of what appears to be the same murder, but gives the victim's name as Captain Hessius.

16. Baurmeister, June 17, 1783, in Uhlendorf, *Revolution in America*, 569. King, "Memoirs of the Life of Boston King," 157.

17. Carelton to North, April 14, and enclosures CO 5/8; CO 5/109, NA. Carleton's orders, April 15, 1783, PRO 30/55/103, NA.

18. For Willoughby, see Petition of Sundry Inhabitants of Norfolk and Princess Anne Counties, April 28, 1783, PRO 30/55/92, NA. Washington to Harrison, April 30, 1783, in Fitzpatrick, *Writings of George Washington*, vol. 26, 364–65. Lund Washington to unknown person, May 10, 1783, Emmett Collection, LOC. Washington to Parker, April 28, 1783, in Fitzpatrick, *Writings of George Washington*, vol. 26, 369–70.

19. British pass for Cato Ramsay, dated April 21, 1783, PANS.

20. Substance of a Conference between General Washington and Sir Guy Carleton, May 6, 1783, in Fitzpatrick, *Writings of George Washington*, vol. 26, 402–6.

21. Washington to Harrison, May 6, 1783; Washington to Carleton, May 6, 1783, to President of Congress, May 8, 1783, in Fitzpatrick, *Writings of George Washington*, vol. 26, 401–14. Evidence of a private meeting in Carleton's cabin comes from the Hessian officer, Baumeister; see Uhlendorf, *Revolution in America*, 557. For Carleton's reply see Carleton to Washington, May 12, 1783, CO 5/109, NA.

22. Madison to Jefferson, May 13, 1783, in Madison, *Papers of James Madison*, vol. 5, 39–40; Izard to Middleton, May 30, 1783, in Smith, *Letters of Delegates to Congress*, vol. 21, 287–88; Notes on Debates, May 26, 1783, in Madison, *Papers of James Madison*, vol. 6, notes on debates, 80. Carleton to North, June 21, 1783, and North to Carleton, August 8, 1783, CO 5/8, NA.

23. King, "Memoirs of the Life of Boston King," 157.

24. A wealth of anecdotal evidence exists for black crews on Royal Navy ships, much of which is documented in Bolster, *Black Jacks*. The majority of the black claimants to the Loyalist Claims Commission were seamen from the Royal

Navy. Nearly every ship in the Royal Navy's American fleet carried a handful of African American crew—some had as many as 20 percent, while on privateers the percentage might be even higher. Captured British ships were found to have between 13 and 30 percent black crew; see Quarles, *The Negro in the American Revolution*, 154–55. For correspondence between the commissioners and Washington, see Washington, *Papers of George Washington, Confederation Series*, vol. 1, 51–56.

25. Washington quote in Fitzpatrick, *Writings of George Washington*, vol. 28, 283.
26. Leslie to Carleton, November 18, PRO CO 5/8/384, PRO 30/55/52, NA. Judith Jackson petition to Dunmore, September 18, 1783, PRO 30/55/81, and Bluecke to Carleton, September 20, 1783, PRO 30/55/40, NA.
27. Details, Book of Negroes.
28. Harrison to Clinton, quoted in Jefferson, *Papers of Thomas Jefferson*, vol. 6, 430. The runaways not accounted for were Peter, Lewis, Thomas, Stephen, James, and Watty, who may have stayed on as free people. At least twenty-four recruits with the Hessian forces chose to stay in New York rather than leave, according to Selig, "The Revolution's Black Soldiers," 15–22. Ira Berlin quotes a 1784 petition from Virginia about a "great number of slaves which were taken by the British army...now passing in this country as free men," in "Revolution in Black Life."
29. For an account of the victory parade and fireworks, see van Buskirk, *Generous Enemies*, 183.

CHAPTER 5

1. For joint petition, see Loyalist Claims Commision, AO 13/79 /744, NA.
2. Petition of John Baptist, AO 12/99/359, NA.
3. Memorial of John Thompson, AO 12/30/290, NA.
4. Memorial of Samuel Burke, AO 12/99/357, NA.
5. Memorial of John Twine, AO 12/54/142, NA.
6. Memorial of Walter Harris, AO 12/99/334, NA.
7. Memorial of Scipio Handley, AO 13/119/431, AO 12/47/117, and AO 12/109/160; Memorial of Benjamin Whitecuff, AO 13/56/628, NA.
8. Memorial of Shadrack Furman, AO 13/29/658 and AO 13/29/658, NA.
9. Quote from West Indian writer William Beckford, in Braidwood, *Black Poor and White Philanthropists*, 32. Memorial of Peter Anderson, AO 12/99/354, NA.
10. Richard Weaver, Peter Anderson, and John Provey, AO 12/100/94; AO 12/99/354; AO 13/27/ 230; AO 12/101/155; NA.

11. Memorial of Shadrack Furman, AO 12/29/658, NA.

12. Long, *Candid Reflections on Judgment*, 75. For the figure of 40,000, see Francklyn, *Observations*. Norton, in "Fate of Some Black Loyalists," 402–26, misjudges the demographics when she suggests a population in London of at least 1,200 in the period immediately after the American War. Braidwood, in *Black Poor and White Philanthropists*, puts the number at 7,500, and Rudé, in *Hanovarian London 1714–1808*, estimates 10,000 or more. Myers analyzed parish records in *Reconstructing the Black Past* to arrive at a number in excess of 10,000.

13. My analysis of records of black baptisms for 1770–1800 for the parishes of Greater London, using data supplied by the London Metropolitan Research Office, indicates that about 1 percent of baptized Londoners were black, but the records underestimate the black population, many of whom were not Christian. Analysis of trial records from the Old Bailey, the Middlesex and Kent assizes in the period immediately after the American War reveals that about 0.9 percent of indictments were identified as black, but racial identity was not always specified in the court documents. In the more detailed records for the prison hulks and transportation ships the percentage of black felons was 2 percent. An average of all three indicators suggests a black population of about 1.3 percent of a general population of 750,000; that is, just under 10,000.

14. For slave servants, see Lorimer, "Black Slaves and English Liberty," 121–31.

15. In June 1780, violent riots broke out in London as Lord George Gordon, the eccentric leader of the Protestant Association, marched on parliament to present an anti-Catholic petition. For an account of the Gordon Riots, see Linebaugh, *London Hanged*, 341–51. For the subsequent trials of Benjamin Bowsey and John Glover, see OBSP June 28, 1780.

16. Trial of Caesar: ASSI 94/1271, ASSI 31/14, NA.

17. To identify one particular Caesar in the revolutionary records would be impossible; every second slaveholder had chattel named Caesar.

18. For further discussion of black seaman: Christopher, "Sons of Neptune and the 'Sons of Ham,'" 31–60; Shyllon, *Black People in Britain*, 101–2; Coquery-Vidrovitch and Lovejoy, *Workers of the African Trade*. For James Williams, see OBSP, 1784–85, 745.

19. For the Royal Navy: Bolster, *Black Jacks*, 32; Equiano, *The Interesting Narrative and Other Writings;* and Duffield, "'I Asked How the Vessel Could Go?'" For Williams, see ASSI 94/1252 and ASSI 31/14, NA.

20. Memorial of David King, and Memorial of Black London, AO 12/99/356, AO 12/19/343, AO 12/99/86, NA.

21. Trial of John Moseley, OBSP, 1873–74, 557.

22. Memorial of Peter Anderson, and Memorial of Walter Harris, AO 12/99/354; AO 12/101/290; NA.

23. Long, *History of Jamaica*, vol. 1, 4. Johnson's friend quoted in Lorimer, *Colour, Class and the Victorians*, 30.

CHAPTER 6

1. For John Martin, see OBSP, 1781–82, 454.

2. For a discussion of the convict trade to America, see Ekirch, *Bound for America*. For hulks see communication with Duncan Campbell, T29/56, NA.

3. For a discussion of eighteenth-century prisons: Linebaugh, *London Hanged*, and Douglas Hay et al., *Albion's Fatal Tree*.

4. Howard, An account of the present state of the prisons.

5. For accounts of the Cape Coast Castle debacle, see Miles to Germain, July 8, 1782, CO 267/20, NA.

6. Miles to the African Committee, February 1, 1783, T 70/33, NA.

7. Roberts to Ross, December 1784, HO 42/5/465–69, NA.

8. Sydney to Africa Company, December 21, 1784, HO 43/1/355, NA.; Calvert to Treasury, January 15, 1785. For the *Recovery* bill of October 16, 1786, see T 1/636. See also HO 42/6; HO 42/6/4370; T 70/69; T 70/145, NA. The *Recovery* bill was for twenty convicts but two more (possibly women) were added at the last moment.

9. For Richard Bradley's mission, see CJ, vol. 43, 411, re £457/10/6 to Bradley per Thomas Cotton. For Camden, Calvert, and King, see T1/614. Draft order, T1/624, NA.

10. *Campbell Letterbooks*, April 2, 1785, A3229, ML.

11. Quote from "Minutes of the House of Commons" PRO HO 7/1, NA.

12. The Sixty-third Regiment, originally raised in Manchester and later reconstituted as the West Suffolk Regiment, still had black drummers on its establishment a decade after 1785. For black drummers in British regiments, see Fryer, *Staying Power*, 81–86. Randall's trial was reported in the *Manchester Mercury*, April 19, 1785.

13. Moseley, OBSP, 1784–85, 532. The baptism record of Jane Moseley, in Marylebone Parish Registers 1785, GLRO.

14. Quote from "Minutes of the House of Commons respecting a plan for transporting felons to the island of Lemaine in the River Gambia," HO 7/1, NA. Gordon, Hampshire Record Office, April 5, 1785. For the *Ceres* convicts, see T1/637, NA.

15. Duncan Campbell's Letterbooks A3227, ML. *Ceres* lists, T1/637, NA.

16. Quote from Burke, CJ, vol. 40, 954–59.

17. Quote from "Minutes of the House of Commons," HO 7/1, NA.

18. Lord Beauchamp's Report from the Committee Enquiring into the Transportation Act of 1784, CJ, vol. 40, 1161–64 and also T1/624, NA.

19. James Mario Matra, "A Proposal for Establishing a Settlement in New South Wales," August 23, 1783, CO 201/5, NA.

20. Banks's evidence to the Committee, May 10, 1786, HO 7/1, NA. Campbell to Nepean, January 22, 1786, HO 42/8, NA.

21. Sydney to Lords of Treasury, August 18, 1786, T1/369, NA. Gordon's Prisoner's Petition, January 8, 1797, was printed by Thos. Wilkins at No. 23 Aldermanbury.

22. For the *Alexander* refit, see Minutes, December 10, 19, 1786, T1/369, NA. Two other black convicts on the *Alexander* were George Francisco and Thomas Orford.

23. See Byrnes, "'Emptying the Hulks,'" 2–23. Phillip's View on the Conduct of the Expedition and the Treatment of Convicts, *Historical Records of New South Wales,* vol. 1, part 2, 56.

24. *Evening Post,* December 19, 1786. The transport ship *Charlotte* in March 1786 had two black convicts: John Coffin, a servant of about twenty-five, sentenced in Exeter in January that year for stealing some china and silverware from the house of his employer; and Samuel Chinery, age twenty, who had been sentenced for stealing a linen shirt. Coffin trial: *Exeter Flying Post,* January 9, 1786. Chinery trial: ASSI 23/8, NA.

25. Phillip to Nepean, January 11, 1787, in *Historical Records of New South Wales.* White, *Journal of a Voyage to New South Wales,* 47–51.

26. Tench, *1788,* 17.

CHAPTER 7

1. Memorial of Whitecuff, AO 13/ 56/628 and AO12/19/148–45, NA. See also London Baptism Registers for Deptford, LMRO.

2. *Public Advertiser,* January 5, 10, 1786; February 17, 1786; January 28, 1786.

3. Adams to Jay, August 15, 1785, and May 25, 1786, in Adams, *Life and Works of John Adams,* vol. 8, 248–50, 394–96. See also Miller, *Wolf by the Ears,* 112.

4. Jefferson to McCaul, April 19, 1786; Jefferson to Jones, January 5, 1787; Jefferson to Gordon, July 16, 1788; in Jefferson, *Papers of Thomas Jefferson,* vol. 9, 388–90; vol. 11, 6; vol. 13, 362–64. Later, when he was secretary of state, Jefferson took the part

of his fellow Virginians in arguing that they should not be required to pay their debts, as the British had made the first infraction of the treaty: see Jefferson to George Hammond, December 15, 1791; Jefferson to George Hammond, May 29, 1792; Notes of a Conversation with George Hammond; in Jefferson, *Papers of Thomas Jefferson*, vol. 22, 409; vol. 23, 568–608; vol. 24, 27.

5. For a closer examination of currents in British opinion, see Brown, *Moral Capital*.

6. Zong case, Prince Hoare, *Memoirs of Granville Sharp*, 236–46.

7. See the *Morning Chronicle*, February 13 and March 10, 1786; *Morning Herald*, February 14, 1786. See also Braidwood, *Black Poor and White Philanthropists*, 63–70. CRBP Minutes, T1/631, NA.

8. Quote from *Morning Post*, March 15, 1786.

9. Memorial of Thomas Johnson, AO 13/70b part 1/301–2, NA.

10. Henry Smeathman, Substance of a Plan of a Settlement, to be made near Sierra Leone, on the Grain Coast of Africa, in Wadstrom, *Essay on Colonization*, 197–209.

11. Granville Sharp, "Memorandum on a Late Proposal for a New Settlement to be Made on the Coast of Africa, August 1, 1783," in Sharp, *Account of the Constitutional English Polity*, 263–81, and *Short Sketch of the Temporary Regulations*.

12. Alphabetical list of black people who have received the bounty, CRBP Minutes, June 28, 1786; CRBP Minutes, June 7, October 6, 1786, T1/638, T1/632, NA.

13. CRBP minutes, June 7, 1786, T1/632, NA.

14. Johnson was last recorded on board the *Atlantic* on February 16, 1787. His attempt at business in England failed, and three years later he was again importuning the Loyalist Claims Commission for money to "settle in the province of New Brunswick": Memorial of Thomas Johnson, to AO 12/102/18 and AO 13/137/384–86, NA.

15. Memorandum of agreement, October 1784, T1/638. CRBP Minutes, October 6, 1786 T1/636, NA.

16. Cugoano, *Thoughts and Sentiments on the Evil of Slavery*, 141–42.

17. For the petition, see CRBP Minutes, August 15, 1876, T1/633, NA. For the issue of arms and documents, see Treasury Minutes, December 1, 1786; CRBP Minutes, August 4, 1786, T29/58 and T1/368; T1/364, NA.

18. Sydney to the Admiralty Lords, December 7, 1786, *House of Commons Sessional Papers of the Eighteenth Century*, vol. 67, 251.

19. CRBP Minutes, October 6, 1786, T1/636, NA.

20. While Wilson and others accepted this order about vagrancy at face value,

Braidwood's meticulous research has shown that it was never acted upon (*Black Poor and White Philanthropists*, 139).

21. Granville Sharp to Lettsom, October 13, 1788, in Hoare, *Memoirs of Granville Sharp*, 316. For the captain's complaints, see Navy Board Minutes, January 1, 1787, ADM 106/2623, NA.

22. Navy Board Minutes, November 29, 1786, ADM 106/2622, NA. Lord George Gordon in *Public Advertiser*, December 18, 1786.

23. For a discussion of this controversy, see Braidwood, *Black Poor and White Philanthropists*, 132–43.

24. For passenger lists, see T1/643, NA. Vassa's reports, Navy Board Minutes, January 8, 1787, ADM 106/2623. Granville Sharp to Lettsom, October 13, 1788, in Hoare, *Memoirs of Granville Sharp*, 316.

25. Navy Board to Vassa, January 29, 1787, ADM 106/2347, NA.

26. Treasury Board Minutes, March 22, 1787, T29/58; Navy Board Minutes, March 23, 24, 1787, ADM 106/2623; Thompson to Navy Board, March 21, 1787, T1/643; Thompson to Navy Board, April 2, 1786, ADM 106/2494; ADM 106/2623, NA. Wilson suggests that as many as thirteen black people left in a purge at Portsmouth (*Loyal Blacks*, 150). This is disputed by Braidwood in *Black Poor and White Philanthropists*, 288–91.

27. The letter in the *Public Advertiser*, April 6, is presumed to be written by Cugoano, since the arguments and the language are nearly identical with those in his subsequent book, *Thoughts and Sentiments on the Evil of Slavery*.

28. Granville Sharp to Lettsom, October 13, 1788, in Hoare, *The Memoirs of Granville Sharp*, 317. "Cession of a Territory on the Banks of the River Sierra Leona for the Accommodation of the Black Poor 11 June 1787" in *House of Commons Sessional Papers of the Eighteenth Century*, vol. 67, 260.

29. For a discussion of the Koya Temne and the land issue, see Fyfe, *History of Sierra Leone*, 19, and Braidwood, *Black Poor and White Philanthropists*, 182–85.

30. Thompson to Admiralty, May 26, 1787, ADM 1/2594, NA. Log of the *Nautilus*, ADM 5/627, NA.

31. Thompson to Admiralty, August 23, 1787, ADM1/2594, NA. Thompson to Stephens, January 23, 1788, in *House of Commons Sessional Papers of the Eighteenth Century*, vol. 67, 255. For deaths, see "List of the Black Poor embarked for Sierra Leone," T1/643, NA. Elliot to Sharp, July 20, 1787, in Hoare, *Memoirs of Granville Sharp*, 320–22.

CHAPTER 8

1. Tench, *1788*, 37.

2. For an account of illness on the *Alexander*, see Log of the *Alexander*, ADM 51/4375, and White, *Journal of a Voyage to New South Wales*, 67.

3. Quotes from King, *Journal of Phillip Gidley King*, 34–35.

4. Bradley, *Voyage to New South Wales*, 62.

5. Quote from Bowes Smith, *Journals of Arthur Bowes Smyth*, 67. Bowes Smith, *Journals of Arthur Bowes Smyth*, 57; King, *Journal of Phillip Gidley King*, 34–35.

6. The fourth black man on the *Scarborough*, James Francisco, was too weak to work; he died the following year. The other black man on the *Alexander* was Thomas Orford. Two black men who had been sentenced in Devon, John Coffin and Samuel Chinery, came off the *Charlotte*.

7. It was Samuel Chinery who made his home in a tree. Quotes from White, *Journal of a Voyage*, 113.

8. Bowes Smith, *Journals of Arthur Bowes Smyth*, 57.

9. Ibid., 68.

10. Phillip to Nepean, July 9, 1788, in *Historical Records of New South Wales*, vol. 1, part 2, 156.

11. For the prim officer's views, see Clark, *Journal and Letters of Lt. Ralph Clark*, 97.

12. For Gordon's reprieve, see White, *Journal of a Voyage to New South Wales*, 116–17.

13. Collins, *Account of the English Colony of New South Wales*, vol. 1, 58.

14. Cook seems to have thought that *kangaroo* was the Aboriginal name for the animal, but he misunderstood. The people indigenous to Sydney Cove called the animal *patagorang*: Tench, *1788*, 56–57.

15. Quote from Worgan, *Journal of a First Fleet Surgeon*, 32.

16. For "iron men" see Hughes, *Fatal Shore*, 429–30. For flogging in the Royal Navy in the Pacific see Dening, *Mr. Bligh's Bad Language*, 116–22, 383–86.

17. Collins, *Account of the English Colony*, 44, 26, 28. When Collins's journal, with its litany of savage punishment, was published in England in 1793, it prompted the penal reformer Jeremy Bentham to protest that the Magna Carta, the Bill of Rights, and Habeas Corpus were all being breached in New South Wales.

18. The description of the king's birthday comes from White, *Journal of a Voyage*, 40.

19. For a discussion of the smallpox epidemic and its likely cause, see Campbell, *Invisible Invaders*.

20. Collins, *Account of the English Colony*, 57. Easty, *Memorandum of a Voyage from England to Botany Bay*, 127.

21. Quote from Scott, *Remarks on a Passage to Botany Bay*, 48. Collins, *Account of the English Colony*, 58–59.

22. Trial of John Calleghan, July 31, 1789, Minutes of the Court of Criminal Judicature, 1147A, ANSW.

23. Trial of Daniel Gordon, August 20, 1789, Minutes of the Court of Criminal Judicature, 1147A, ANSW. Collins, *Account of the English Colony*, 65.

24. Collins, *Account of the English Colony*, 73, 76. William Bradley's journal entry of January 31, 1790, in Bradley, *Voyage to New South Wales*, 186. Quote from Tench, *1788*, 116.

25. Collins, *Account of the English Colony*, 58, 91.

26. Clark, *Journal and Letters of Lt. Ralph Clark*, 117, 122.

27. For the daily bird count, see ibid., 118–47.

28. Collins, *Account of the English Colony*, 83. Tench, *1788*, 120. The flights of fancy come from a letter of April 14, 1790, quoted in Colby, *Sydney Cove*, 183.

CHAPTER 9

1. Thompson to Stephens, January 23, 1788, in *House of Commons Sessional Papers of the Eighteenth Century*, vol. 67, 255. Elliot to Sharp, July 20, 1787, in Hoare, *Memoirs of Granville Sharp*, 320–22.

2. Bance Island was now owned by Richard Oswald's nephews. Weaver to Sharp, April 23, 1788, in ibid., 321–22. The sale of the five settlers was subsequently investigated by a House of Commons inquiry into the slave trade: Braidwood, *Black Poor and White Philanthropists*, 199–200. Weaver to Sharp, April 23, 1788, in Hoare, *Memoirs of Granville Sharp*, 321–22.

3. Quote from Old Settlers at Sierra Leone to Granville Sharp, September 3, 1788, in Hoare, *Memoirs of Granville Sharp*, 331–33. Sharp was able to get the Treasury to reimburse him for the outlay on the treaty: Sharp to Steele, May 18, 1789, T1/669. For accounts of the new treaty, see Sharp to Jay, March 7, 1789, in Hoare, *Memoirs of Granville Sharp*, 334–36. For a discussion of land in Sierra Leone, see Dorjahn and Fyfe, "Landlord and Stranger," 391–97.

4. Granville Sharp was able to recover the four men sold to the West Indies before they reached Martinique: Granville Sharp to the Worthy Inhabitants of Granville Town, in Hoare, *Memoirs of Granville Sharp*, 344–47. The response of the Bance

Island agents is in the report of Captain Savage of HMS *Pomona*, May 27, 1790, ADM1/2488, NA.

5. This account is based on the report of Captain Savage of HMS *Pomona*, ADM1/ 2488; Tilley to Anderson, April 12, 1790, and Bowie to Anderson, December 22, 1789, in Chatham Papers, PRO 30/8/363, NA.

6. Sharp to Lettsom, October 31, 1787, in Hoare, *Memoirs of Granville Sharp*, 313. The company was originally called the St. George's Bay Company. Most of its directors were members of the Clapham sect. For opposition to the company see "Reasons Against Giving a Territorial Grant to a Company of Merchants to Colonize and Cultivate the Peninsula of Sierra Leone on the Coast of Africa" 1791, Sierra Leone Collection, UIC.

7. Sharp to the Worthy Inhabitants of the Territory Purchased by the King of Great Britain in Sierra Leone, called the Province of Freedom, January 22, 1791, in Hoare, *Memoirs of Granville Sharp*, 359–61.

8. Falconbridge to Sharp, April 18, 1791, PRO 30/8/310. Quotes from Tilley to Anderson and Bowie to Anderson, December 22, 1789, April 12, 1790, PRO 30/8/363, NA.

9. Falconbridge, *Two Voyages to Sierra Leone*, 70.

10. Ibid., 69–70.

11. Quote from Sharp, October 5, 1791, in Hoare, *Memoirs of Granville Sharp*, 362.

12. Falconbridge, *Two Voyages*, 71.

13. Ecstasy, convulsions, and a reliance on direct intervention of the spirit were denounced as "enthusiasms" by the Anglican clergy and were also frowned on by the dissenting elements within the Anglicans, such as Wesleyan Methodists and other Evangelicals.

14. George details his ministry in Nova Scotia in "An Account of the Life of Mr. David George," in Rippon, *Baptist Annual Register 1790–1793*, 478–82.

15. Methodist preacher William Black quoted in Wilson, *The Loyal Blacks*, 124. Boston King's conversion, detailed in King, "Memoirs of Boston King," 159–161, finds echoes in the black narratives of period, all of which emphasize the essential connection between the liberation from bondage of both body and soul: Carretta, *Unchained Voices*.

16. The term "pious frenzy" was used by a disapproving Anglican missionary, but it could easily have been applied by the Wesleyan Methodists: Wilson, *Loyal Blacks*, 120. Adam Potaky and Sandra Burr observe that black converts gave evangelical religion a new resonance by revealing how "each Christian self is

rooted in cultural pasts that cannot and ought not be forgotten" (*Black Atlantic Writers of the Eighteenth Century*). W. E. B. Du Bois has identified the "frenzy" as one of the three fundamental elements of black religion (*Souls of Black Folk,* 191).

17. Bangs, *Life of the Rev. Freeborn Garrettson,* 144, 152. Marrant, *Journal of the Rev. John Marrant,* 11–12, 33–34.

18. Quotes about Birchtown from T. Watson Smith, in Wilson, *Loyal Blacks,* 94, and King, "Memoirs of Boston King," 209.

19. Petition of Thomas Peters, CO 217/63, NA. Ellen Gibson Wilson believed Peters traveled to England on the *Lord Dorchester,* which arrived at Spithead in October 1790. He probably borrowed the money for his passage, as he was in debt in 1791.

20. Clinton to Grenville, December 26, 1790, FO 4/1, NA.

21. Petition of Thomas Peters, FO 4/1/419, NA.

22. Free Settlement on the Coast of Africa signed by the Directors dated August 2, 1791, and placed as an advertisement at Shelburne, signed by John Clarkson October 29, 1791, Sierra Leone Collection, UIC.

23. John Clarkson's Journal of his Mission to America, and parts of his Sierra Leone Journal are held by the NYHS.

24. "List of blacks who gave their names for Sierra Leone in November 1791," CO 217/63, NA.

25. Falconbridge, *Two Voyages,* 93.

26. Quote from Clarkson's Journal, May 19, 1792, NYHS. The account of this hymn singing is described in Elliott, *Lady Huntingdon's Connexion in Sierra Leone,* 15. The words given differ from the original by Charles Wesley. John Clarkson's Journal, March 11, 1792, also refers to the hymn being sung and he describes it again a letter to William Wilberforce, n.d., Clarkson Papers Add MSS 41263, BL.

27. Clarkson Journal, March 19, 30, 1792, NYHS.

28. Clarkson Journal, April 11, 1792, NYHS.

29. Clarkson Journal, April 8, May 19, April 9, 1792, NYHS. Clarkson to Thornton, April 18, 1792, Add MSS 41262A, BL. Clarkson to Hartshorne, August 4, 1793, Clarkson Papers, Add MSS 41263, BL.

30. Clarkson Journal, April 2, 1792. Falconbridge, *Two Voyages,* 102.

31. Clarkson Journal, June 26, 1792. Letter from Clarkson, *Journal,* June 26. Beverhout Petition of June 26, 1792, in Fyfe, *Our Children Free and Happy,* 25–26.

32. Strand Journal, July 28, 1792, Add MSS 12131, BL.

CHAPTER 10

1. Tench, *1788*, 124–25.

2. Collins, *Account of the English Colony*, 91. Dawes's criminal behavior was discussed in Phillip to Grenville, November 7, 1791, while the refusal of marine officers to be tried was outlined in Campbell to Ross, October 13, 1788, enclosing Officer's Objections, *Historical Records of Australia*, vol. 1, 290–94, 92–94.

3. Trial of Williams, April 12, 1790, Minutes of the Court of Criminal Judicature 1147A, ANSW. Tench quote from *1788*, 125.

4. Collins, *An Account of the English Colony*, 87, 116.

5. Ibid., 94–97. Tench, *1788*, 127.

6. For the quote from the chaplain, Richard Johnson, refer to Flannery, *Birth of Sydney*, 100–101.

7. For an account of the infamous Second Fleet, see Flynn, *The Second Fleet*. Camden, Calvert, and King also had the contract for the equally infamous Third Fleet, on which hundreds of Irish convicts died from gross brutality and starvation. Captain William Hill quoted in Cobley, *Sydney Cove*, 251. Quote on selling rations in Tench, *1788*, 132.

8. Tench, *1788*, 135.

9. The best eyewitness account of the punitive expedition is in ibid., 164–76.

10. Quote from Easty, *Memorandum of a Voyage from England to Botany Bay*, 123.

11. Mary Ann Poore's father is not registered, but the most authoritative source, Gillen, *Founders of Australia*, names Caesar. Quote from Collins, *Account of the English Colony*, 232. The conflict with soldiers over the few available women eventually led to mutiny on Norfolk Island: *Historical Records of New South Wales*, vol. 2, 103–10, 136–37.

12. Tench gives a sardonic account of the idiocy of these "Chinese travelers" in light of the fact that they were Irish in *1788* (211).

13. Marriage of Martin and Toy, Register of St. Johns Anglican Church, Parramatta.

14. Quote from Collins, *Account of the English Colony*, 184.

15. Richard Atkins, Journal, April 18, 1792, June 26, 1792, ML. Convict Henry Hale quoted in Hughes, *Fatal Shore*, 107.

16. Richard Atkins, Journal, April 18, 1792, May 21, June 26, 1792, ML.

17. Ryan, *Land Grants 1788–1809*, book 1a, 12.

18. Tench, *1788*, 220.

19. Collins, *Account of the English Colony*, 217.

20. Atkins's Journal for 1792–93 gives the daily weather reading (ML).

21. Quote from Atkins's Journal, December 7, 1792, ML.
22. Lydia Randall's burial is recorded at St. Johns Church, Parramatta, February 13, 1793.
23. See entry for John Martin and John Randall in Gillen, *Founders of Australia*. The Irish radical Joseph Holt, who bought Randall's farm, described him as shooter for the governor, "about six feet high, well made and straight." Holt, *A Rum Story*, 66–67.

CHAPTER 11

1. Wilberforce to Clarkson, September 1793, Clarkson Papers, Add MSS 41262A, BL.
2. Falconbridge quote in *Two Voyages*, 122.
3. Clarkson Journal, November 27, 1792, quoted in Wilson, *Loyal Blacks*, 346.
4. For an account of this dispute, see Clarkson Journal, July 30 to August 1, 1792, NYHS.
5. Clarkson Journal, July 30, 1792, NYHS.
6. The description of Dawes is in Thornton to Clarkson, July 12, 1792, Clarkson Papers, Add MSS 41262A, BL. Quote from Clarkson, "Diary of Lieutenant Clarkson R.N.," 31.
7. David George et al., Farewell Petition, November 28, 1792, in Fyfe, *Our Children Free and Happy*, 29–32. Falconbridge quotes from *Two Voyages*, 113, 116.
8. Thornton to Clarkson, November 20, 1792, Clarkson Papers, Add MSS 41262A, BL. Zachary Macaulay, Journal, September 13, 1793, Zachary Macaulay Papers, MSS MY 418, HL.
9. Falconbridge, *Two Voyages*, 123–24. References to Discontented Row occur throughout Macaulay's Journal in Sierra Leone (HL).
10. Macaulay was converted through the influence of his uncle Thomas Babington, who was a member of the Clapham sect. Thornton to Clarkson, November 20, 1792, Clarkson Papers, Add MSS 41262A, BL.
11. Falconbridge, *Two Voyages*, 123, 131. Macaulay Journal, September 13, 1793, HL.
12. Perkins and Anderson to Clarkson, October 26, 1793, in Fyfe, *Our Children Free and Happy*, 35.
13. Perkins and Anderson to Chairman and Court of Directors, n.d., in ibid., 35–39.
14. Thornton to Clarkson, September 16, 1793, Clarkson to Thornton, September 24, 1793, Clarkson to Perkins and Anderson, November 3, 1793, Clarkson Papers, Add MSS 41263, BL.

15. Perkins and Anderson petition, November 1793, in Falconbridge, *Two Voyages,* 143–44. Anderson and Perkins to Clarkson, November 9, 1793, in Fyfe, *Our Children Free and Happy,* 41.

16. Clarkson to DuBois, July 1, 1793, Clarkson Papers, Add MSS 41263, BL. Sierra Leone Company, *An account of the colony of Sierra Leone,* 24–65.

17. Falconbridge, *Two Voyages,* 118. Luke Jordan and Isaac Anderson to John Clarkson, June 28, 1794, in Fyfe, *Our Children Free and Happy,* 42. Macaulay Journal, August 31, 1793, HL.

18. For the Patrick case see DuBois Journal, January 22, 1793, Clarkson Papers, Add MSS 41262, BL. Macaulay Journal, August 31, 1793, HL.

19. Macaulay Journal, September 3, November 16, November 30, 1793, HL. Reference to carelessness is from the log of the *Sandown,* January 1794, quoted in Schwartz, *Zachary Macaulay and the Development of the Sierra Leone Company,* vol. 2, 227.

20. The riot is discussed in Council Minutes, June 16–July 9, 1794, CO 270/2, NA.

21. Jordan and Anderson to Clarkson, June 28, 1794, in Fyfe, *Our Children Free and Happy,* 42–43. Council Minutes, June 22, 1794, CO 270/2, NA.

22. The accused men were Scipio Channel, James Jackson, Ralph Henry, Lewis Kirby, Samuel Goodwin, Joseph Tybee, John Manuel, and Simon Johnson; see Macaulay Journal, November 26, 1794, September 13, 1793, HL.

23. Sharp to Thornton, November 26, 1794, in Hoare, *Memoirs of Granville Sharp,* 179–80; Clarkson to Thornton, December 11, 1796, and Allison to Clarkson, n.d., Clarkson Papers, BL. There are records of Kirby, Manuel, and Tybee returning to Sierra Leone, although Tybee was again banished as a result of a decision taken at the Quarter Sessions in Freetown in April 1796: Sierra Leone Company, *Substance of the report,* 18.

24. "An Account of the Life of David George," in Rippon, *Baptist Annual Register, 1790–1793,* 484. Macaulay Journal, October 10, 1794, HL.

25. Eli Akim, evidence to Commission of Enquiry into Sierra Leone, 1826, CO 267/92, NA.

26. Macaulay to Directors, November 15, 1794, Macaulay Papers, HL. Jordan, Willkinson, et al. to Clarkson, November 19, 1794, in Fyfe, *Our Children Free and Happy,* 40–47.

27. Methodist petition to Governor, April 16, 1795, and Jordan, Wilkinson, et al. to Clarkson, November 19, 1794, in Fyfe, *Our Children Free and Happy,* 43, 45–47. Macaulay to Directors, November 15, 1795, Macaulay Papers, HL.

CHAPTER 12

1. Liaster to Clarkson, March 30, 1796; Hutcherson and Murray to Clarkeson, May 24, 1796, in Fyfe, *Our Children Free and Happy,* 49–51.

2. Macaulay Journal, March 19, 1796, HL.

3. Macaulay Journal, September 16, 1796, HL.

4. Macaulay Journal, July 20, 1796, HL.

5. Snowball and Hutcherson to Clarkson, June 1, 1797, King to Clarkson, January 16, 1798, in Fyfe, *Our Children Free and Happy,* 52–55; Clarkson to King, October 2, 1897, Clarkson Papers, Add MSS 41263, BL.

6. Macaulay to Mills, May 20, 1796, HL. Macaulay Journal, October 13, 1793; November 23, June 26, April 23, October 6, 1796, HL.

7. Macaulay Journal, October 5, May 22, 1796, HL.

8. Macaulay Journal, April 23, June 17, 1796, HL. Quote on Mary Perth from "Letter from the Rev. Mr. Clark," 463.

9. Macaulay Journal, May 30, July 8, 1796, HL.

10. Methodist petition reprinted in Knutsford, *Life and Letters of Zachary Macaulay,* 145.

11. Macaulay Journal, July 14, July 21, 1796, HL.

12. Jordan and Snowball to Clarkson, July 29, 1796, in Fyfe, *Our Children Free and Happy,* 53. Macaulay to Mills, October 5, 1796, Macaulay Papers, HL.

13. Macaulay Journal, July 10, December 18, November 21, 1796, HL.

14. Macaulay Journal, September 16, 1796, HL.

15. Macaulay Journal, December 10, September 16, December 15, December 19, December 21, 1796, January 3, 1797, HL.

16. Anderson to Clarkson, January 21, 1798, in Fyfe, *Our Children Free and Happy,* 56.

17. Macaulay Journal, January 5, February 13, 1797, HL.

18. Sierra Leone Council Minutes, August 17, 1797, CO 270/4, NA.

19. Macaulay Journal, August 21, 1797, HL.

20. Macaulay Journal, August 26, 1797, HL.

21. Macaulay Journal, September 30, October 2, 1797, HL.

22. York, Peters, and Anderson to Captain Ball, January 16, 1797, in Fyfe, *Our Children Free and Happy,* 57–58.

23. King to Clarkson, January 16, 1797, in Fyfe, *Our Children Free and Happy,* 55.

24. Macaulay Journal, December 21, 1796, December 1, 1797, May 5, 1798, HL. Ludlam, report, November 17, 1801, CO 270/6, NA.

25. Council Minutes, February 1799, CO 270/5. Macaulay to Mills, January 27, 1799, Macaulay Papers, HL.

26. Thornton to More, October 26, 1798, quoted in Wilson, *Loyal Blacks,* 256.

27. Sierra Leone Company Report, 1801.

28. Sierra Leone Company, Minutes, November 4, 1799, CO 270/4, NA.

29. Sierra Leone Company, Minutes, December 16, 1799, CO 270/4, NA. Wansey to Ludlam, February 13, 1800, in Fyfe, *Our Children Free and Happy,* 61.

30. Ludlam was ill and his written speech was delivered by another white employee. Council Minutes, May 20, 1800, CO 270/5, NA.

31. Sierra Leone Company Report, 1801. Paper of Laws, September 3, 1800, in Fyfe, *Our Children Free and Happy,* 63.

32. Ludlam's post facto account of this whole episode was printed as an appendix to Sierra Leone Company Report for 1800, CO 270/5, NA. Eli Akim and John Kizell gave evidence about this episode to the Commission of Enquiry into Sierra Leone in 1826: CO 267/92. The new laws were authorized by the elected representatives Isaac Anderson, James Robinson, Nathaniel Wansey, and Ansel Zizer.

33. Appendix, CO 270/5, NA. Unsigned, undated letter said to come from Isaac Anderson, in Fyfe, *Our Children Free and Happy,* 67.

34. Appendix, CO 270/5, NA.

35. Ibid. George Ross quoted in Campbell, *Back to Africa,* 16.

36. Thornton to More, February 16, 1801, quoted in Wilson, *Loyal Blacks,* 393.

37. George Ross in Campbell, *Back to Africa,* 17. Ludlam's account: Appendix, CO 270/5, NA.

38. George Ross in Campbell, *Back to Africa,* 16–19.

39. Appendix, CO 270/5, NA.

40. Ibid.

41. The third of the rebels wanted for treason, Nathaniel Wansey, led Koya Temne chiefs and their warriors to attack Freetown on November 18, 1801, and again on April 11, 1902. They were beaten back and several settlers were killed: *Times,* February 12, 1802. After Dawes successfully negotiated with the Mandinka, who were harboring Wansey, he was handed over: *Times,* February 12, 1802. Presumably, he too was executed.

42. Sierra Leone Company Report for 1801, 8, BL. Wilberforce to Dundas, April 1, 1800, Melville Papers, Add MSS 41085, BL.

EPILOGUE

1. Collins, *Account of the English Colony of New South Wales,* 381.

2. General Orders, January 8,1806, May 17, 1807, March 24, 1808, in *Historical Records of Australia,* series 3, vol. 1, 537, 555, 564. The quote is from the chorus of the famous Australian ballad "The Wild Colonial Boy," a celebration of bushrangers, second only to "Waltzing Matilda" as Australia's national folk song. Though the bushranger became associated with the Irish convict's rebellion against the British, reaching its apotheosis with Ned Kelly, black bushrangers continued Caesar's tradition, including "Black" John Goff, who was possibly the son a black refugee of the American Revolution listed as receiving the bounty for the Black Poor in London in 1786.

3. See Gillen, *Founders of Australia,* 255.

4. The information that "after a few years of probation" the exiled men were given amnesty to return comes from Hoare, *Life of Granville Sharp,* 302. Harry Washington may have been among them, but he is not mentioned in the cases of returning exiles discussed in council minutes, CO 270/13, NA, or in any subsequent documentation. His election as one of two leaders of the exiles on the Bullom Shore is reported in council minutes of April 7, 1801, CO 270/5, NA.

5. Thompson to Castlereagh, February 8, 17, 1809, CO 270/10 and CO 267/25, NA. Thompson, November 2, 1808, quoted in Wilson, *Loyal Blacks,* 405.

ARCHIVAL AND MANUSCRIPT SOURCES
National Archives, UK (NA)
      Records of Colonial Office (CO) 1774–1801
      Records of War Office (WO) 1775–84
      Records of Admiralty (ADM) 1775–93
      Records of Treasury (T) 1776–87
      Records of Home Office (HO) 1787–90
      Records of Foreign Office (FO) 1774–1808
      Records of the Auditor (AO) 1783–86
      Records of the Justices of Assizes (ASSI) 1785–87
      Chatham Papers (PRO 30)
      Carleton Papers (PRO 30)
      Cornwallis Papers (PRO 30)

Greater London Records Office (GLRO)
      Court Records of the Middlesex and Westminster Sessions
      Anglican Parish Records for Greater London
      Records of the Boards of Guardians of the Poor

British Library, London (BL)
      Clarkson Papers
      Melville Papers
      Peel Papers
      Boulden-Thompson Papers
      DuBois Journal
      Proceedings of the Committee for the Abolition of the Slave Trade

The Guildhall, London
      Parish Records for Inner London

Clements Library, University of Michigan (CL)
        Henry Clinton Papers
        Howe Orderly Books
        George Wray Papers
        Frederick Mackenzie Papers
        Richard Oswald Papers
        Miscellaneous Revolutionary Papers

Manuscript Division, Library of Congress (LOC)
        Peter Force Collection
        Force Historical Manuscripts
        Rochambeau Collection
        George Washington Papers
        Papers of the Members of Congress
        Henry Willard Papers
        Benjamin Harrison Papers
        Diary of Robert Honyman
        British Army Regimental Order Book, July 2–October 2, 1779

University of Illinois at Chicago (UIC)
        Sierra Leone Company Documents 1787–92
        John Clarkson Diary, March 19–August 4, 1792
        Letters from Freetown Settlers, 1792–93

New-York Historical Society (NYHS)
        John Clarkson Journal, August 6–March 18,1792
        Beekman Family Papers

Huntington Library (HL)
        Zachary Macaulay Papers

Virginia State Library (VSL)
        Virginia Assembly House of Delegates: Report of Losses Sustained From
        the British, 1782–83

Virginia Assembly House of Delegates: Losses in Norfolk, 1777–1836
Papers of the House of Delegates, May 1782
Virginia Assembly House of Delegates: Petitions

College of William and Mary
Journal of St. George Tucker

University of Virginia
Ralph Wormeley Papers
Lee Family Papers

Mount Vernon Ladies Association Archives (ViMtV)
Letters of Lund Washington
Mt. Vernon Account Books

Boston Public Library
Cornwallis Orderly Book, June 28–October 19, 1781

The Public Archives of Nova Scotia (PANS)
White Collection
Letters of Bishop Charles Inglis
Diary of Alex Huston, 1778–88
Ward Chipman Papers
Army Muster Books
Notes on Service of Negroes in Militia and Army
Commissary General's Department Receipts for Provisions, 1784
List of Loyalist Refugees to Halifax
Poll Tax Records
Land Grants 1783–1845
List of Black Loyalist Settlers at Digby, Annapolis and Granville, 1784
Birchtown Muster, 1784
Annapolis Muster, 1784
Tax Assessor's Statements and Accounts
British Military and Naval Records

Returns of Prisoners and Warrants for Gaol and Workhouse
Records of Enlistment in the Black Carolina Corps
Judicial Records of Court of General Sessions, Shelburne County
Phyllis Blakeney Collection
Marion Robertson Papers

Mitchell Library, State Library of New South Wales (ML)
Richard Atkins Journal
Phillip Gidley King Letterbook, 1788–99
Phillip Gidley King, Norfolk Island Journal, 1791–94
Register from St. John's Church, Parramatta
Register from St. Phillip's Church, Sydney
Letters of Rev. Richard Johnson
Mrs. John Macarthur Correspondence

Archives of New South Wales (ANSW)
Proceedings of the Bench of Magistrates, 1788–92
Proceedings of the Court of Civil Jurisdiction, 1788–1809
Proceedings of the Court of Criminal Jurisdiction, 1788–1800
Colonial Secretary's Papers
Register of Pardons

Contemporary Newspapers
Morning Chronicle (London)
Morning Post (London)
Morning Herald (London)
Public Advertiser (London)
Mercury (Manchester)
Rivington's *Royal Gazette* (New York)
Royal Georgia Gazette
Virginia Gazette (Dixon and Hunter)
Virginia Gazette (Purdie)
Virginia Gazette (Purdie and Dixon)
Pennsylvania Evening Post
Pennsylvania Gazette and Weekly Advertiser

PRINTED PRIMARY SOURCES

Adams, Charles Francis, ed. *The Works of John Adams*. Vol. 8. Boston: Little, Brown and Company, 1850–56.

Afzelius, Adam. *Sierra Leone Journal*. Edited by A. P. Kup. Uppsala: Studia Ethnographica Upsaliensia, 1967.

Ballagh, James Curtis, ed. *The Letters of Richard Henry Lee*. Vol. 2. New York: Macmillan Company, 1911.

Bangs, Nathan, ed. *The Life of the Rev. Freeborn Garrettson*. New York: Mason and Lane, 1839.

Betts, Edwin Morris, ed. *Thomas Jefferson's Farm Book: With Commentary and Relevant Extracts from Other Writing*. Charlottesville: University Press of Virginia, 1953.

Bowes Smyth, Arthur. *The Journal of Arthur Bowes Smyth: Surgeon, Lady Penryn 1787–1789*. Edited by Paul Fidlon and R. J. Ryan. Sydney: Australian Documents Library, 1979.

Bradley, William. *A Voyage to New South Wales: The Journal of Lieutenant, William Bradley RN of HMS Sirius, 1786–1792*. Sydney: Ure Smith, 1969.

Butterfield, L. H., ed. *The Diary and Autobiography of John Adams*. Vol. 2. Cambridge: Belknap Press, 1961.

Campbell, Archibald. *Journal of an Expedition against the Rebels of Georgia in North America under the Orders of Archibald Campbell Esquire Lieut. Colol. of His Majesty's 71st Regimt. 1778*. Edited by Colin Campbell. Darien: Ashantilly Press, 1981.

Cappon, Lester J., ed. *The Adams–Jefferson Letters: The Complete Correspondence Between Thomas Jefferson and Abigail and John Adams*. Chapel Hill: University of North Carolina Press, 1959.

Carter, Landon. *The Diary of Colonel Langdon Carter of Sabine Hall, 1752–1778*. Edited by Jack P. Greene. Charlottesville: University Press of Virginia, 1965.

Clark, Ralph. *The Journal and Letters of Ralph Clark, 1787–1792*. Edited by Paul Fidlon and R. J. Ryan. Sydney: Australian Documents Library, 1981.

Clark, William Bell, William James Morgan, and Michael J. Crawford, eds. *Naval Documents of the American Revolution*. Vols. 3–10. Washington, D.C.: Naval History Division, 1968–96.

Clarkson, John. "Diary of Lieutenant Clarkson R.N." *Sierra Leone Studies* 8 (March 1927): 1–114.

Clinton, Henry. *The American Rebellion: Sir Henry Clinton's Narrative of His Cam-paigns, 1775–1782.* Edited by William B. Willcox. New Haven: Yale University Press, 1954.

Cobbett's Parliamentary History of England from the Earliest Period to the Year 1803. London: Hansard, 1806–20.

Cobley, John, ed. *Sydney Cove: 1788–1792.* 3 vols. Sydney: Angus & Robertson, 1962–65.

Collier, George. *A Detail of Some Particular Services Performed in America During the Years 1776–1779.* New York: I. Town, 1835.

Collins, David, *An Account of the English Colony of New South Wales: With remarks on the Dispositions, Customs, Manners, etc, of the Native Inhabitants of that Country.* Vol. 1. Edited by Brian Fletcher. Sydney: Reed, 1975.

Cornwallis, Charles. *An answer to that part of the narrative of Lieutenant-General Sir Henry Clinton, K.B. which relates to the conduct of Lieutenant-General Earl Cornwallis, during the campaign in North-America, in the year 1781,* London: J. Debrett, 1783.

———. *Correspondence of Charles, First Marquis of Cornwallis.* 3 vols. Edited by Charles Ross and John Murray. London, 1859.

Cugoano, Ottobah. *Thoughts and Sentiments on the Evil of Slavery.* Edited by Vincent Carretta.London: Penguin, 1999.

Davies, K. G., ed. *Documents of the American Revolution 1770–1783.* Vols. 19–22. Shannon: Irish University Press, 1978–82.

Easty, John. *Memorandum of a Voyage from England to Botany Bay, 1787–1793: A First Fleet Journal.* Sydney: Angus & Robertson, 1965.

Equiano, Olaudah. *The Interesting Narrative and Other Writings.* Edited by Vincent Carretta. London: Penguin, 2003.

Ewald, Johann. *Diary of the American War: A Hessian Journal.* Translated and edited by Joseph P. Tustin. New Haven: Yale University Press, 1979.

Falconbridge, Anna Maria. *Two Voyages to Sierra Leone.* In *Maiden Voyages and Infant Colonies: Two Women's Travel Narratives of the 1790s,* edited by Deirdre Coleman. London: Leicester University Press, 1999.

Fitzpatrick, John C., ed. *The Writings of George Washington.* Vols. 23–28. Washington, D.C.: Government Printing Office, 1937–38.

Francklyn, Gilbert. *Observations, occasioned by the attempts made in England to effect the abolition of the Slave Trade.* London: Logographic Press, 1789.

Fyfe, Christopher, ed. *Our Children Free and Happy: Letters from Black Settlers in Africa in the 1790s.* Edinburgh: Edinburgh University Press, 1991.

Green, Nathanael. *The Papers of Nathanael Green.* Vols. 1–9. Edited by Richard K. Showman. Chapel Hill: University of North Carolina Press, 1976–2000.

Historical Records of Australia. Series 1, vol 1. Canberra: Commonwealth Parliament, 1914.

Historical Records of New South Wales. Vols. 1–3. Sydney: Government Printer, 1892–95.

Hoare, Prince, ed. *The Memoirs of Granville Sharp.* London, Henry Colburn, 1820.

Holt, Joseph. *A Rum Story: The Adventures of Joseph Holt, Thirteen Years in New South Wales, 1800–1812.* Edited by Peter O'Shaughnessy. Sydney: Kangaroo Press, 1988.

House of Commons Sessional Papers for the Eighteenth Century. Wilmington, N.C.: Scholarly Resources, 1975.

Howard, John. *An account of the present state of the prisons, houses of correction, and hospitals in London and Westminster.* London: The Society lately instituted for giving effect to his Majesty's proclamation against vice and immorality, 1789.

Idzerda, Stanley J., ed. *Lafayette in the Age of the American Revolution: Selected Letters and Papers, 1776–1790.* Vol. 4. Ithaca, N.Y.: Cornell University Press, 1981.

James, Bartholomew. *Journal of Rear Admiral Bartholomew James, 1752–1828.* London: Navy Records Society, 1896.

Jefferson, Thomas. *The Papers of Thomas Jefferson.* Vols.1–24. Edited by Julian P. Boyd. Princeton: Princeton University Press, 1950–90.

Jones, Thomas. *A History of New York During the Revolutionary War, and of the Leading Events in the Other Colonies at That Period.* New York: New-York Historical Society, 1879

Journal of the House of Delegates of the Commonwealth of Virginia. Richmond: Thomas White, 1827.

King, Boston. "Memoirs of the Life of Boston King, a Black Preacher Written by Himself During His Residence at Kingswood School." *Methodist Magazine* 21 (1789).

King, Phillip Gidley. *The Journal of Phillip Gidley King, Lieutenant RN, 1787–1790.* Edited by Paul Fidlon and R. J. Ryan. Sydney: Australian Documents Library, 1981.

Laurens, Henry. *The Papers of Henry Laurens.* Vols. 10–16. Edited by David R. Chesnutt. Columbia: University of South Carolina Press, 1985–2003.

"A Letter from the Rev. Mr. Clark, July 29, 1796." *Evangelical Magazine* 4 (1796): 463.

Lists and Returns of Connecticut Men in the Revolution. Bowie: Heritage Books, 1995.

Long, Edward. *Candid Reflections on the Judgment Lately awarded by the Court of the King's Bench in Westminister Hall on what is commonly called the Negroe-Cause.* London: T. Lowndes, 1772.

———. *A History of Jamaica.* Vol.1. New York: Arno Press, 1972.

Mackenzie, Frederick. *Diary of Frederick Mackenzie.* Vol. 2. Cambridge: Harvard University Press, 1930.

Madison, James. *The Papers of James Madison.* Vols.1–7. Edited by William T. Hutchinson and William M. E. Rachal. Chicago: University of Chicago Press, 1962–71.

Marrant, John. *A Journal of the Rev. John Marrant, From August the 18th, 1785, to The 16th of March, 1790.* London: printed for the author, 1790.

Matthews, John. *A Voyage to the River Sierra Leone on the Coast of Africa,* London: White & Son, 1788.

McIlwaine, H. R., ed. *Official Letters of the Governors of the State of Virginia: The Letters of Patrick Henry.* Richmond: Virginia State Library, 1926.

Newsome, A. R. "A British Orderly Book, 1780–1781." *North Carolina Historical Review* 9 (January–October 1932).

Old Bailey Session Papers: The Proceedings on the King's commission of the peace for the city of London, 1782–1787. 32 vols. London: E. Hodgson, 1782–87.

Palmer, William P. *Calendar of Virginia State Papers and Other Manuscripts.* Richmond, 1881.

Pendleton, Edmund. *The Letters and Papers of Edmund Pendleton.* Vols.1–2. Edited by David John Mays. Charlottesville: University Press of Virginia, 1967.

Perkins, Simeon. *The Diary of Simeon Perkins, 1780–1789.* Edited by D. C. Harvey and Bruce Fergusson. Toronto: Champlain Society, 1958.

Rippon, John. *The Baptist Annual Register, 1790–1802, including sketches of the state of religion among denominations of good men at home and abroad.* 4 vols. London, 1803.

Ryan, R. J. *Land Grants 1788–1809: A Record of the Registered Grants and Leases in New South Wales and Norfolk Island.* Book 1A. Sydney: Australian Documents Library, 1972.

Scott, James. *Remarks on a Passage to Botany Bay: A First Fleet Journal, 1787–1792.* Sydney: Angus and Robertson, 1963.

Scribner, Robert L., ed. *Revolutionary Virginia: The Road to Independence.* Vols. 2–7, Charlottesville: University Press of Virginia, 1976–83.

Sierra Leone Company. *An account of the colony of Sierra Leone, from its first establishment in 1793: Being the substance of a report delivered to the proprietors.* London: James Philips, 1795.

———. *Substance of the report of the Court of Directors of the Sierra Leone Company to the General Court, held at London on Wednesday the 19th of October, 1791.* London: James Phillips, 1792.

———. *Substance of the report, delivered, by the Court of Directors of the Sierra Leone Company, to the General Court of Proprietors, on Thursday the 29th of March.* London: James Phillips & Son, 1798.

Simcoe, Lt. Col. J. G. *Simcoe's Military Journal: A History of the Operations of a Partisan Corps called The Queen's Rangers, Commanded by Lieut. Col. J. G. Simcoe During the War of the American Revolution.* New York: Bartlett and Welford, 1844.

Smeathman, Henry. *A Short Sketch of the Temporary Regulations for the Intended Settlement on the Grain Coast near Sierra Leone.* London: H. Baldwin, 1788.

Smith, James Morton, ed. *The Republic of Letters: The Correspondence Between Thomas Jefferson and James Madison, 1776–1826.* New York: Norton, 1995.

Smith, Paul H., ed. *Letters of Delegates to Congress, 1774 to 1789.* Vols. 19–20. Washington, D.C.: Library of Congress, 1992–93.

Smith, William. *Historical Memoirs of William Smith, 1778–1783.* Edited by William H. W. Sabine. New York: New York Public Library, 1971.

Tarleton, Banastre. *A History of the Campaigns of 1780 and 1781.* London: Cadell, 1787.

Tench, Watkin. *1788: Comprising a Narrative of the Expedition to Botany Bay and A Complete Account of the Settlement at Port Jackson.* Edited by Tim Flannery. Melbourne: Text Publishing, 1996.

Tilden, Robert J. trans. "The Doehla Journal." *William and Mary Quarterly,* 2nd series, Vol. 22 (1942).

Uhlendorf, Bernhard A., trans. *Revolution in America: Confidential Letters and Journals, 1776–1784 of Adjutant General Major Baurmeister of the Hessian Forces.* New Brunswick, N.J.: Rutgers University Press, 1957.

———, trans. *The Siege of Charleston: With an Account of the Province of South Carolina: Diaries and Letters of Hessian Officers.* Ann Arbor: University of Michigan Press, 1938.

Wadstrom, C. B. *An Essay on Colonization, particularly applied to the Western Coast of Africa.* London: Edgerton, 1792.

Washington, George. *The Diaries of George Washington*. Vols. 2–3. Edited by Donald
    Jackson. Charlottesville: University Press of Virginia, 1976–78.

———. *The Papers of George Washington: Colonial Series*. Vols. 7–10. Edited by W. W.
    Abbott and Dorothy Twohig. Charlottesville: University Press of Virginia,
    1990–95.

———. *The Papers of George Washington: Confederation Series*. Vol. 1. Edited by
    W. W. Abbott and Dorothy Twohig. Charlottesville: University Press of
    Virginia, 1992.

———. *The Papers of George Washington: Revolutionary War Series*. Vols. 2–3. Edited
    by W. W. Abbott and Dorothy Twohig. Charlottesville: University Press of
    Virginia, 1987–88.

Wharton, Francis, ed. *The Revolutionary Diplomatic Correspondence of the United
    States*. Vol. 6. Washington, D.C.: Government Printing Office, 1889.

White, John. *Journal of a Voyage to New South Wales*. Sydney: Angus & Robertson,
    1962.

Worgan, George. *Journal of a First Fleet Surgeon*. Sydney: Library of Australian His-
    tory, 1978.

ESSENTIAL SECONDARY SOURCES

Andrews, William L. *To Tell a Free Story: The First Century of African American Au-
    tobiography*. Urbana: University of Illinois Press, 1986.

Anstey, Roger. *The Atlantic Slave Trade and British Abolition, 1760–1810*. Atlantic
    Highlands: Humanities Press, 1975.

Aptheker, Herbert. *A History of the American People: An Interpretation. The American
    Revolution, 1763–1783*. New York: International Publishers, 1960.

Atkinson, Alan. *The Europeans in Australia: A History*. Vol. 1. Melbourne: Oxford
    University Press, 1997.

Barnwell, Joseph W. "The Evacuation of Charleston by the British in 1782." *South
    Carolina Historical and Genealogical Magazine* 11 (1910): 8–26.

Bear, James A., ed. *Jefferson at Monticello*. Charlottesville: University of Virginia
    Press, 1967.

Berlin, Ira. *Many Thousands Gone: The First Two Centuries of Slavery in North Amer-
    ica*. Cambridge, Belknap Press, 1998.

———. "The Revolution in Black Life." In *The American Revolution*, edited by Al-
    fred F. Young. DeKalb: Northern Illinois University Press, 1976.

Blackburn, Robin. *The Overthrow of Colonial Slavery, 1776–1848.* London: Verso, 1988.

Boas, Norman. *Stonington During the American Revolution.* Mystic, Conn.: Seaport Autographs, 1990.

Bolster, W. Jeffrey. *Black Jacks: African American Seamen in the Age of Sail.* Cambridge: Harvard University Press, 1997.

Bowler, R. Arthur. *Logistics and the Failure of the British Army in America, 1775–1783.* Princeton: Princeton University Press, 1975.

Braidwood, Stephen. *Black Poor and White Philanthropists: London's Blacks and the Foundations of the Sierra Leone Settlement, 1786– 1791.* Liverpool: Liverpool University Press, 1994.

Brown, Christopher L. "Empire Without Slaves: British Concepts of Emancipation in the Age of the American Revolution." *William and Mary Quarterly* 56, 3rd series (April 1999).

———. *Moral Capital: Foundations of British Abolitionism.* Chapel Hill: University of North Carolina Press, 2006.

Byrnes, Dan. "'Emptying the Hulks': Duncan Campbell and the First Three Fleets to Australia." *Push from the Bush* 24 (1987).

Campbell, Judy. *Invisible Invaders: Smallpox and Other Diseases in Aboriginal Australia, 1788–1880.* Melbourne: Melbourne University Press, 2002.

Campbell, Mavis C. *Back to Africa: George Ross and the Maroons from Nova Scotia to Sierra Leone.* Trenton, N.J.: Africa World Press, 1993.

Carretta, Vincent. "Olaudah Equiano or Gustavus Vassa: New Light on an Eighteenth-Century Question of Identity." *Slavery and Abolition* 20, no. 3 (1999).

———, ed. *Unchained Voices: An Anthology of Black Authors in the English-Speaking World of the Eighteenth Century.* Lexington: University Press of Kentucky, 1996.

Carter, Paul. *The Road to Botany Bay: An Essay in Spatial History.* London: Faber & Faber, 1987.

Christopher, Emma. "The Sons of Neptune and the 'Sons of Ham': Slave Trade Sailors and the African Seaboard Proletariat." Ph.D. thesis, London University, 2002.

Cobley, John. *The Crimes of the First Fleet Convicts.* Sydney: Angus & Robertson, 1970.

Coleman, Deirdre. *Romantic Colonization and British Anti-Slavery.* Cambridge: Cambridge University Press, 2005.

Coleman, Kenneth. *The American Revolution in Georgia: 1763–1789.* Athens: University of Georgia Press, 1958.

Coquery-Vidrovitch, R. Catherine, and Paul E. Lovejoy, eds. *The Workers of the African Trade.* Beverly Hills: Sage, 1985.

Crow, Jeffrey J. *The Black Experience in Revolutionary North Carolina.* Raleigh: North Carolina Department of Cultural Resources, 1977.

Curry, John. *David Collins: A Life.* Melbourne: Melbourne University Press, 2000.

Curtin, Philip. *The Image of Africa: British Ideas and Action, 1780–1850.* Madison: University of Wisconsin Press, 1964.

Dalzell, Robert E., and Lee Baldwin Dazell. *George Washington's Mt. Vernon: At Home in Revolutionary America.* New York: Oxford University Press, 1998.

Dening, Greg. *Mr. Bligh's Bad Language: Passion, Power and Theatre on the Bounty.* Cambridge: Cambridge University Press, 1993.

Dorjahn, V. R., and Christopher Fyfe. "Landlord and Stranger: The Change in Tenancy Relations in Sierra Leone." *Journal of African History* 3 (1962).

Drescher, Seymour, and Christine Bolt, eds. *Anti-Slavery, Religion and Reform: Essays in Memory of Roger Anstey.* Hamden: Archon Books, 1980.

Du Bois, W. E. B. *Souls of Black Folk.* Chicago, University of Chicago Press, 1903.

Duffield, Ian. "Constructing and Reconstructing 'Black' Caesar." In *Romanticism and Wild Places,* edited by Paul Hullah. Edinburgh: Edinburgh University, 1999.

———. " 'I Asked How the Vessel Could Go?' " In *Language, Labour and Migration,* edited by Anne Kershen. Aldershot, England: Ashgate, 2000.

Ekirch, Roger. *Bound for America: Transportation of British Convict to the Colonies, 1716–1775.* Oxford: Oxford University Press, 1987.

Elliott, J. B. *The Lady Huntingdon's Connexion in Sierra Leone.* London, 1851.

Fenn, Elizabeth. *Pox Americana: The Great Smallpox Epidemic of 1775–82.* New York: Hill and Wang, 2001.

Flannery, Tim, ed. *The Birth of Sydney.* Melbourne: Text Publishing, 1999.

Flynn, Michael. *The Second Fleet: Britain's Grim Convict Armada of 1790.* Sydney: Library of Australian History, 1993.

Frey, Sylvia. *Water from the Rock: Black Resistance in a Revolutionary Age.* Princeton: Princeton University Press, 1991.

Frey, Sylvia, and Betty Wood. *Come Shouting to Zion: African American Protestantism in American South and the British Caribbean to 1830.* Chapel Hill: University of North Carolina Press, 1998.

Fryer, Peter. *Staying Power: The History of Black People in Britain.* London: Pluto Press, 1984.

Fyfe, Christopher. *A History of Sierra Leone.* London: Oxford University Press, 1962.

Gillen, Mollie. *Founders of Australia: A Biographical Dictionary of the First Fleet.* Sydney: Library of Australian History, 1989.

Hay, Douglas, et al. *Albion's Fatal Tree: Crime and Society in Eighteenth-Century England.* New York: Pantheon Books, 1975.

Hirschfeld, Fritz. "'Burn All Their Houses': The Log of HMS *Savage* During a Raid up the Potomac River, Spring 1781." *Virginia Magazine of History and Biography* 99 (1991).

Hodges, Graham Russell, ed. *The Black Loyalist Directory: African Americans in Exile After the American Revolution.* New York: Garland Publishing, 1996.

———. *Root and Branch: African Americans in New York and East Jersey, 1613–1863.* Chapel Hill: University of North Carolina Press, 1999.

———. *Slavery and Freedom in the Rural North: African Americans in the Monmouth County, New Jersey, 1665–1865.* Madison: Madison House, 1997.

Hodges, Graham Russell, and Alan Edward Brown, eds. *"Pretends to Be Free": Runaway Slave Advertisements from Colonial and Revolutionary New York and New Jersey.* New York: Garland Publishing, 1994.

Hoffman, Ronald. "The 'Disaffected' in the Revolutionary South." In *The American Revolution: Explorations in the History of American Radicalism,* edited by Alfred E. Young. Dekalb: Northern Illinois University Press, 1976.

Hoffman, Ronald, and Peter J. Albert. *Peace and the Peacemakers: The Treaty of 1783.* Charlottesville: University of Virginia Press, 1986.

Holton, Woody. *Forced Founders: Indians, Debtors, Slaves, and the Making of the American Revolution in Virginia.* Chapel Hill: University of North Carolina Press, 1999.

Hughes, Robert. *The Fatal Shore: A History of the Transportation of Convicts to Australia, 1787–1868.* London: Collins Harvill, 1987.

Isaac, Rhys. *The Transformation of Virginia, 1740–1790.* Chapel Hill: University of North Carolina Press, 1982.

———. *Landon Carter's Uneasy Kingdom.* New York: Oxford University Press, 2004.

Jones, Eldon. "The British Withdrawal from the South, 1781–85." In *The Revolutionary War in the South: Power, Conflict, Leadership,* edited by W. Robert Higgins. Durham, N.C.: Duke University Press, 1979.

Jones, George Fenwick. "The Black Hessians: Negroes Recruited by the Hessians in

South Carolina and Other Colonies." *South Carolina Historical Magazine* 83 (1982).

Kaplan, Sidney, and Emma Nogrady Kaplan. *The Black Presence in the Era of the American Revolution.* Rev. ed. Amherst: University of Massachusetts Press, 1989.

Knutsford, Viscountess. *Life and Letters of Zachary Macaulay.* London: Edward Arnold, 1900.

Kroger, Larry. *Free Black Slave Masters in South Carolina.* Columbia: University of South Carolina Press, 1985.

Kulikoff, Allan. *Tobacco and Slaves: The Development of Southern Cultures in the Chesapeake, 1680–1800.* Chapel Hill: University of North Carolina Press, 1986.

———. "Uprooted Peoples: Black Migrants in the Age of the American Revolution, 1790–1820." In *Slavery and Freedom in the Age of the American Revolution,* edited by Ira Berlin and Ronald Hoffman. Charlottesville: University Press of Virginia, 1983.

Landers, Jane. "Spanish Sanctuary: Fugitive Slaves in Florida, 1687–1790." *Florida Historical Quarterly* 62 (1984).

Linebaugh, Peter. *The London Hanged: Crime and Civil Society in the Eighteenth Century.* Cambridge: Cambridge University Press, 1992.

Linebaugh, Peter, and Marcus Rediker. *The Many-Headed Hydra: Sailors, Slaves, Commoners, and the Hidden History of the Revolutionary Atlantic.* Boston: Beacon Press, 2000.

Little, Thomas J. "George Liele and the Rise of Independent Black Baptist Churches in the Lower South and the Jamaica." *Slavery and Abolition* 16, no. 2 (1995).

Lockett, James D. "The Deportation of the Maroons of Trelawny Town to Nova Scotia, Then Back to Africa." *Journal of Black Studies* 30, no. 1 (1999).

Lorimer, Douglas. "Black Slaves and English Liberty: A Re-Examination of Racial Slavery in England." *Immigrants and Minorities* 3, no. 2 (July 1984).

———. *Colour, Class and the Victorians: English Attitudes to the Negro in the Mid-Nineteeth Century.* Leicester: University of Leicester Press, 1978.

McCowen, George Smith. *The British Occupation of Charleston, 1780–1782.* Columbia: University of South Carolina Press, 1972.

Meade, Robert Douhat. *Patrick Henry: Practical Revolutionary.* New York: J. B. Lippencott, 1969.

Miller, John Chester. *Wolf by the Ears: Thomas Jefferson and Slavery.* Charlottesville: Free Press, 1991.

Morgan, Philip D. *Slave Counterpoint: Black Culture in the Eighteenth-Century Chesapeake and Lowcountry.* Chapel Hill: University of North Carolina Press, 1998.

Morris, Richard B., ed. *John Jay: The Winning of the Peace, 1780–1784.* New York: Harper and Row, 1980.

Mullin, Gerald W. *Flight and Rebellion: Slave Resistance in Eighteenth-Century Virginia.* New York: Oxford University Press, 1972.

Myers, Norma. *Reconstructing the Black Past: Blacks in Britain, 1780–1830.* London: Frank Cass, 1996.

Nash, Gary B. *Forging Freedom: The Formation of Philadelphia's Black Community, 1720–1840.* Cambridge: Harvard University Press, 1988.

———. "Thomas Peters: Millwright and Deliverer." In *Struggle and Survival in Colonial America,* edited by David G. Sweet and Gary B. Nash. Berkeley: University of California Press, 1981.

Norton, Mary Beth. "The Fate of Some Black Loyalists of the American Revolution." *Journal of Negro History* 58 (1973).

Olwell, Robert. "Becoming Free: Manumission and the Genesis of a Free Black Community in South Carolina, 1740–1790." *Slavery and Abolition* 17 (1996).

———. *Masters, Slaves and Subjects: Culture and Power in the South Carolina Low Country, 1740–1790.* Ithaca, N.Y.: Cornell University Press, 1998.

Potkay, Adam, and Susan Burr, eds. *Black Atlantic Writers of the 18th Century: Living the Exodus in England and the Americas.* New York: St. Martin's Press, 1996.

Pulis, John W., ed. *Moving On: Black Loyalists in the Afro-American World.* New York: Garland Publishing, 1999.

Pybus, Cassandra. "Jefferson's Faulty Math: The Question of Slave Defections in the American Revolution." *William and Mary Quarterly* 62, 3rd series (April 2005).

———. "The Many Escapes of John Moseley." *Journal of Australian Colonial Studies* 7 (2005).

———. "The World Is All of One Piece: The African Diaspora and Transportation to Australia." in *Routes of Passage: Rethinking the African Diaspora,* edited by Ruth Hamilton. Lansing: Michigan State University Press, 2005.

Quarles, Benjamin. *The Negro in the American Revolution* [1961]. Chapel Hill: University of North Carolina Press, 1996.

Raboteau, Albert J. *Fire in the Bones: Reflections on African American Religious History.* Boston: Beacon Press, 1995.

————. "The Slave Church in the Era of the American Revolution." In *Slavery and Freedom in the Age of the American Revolution,* edited by Ira Berlin and Ronald Hoffman. Charlottesville: University Press of Virginia, 1983.

Ramsay, David. *History of the Revolution in South Carolina* [1858]. Vol. 2. Spartanburg, S.C.: Reprint Company, 1960.

Ranlet, Phillip. "The British, Slaves, and Smallpox in Revolutionary Virginia." *Journal of Negro History* 84 (1999).

Rawley, James A. *London, Metropolis of the Slave Trade.* St. Louis: University of Missouri Press, 2003.

Rawlyk, George A. *The Canada Fire: Radical Evangelicalism in British North America 1775–1812.* Kingston: Queens University Press, 1994.

Rediker, Marcus. *Between the Devil and the Deep Blue Sea: Merchant Seamen, Pirates, and the Anglo-American Maritime World, 1700–1750.* Cambridge: Cambridge University Press, 1987.

Rice, Howard C., Jr., and Anne S. K. Brown, eds. *The American Campaigns of Rochambeau's Army.* Vol. 2. Princeton: Princeton University Press, 1972.

Richardson, David. "The British Slave Trade to Colonial South Carolina." *Slavery and Abolition* 12, no. 3 (1991).

Royster, Charles. *The Fabulous History of the Dismal Swamp Company: A Story of George Washington's Times.* New York: Knopf, 1999.

Rudé, George. *Hanoverian London, 1714–1808.* London: Secker and Warburg, 1971.

Saillant, John. "'Wipe Away All Tears from Their Eyes': John Marrant's Theology in the Black Atlantic, 1785–1808." *Journal of Millennial Studies* 1, no. 2 (1999).

Schwartz, Suzanne, ed. *Zachary Macaulay and the Development of the Sierra Leone Company.* Vols. 1–2. Leipzig: University of Leipzig Papers on Africa, 2001–2.

Schwarz, Philip J., ed. *Slavery at the Home of George Washington.* Mount Vernon, Va.: Mount Vernon Ladies Association, 2001.

Selig, Robert. "The Revolution's Black Soldiers." *Colonial Williamsburg* 19, no. 4 (1997).

Shepherd, Verene, ed. *Working Slavery, Pricing Freedom: Perspectives from the Caribbean, Africa and the African Diaspora.* New York: Dalgrave, 2001.

Shyllon, F. O. *Black People in Britain, 1555–1833.* Oxford: Oxford University Press, 1977.

Siebert, Wilbur Henry. *The Legacy of the American Revolution to the British West Indies and Bahamas: A Chapter out of the History of the American Loyalists.* Columbus: Ohio State University, 1913.

Simpson, Bland. *The Great Dismal Swamp: A Carolinian's Memoir.* Chapel Hill: University of North Carolina Press, 1990.

Sobel, Mechal. *The World They Made Together: Black and White Values in Eighteenth-Century Virginia.* Princeton: Princeton University Press, 1987.

Stanton, Lucia C. *Free Some Day: The African-American Families of Monticello.* Charlottesville: Thomas Jefferson Memorial Foundation, 2000.

———. *Slavery at Monticello.* Monticello, Va.: Thomas Jefferson Memorial Foundation, 1996.

Sweig, Donald M. "The Importation of African Slaves to the Potomac River, 1732–1772." *William and Mary Quarterly* 42, 3rd series (October 1985).

Toth, Charles W., ed. *The American Revolution in the West Indies.* Port Washington: Kennikat Press, 1975.

Tyson, George. "The Carolina Black Corps: Legacy of Revolution, 1783–1798." *Revista/Review Interamericana* 5 (1975–76).

van Buskirk, Judith L. *Generous Enemies: Patriots and Loyalists in Revolutionary New York.* Philadelphia: University of Pennsylvania Press, 2002.

Walker, James W. St. G. *The Black Loyalists: The Search for the Promised Land in Nova Scotia and Sierra Leone, 1783–1870.* New York: Africana Publishing Co., 1976.

Walvin, James. *Questioning Slavery.* London: Routledge, 1996.

———, ed. *Slavery and British Society, 1776–1846.* Baton Rouge: Louisiana State University Press, 1982.

White, David O. *Connecticut's Black Soldiers.* Chester, Conn.: Pequod Press, 1973.

White, Shane. *Somewhat More Independent: The End of Slavery in New York City, 1770–1810.* Athens: University of Georgia Press, 1991.

Wiencek, Henry. *An Imperfect God: George Washington, His Slaves, and the Creation of America.* New York: Farrar, Straus, Giroux, 2003.

Wigger, John H. *Taking Heaven by Storm: Methodism and the Rise of Popular Christianity in America.* New York: Oxford University Press, 1988.

Wilson, Ellen Gibson. *The Loyal Blacks.* New York, Capricorn Books, 1976.

Windley, Lathan A. *A Profile of Runaway Slaves in Virginia and South Carolina from 1730 through 1787.* New York: Garland Publishing, 1995.

Wood, Peter H. "The Changing Population of the Colonial South: An Overview by

Race and Region, 1685–1790." In *Powhatan's Mantle: Indians in the Colonial Southeast,* edited by Peter H. Wood et al. Lincoln: University of Nebraska Press, 1989.

———. "'The Dream Deferred': Black Freedom Struggles on the Eve of White Independence." In *In Resistance: Studies in African, Caribbean, and Afro-American History,* edited by Gary Y. Okihiro. Amherst: University of Massachusetts Press, 1986.

Wright, J. Leitch, Jr., "Blacks in East Florida." *Florida Historical Quarterly* 54 (1976).

Wrike, Peter J. *The Governor's Island.* Gwynn: Gwynn Island Museum, 1993.